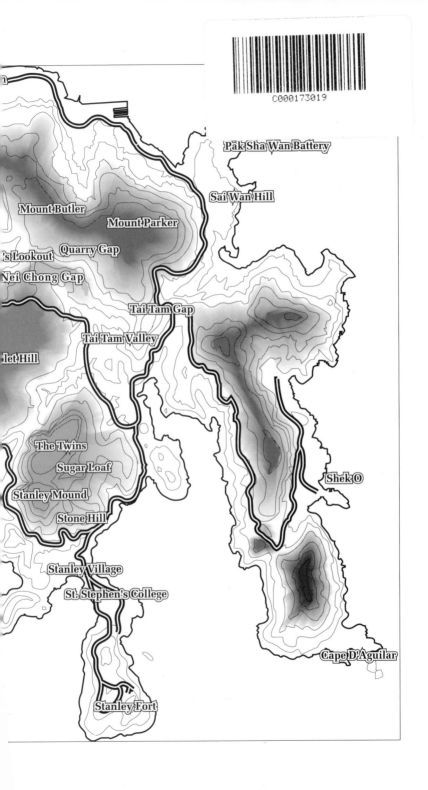

Pak Sha Wan Battery

Sai Wan Hill

Mount Butler

Mount Parker

Quarry Gap

's Lookout

Nei Chong Gap

Tai Tam Gap

Tai Tam Valley

let Hill

The Twins

Sugar Loaf

Stanley Mound

Stone Hill

Shek O

Stanley Village

St. Stephen's College

Cape D'Aguilar

Stanley Fort

SECOND TO NONE

THE STORY OF THE HONG KONG VOLUNTEERS

SECOND TO NONE
The Story of the Hong Kong Volunteers

PHILLIP BRUCE

HONG KONG
OXFORD UNIVERSITY PRESS
OXFORD NEW YORK
1991

Oxford University Press

Oxford   New York   Toronto
Petaling Jaya   Singapore   Hong Kong   Tokyo
Delhi   Bombay   Calcutta   Madras   Karachi
Nairobi   Dar es Salaam   Cape Town
Melbourne   Auckland

and associated companies in
Berlin Ibadan

First published 1991
Published in the United States
by Oxford University Press, Inc., New York

British Library Cataloguing in Publication Data

Bruce, Phillip, 1950–
Second to none : the story of the Hong Kong Volunteers.
I. Title
356.162095125
ISBN 0-19-585518-3

Library of Congress Cataloging-in-Publication Data

Bruce, Phillip, 1950–
Second to none : the story of the Hong Kong Volunteers/Phillip Bruce.
p. cm.
Includes bibliographical references and index.
ISBN 0-19-585518-3 : $29.00 (est.)
1. Hong Kong. Royal Hong Kong Defence Force. Hong Kong Regiment-History.
I. Title.
UA853. H85B78 1991
355.3'51'095125–dc20
91-36517
CIP

Printed in Hong Kong by Kings Time Printing Press Ltd.
Published by Oxford University Press, Warwick House, Hong Kong

Contents

Abbreviations

AA	Anti-Aircraft
ACS	Armoured Car Section
ADC	Aide-de-Camp
ASC	Army Service Corps
BAAG	British Army Aid Group
CBF	Commander British Forces
CRA	Commander Royal Artillery
DSO	Distinguished Service Order
GOC	General Officer Commanding
GSO	General Staff Officer
HKAAF	Hong Kong Auxiliary Air Force
HKR	Hong Kong Rifles
HKRNVR	Hong Kong Royal Naval Volunteer Reserve
HKVDC	Hong Kong Volunteer Defence Corps
HKSRA	Hong Kong and Singapore Royal Artillery
HM Government	Her Majesty's Government
HMS	Her Majesty's Ship
KCMG	Knight Commander of the Order of St. Michael and St. George
MC	Military Cross
MM	Military Medal
MMG	Motor Machine Gun
MTB	Motor Torpedo Boat
NCO	Non-Commissioned Officer
OBE	Officer of the Order of the British Empire
OC	Officer Commanding
ORs	Other Ranks
POW	Prisoner of War
RA	Royal Artillery
RAF	Royal Air Force
RAMC	Royal Army Medical Corps
RAOC	Royal Army Ordinance Corps
RASC	Royal Army Service Corps
REME	Royal Electrical and Mechanical Engineers
RHKDF	Royal Hong Kong Defence Force
RN	Royal Navy
RSM	Regimental Sergeant Major
TF	Territorial Force

1

The First Volunteers

Hong Kong Government Gazette, No 37, of June 3rd, 1854

Government Notification

The following extract from a Circular lately addressed to the inhabitants of Hong Kong is published for general information.

C.B. Hillier
Officiating Colonial Secretary

Colonial Secretary's Office
Victoria, Hong Kong, 3rd June, 1854.

Circular

Colonial Secretary's Office
Hong Kong, 30th May, 1854.

The exigencies of the public service having compelled His Excellency, the Rear-Admiral to withdraw for a time the protection afforded by a Naval Force, the Honourable the Lieutenant Governor has had under his anxious consideration the defenceless state of the colony and the calamities that might ensue were it attacked in its present condition by the Naval Power of an enemy or by one of the formidable piratical Fleets known to be in the neighbourhood.

The peculiar composition of the Chinese population of the place renders probable also another danger of no minor importance, that of a combination of the vagrant Inhabitants for purposes of plunder whenever they may find the Police and the Troops engaged by the absorbing occupation of preparation for an enemy.

Under these circumstances, the Lieutenant Governor calls upon the faithful inhabitants of this Colony to lend him their aid in this emergency by forming themselves into a Corps of Volunteers for the defence of the lives and property of themselves and their families on the occurrence of any of the above mentioned contingencies.

The Honourable Colonel Griffin, Commanding the Forces, has kindly promised to make the requisite arrangements for the equipment and training of the Corps.

By Order,
C.B. Hillier,
Officiating Colonial Secretary

— * —

The Volunteer Corps which has been resolved on will never be organised; that is to say organised so as to be of use; and whatever our Honourable Lt Governor may know of the 'peculiar composition of the Chinese population,' he evinces very little knowledge of the 'peculiar composition of the European population' in entertaining the fond delusion that any corps of the kind will ever find a *volunteer* existence.

Friend of China newspaper, 7 June 1854.

HONG Kong has always stood at the crossroads of east and west. Its history as a British colony can be dated from the landing in January 1841 when the Union Flag was raised at Possession Point, though the legalities took a few more years to tie up.

The story of volunteering in Hong Kong is the story of the territory. The civilian soldiers, sailors and airmen whose names appear in the rolls have never been a force apart from the general life of the colony.

The first Volunteers appeared only 13 years after the foundation of Hong Kong, and today their successors still play an active and important part in the life of the colony. The story will move into a different phase in the 1990s when the Royal Hong Kong Regiment is disbanded prior to the return to Chinese sovereignty of Hong Kong.

There are now nearly six million people crammed into the crowded urban areas of Hong Kong and the territory lays strong claim to possessing some of the most densely populated areas on earth.

Amid the high-rise towers, the busy roads, the harbour criss-crossed by ships and ferries, the noise of the streets, and the constant demolition and construction work, it is difficult to conceive of the small town which existed in 1854 when the Volunteers first appeared on this speck on the coastline of China.

To see why a volunteer force was called into being it is necessary to go back to before the establishment of the colony in 1841.

The British government did not want Hong Kong. Charles Elliot, the man who accepted it as part of the settlement of the First China War, was recalled to Britain in disgrace and given the ignominious appointment of British Consul-General to Texas. Many people felt that the new settlement should have been on the Chusan (Zhousan) Islands off the mouth of the Yangtze River. From there, the heart of China would have been open.

Though China had been compelled by force of arms to cede Hong Kong, every obstacle was placed in the way of its development. What the Treaty of Nanking permitted theoretically, and what the Chinese were prepared to see develop, were entirely separate matters.

The young colony was small, a long way from Britain and perched on the edge of the vast nation of China, in which other European powers and the United States were increasingly taking an interest. From a defensive point of view, Hong Kong had big problems.

Adding to those problems was the fact that Hong Kong was, above all, a trading centre. The stream of settlers, administrators, camp-followers and entrepreneurs which flowed into other colonies never reached Hong Kong. While colonists were moving out across the expanses of Canada, Africa or Australia, Hong Kong remained a place where the British came to do business and, with luck, make money, before returning gratefully home on retirement.

The Chinese who moved to the island after 1841 had a very similar outlook, retaining strong family ties with their native villages, returning there in time of sickness or disturbance, with relatives on the mainland used by the mandarins for exerting influence on their countrymen in the new British colony.

Early census figures show a population of 24,175 people in Hong Kong in 1845. By 1853, this figure had grown to 39,017. A typical modern development, at Taikoo Shing, on Hong Kong Island, today houses 60,000 people.

The perception of the British and other European residents of the threat to Hong Kong was as important as the reality of that threat in determining defensive planning. The plain fact was that there were very, very few Europeans in early Hong Kong. The 1853 census counted only 476 British and Americans. Of these, 86 were women, and 78 children — leaving only 312 men. Within this figure, allowance must be made for the sick, for clergymen, and for others not available for military service.

Hong Kong was a wild and raucous town in its early days. Throughout the 1840s there were alarms, pirate attacks, expeditions, deadly outbreaks of disease, scandals, murderous assaults, and dissension in civil, military and ecclesiastical circles. The colony gained such a reputation that an old curse in use in Britain was modified especially for it. 'Go To Hong Kong!' became an alternative to 'Go To Halifax', the latter stemming from an an old gibbet law, said to have seen alleged miscreants executed first and then tried.

The two main categories of European in Hong Kong in the 1840s and 1850s were the traders and the military and naval men. Both were concerned about defending the colony. How this should best be done was the problem. British naval power was unquestioned, and Hong Kong was the major base in Chinese waters. While the fleet was in harbour, the colony was unassailable. The problem was that fleets do not fulfill their primary role when they are in harbour. Royal Navy ships had the job of projecting British influence and to do that they had to sail. Once the fleet left to do its job, Hong Kong was completely undefended.

Throughout the 1840s there was constant concern at the lack of an effective defence for Hong Kong in the absence of the fleet. Small forts and defensive works went up along the northern shore of the island at such places as Murray Battery, Kellett Island, and elsewhere, but these were close-in defences mounting small guns of limited range. An early attempt to establish a military presence at Lyemun, at the narrow eastern entrance to the harbour had been a disaster. Within five weeks, of the 20 soldiers sent out, five were dead, three were in a dangerous condition and three were convalescent.

The British saw the threat to Hong Kong as coming not from the weakened and militarily ineffective China, but from the Western powers. The French and the Russians were suspected of casting envious eyes on British territory and they had the military and naval potential to cause trouble.

However, there was a fundamental difference of opinion between the British residents of Hong Kong and the home government over who should pay for the colony's defence. The Hong Kong view was that the existence of the colony was of benefit to British interests in the region, providing a base for the fleet and a British settlement which underpinned trade and prestige elsewhere. The cost of its defence should, therefore, be largely an

Imperial responsibility. The London view, however, inclined towards a 'You Live There — You Pay For It' line. This squabble was to continue throughout the history of Hong Kong.

In the late 1840s, when defence was entirely paid for by Britain, Hong Kong went through a financial crisis and a savage cost-cutting exercise was ordered. London was extremely concerned at the cost of the colony and a thorough review ensued which saw the Governor, Sir George Bonham, recommending in early 1849 that six companies of British troops and three of Ceylon Rifles, about 1,200 men, would be enough for defence, and that a colonel, rather than a major-general, could command. He also recommended big reductions in support troops. Bonham felt that the ultimate defence of Hong Kong should lie with the navy, rather than with the army.

Bonham's economies saw the cost of the military fall from 80,778 pounds in 1848 to 50,346 pounds in 1853. This no doubt pleased London, but the reductions must have concerned Hong Kong residents who saw threats on all sides.

In China, the cataclysm of the Tai Ping Rebellion had begun. The humiliations of the first war with the British had resulted in a lessening of the prestige of the central government. Bands of militia had been called out to assist the Imperial forces and this had helped the people to realize the extent of their potential power.

The ruling Ch'ing Dynasty was not Chinese, but Manchu, and military humiliation, together with other factors including political corruption, natural disasters such as the flooding of the Yangtze River, famine in Kwangsi in 1847, the change in the course of the Yellow River in 1852, and economic and social pressures, lead to an increase in patriotic activity, disturbances and unrest. However, the flame that was to explode into the Tai Ping Rebellion was lit by Christianity.

Over the decade and a half of the Tai Ping Revolution, China was thrown into turmoil, 20 million died, either as a direct or indirect result, more than 600 cities were destroyed and the dynasty was brought almost to its knees.

The few European residents of Hong Kong looked across a narrow stretch of water to the shores of Kowloon — still Chinese territory — and watched and wondered. Press reports of the rebellion were sketchy at first. But by 1854 rebels, or people calling themselves rebels, had taken Kowloon City.

The prime impetus for the birth of Hong Kong's first Volunteers came, however, not from nearby China, but from a war that had broken out in the Crimea. Britain and France declared war on Russia in March 1854.

The outbreak of war with Russia had serious implications for Hong Kong. To the north of China lay the Russian coastline from which the Tsarist navy operated in Asian waters. The enemy fleet posed a threat in a wide arc and the British government was naturally concerned that every effort should be made to hunt it down, or blockade it in a port. Defensive preparations began even in Australia and New Zealand. Pundits put the enemy fleet as being anywhere from Indian waters to far out in the Pacific.

The Royal Navy force based in Hong Kong set out on May 25, 1854, to scour the ocean for the Russians. An estimate of British ships in Asian waters showed a total of 15 major war vessels mounting 244 guns. The departure of the Hong Kong naval element had serious implications because in the absence of the navy, the colony was virtually undefended. The garrison was weak and fixed defences were regarded as grossly inadequate.

The Lieutenant Governor, William Caine, wrote to London on 5 June 1854, saying that news of the outbreak of war with Russia had arrived on 25 May: 'The Rear Admiral left with the Ships of War *Winchester*, *Spartan* and *Barracouta* a few hours afterwards for the northern ports, having on board Sir John Bowring and suite.'

Caine also referred to a recent case of piracy of a Dutch vessel where the head pirate had informed the mate that, had he been English instead of Dutch, the ship would have been burnt and all on board murdered.

This created some little alarm in the colony. It shewed that a fleet of 19 heavily armed piratical vessels were in the neighbourhood, the monsoon being fair for Hong Kong, and we were in a few hours to be unprotected by a single British ship of war without any Colonial vessel larger than a common boat for our defence.

The Attorney General, W.T. Bridges, put forward the idea of a volunteer force — not in his official capacity but as an ordinary member of the community.

Caine wrote that much responsibility had devolved upon him. A formidable Russian fleet was in the vicinity, while a fleet of pirates with a grudge against the British in view of the action taken against them by the Royal Navy, was also around.

At the same time a vagabond population bound together by the ties of secret association was living in our midst — I deemed it necessary to consult without delay the Honourable Colonel Griffin, Commanding the Forces, and to aid him by every means in my power to concert effective measures of defence as well against a foreign enemy and piratical fleets as against insubordination among the native population of which the recent disturbances at Singapore in the beginning of the month had given us a very melancholy example. I am happy to say that our views as to the most prudent steps to take in the emergency entirely coincided.

As the interests of the European residents were of course much involved in the measures proposed; I gave verbal notification to the principal merchants of the place that their advice and assistance would be very acceptable and accordingly on Monday 29th May seven of those gentlemen attended me and the Executive Council, and I explained to them the projects of the government in aid of the military forces. The nature of my address will more clearly appear from the enclosed memorandum made at the time; and the attached minutes of their subsequent proceedings will inform you Grace how cordially they assented to my propositions.

These measures I may expand to Your Grace in brief to be the formation of a Volunteer Corps from among the European inhabitants and the immediate raising of an Auxiliary Police well armed and drilled. Both bodies to be equipped by the Colonel Commanding the Forces from the arms and accoutrements in the ordnance store and the Auxiliary Force to be paid for by a rate upon the Police Assessment. It was also necessary to hire for the purposes of a battery the house and garden at West Point known as 'Edger's Bungalow', a commanding position and the only one in the opinion of the Senior Artillery Officer which at that extremity of the town can be made available for efficient protection.

I did besides take the precaution of establishing a signal station at each side of the island that during the day at least the presence of an enemy's squadron or of a piratical fleet might be known without delay, and for the out Police Stations, reinforced by Europeans, horses were purchased that intelligence might be communicated with the least possible delay. A reward was promised for any intelligence brought by fishermen and a watch is kept by the Harbour Master and the Water Police to prevent the equipment of privateers. This with a couple of look out boats, one on the east and one on the south side of the island, seemed all that was necessary to prevent surprises.

Caine went on to note that the *Spartan* had returned unexpectedly to Hong Kong on May 28, having sprung a main yard. However, he did not feel that the presence of the warship justified him making any changes to his plans for improvements to defence.

Detailing the formation of a volunteer force he went on to explain:

A circular was sent round to the community inviting them to form themselves into a Volunteer Corps for the defence of themselves and their property, and after this had been signed by such a number of inhabitants as assured me that the principle of the measure was approved and its necessity acknowledged, a public meeting was called by the Sheriff that an opportunity might be afforded of having the matter fully discussed and the opinions of the residents unreservedly expressed. I purposely abstained from accrediting any person to represent the government at this meeting being unwilling to exhibit the semblance of a wish to obstruct the freedom of action.

It appeared, however, that some one or two persons of the meeting objected to the formation of a Volunteer Corps on two grounds, first that in all such volunteer associations the willing were made to work for and protect the unwilling, and secondly because the residents who owed allegiance to foreign states at peace with Russia might in the presence of a Russian enemy object to bear arms. This objection was not propounded by the foreign residents themselves, for several of these had signed the Circular, and many more were willing to do so, but by two or three Englishmen. The point had of course not escaped the notice of the Government, as the cautious wording of the Circular itself will demonstrate. It was proposed to form a Militia, an altercation ensued, which was abruptly terminated by the adjournment of the meeting till next day, on a resolution that the Government should be requested to send some person to state its views and wishes.

Next day Mr Hillier, the Officiating Colonial Secretary, attended the meeting and explained the reasons of the government in proposing the measure and the advice anticipated from its adoption. There was a full attendance. The proposition for a militia was again brought forward and discussed; but on being put to the meeting it was found that only six persons, including the proposer and seconder, were in its favour, and the Chairman was vociferously requested by those who were not yet enrolled to lay the circular on the table at once that they might sign it without further delay. A committee of three was then balloted for that steps might be taken for the immediate organisation of the Corps. The persons chosen were three of the most respectable residents, one Mr Antrobus, is the representative of the firm of Lindsay and Co.

Caine went on:

The present garrison though numbering 570 non-commissioned officers and privates cannot, owing to its weakened condition through sickness produce at this moment more than 400 men really fit for duty. With these assisted by a Volunteer Corps and the temporary and permanent Police force we may humbly trust to make a firm and successful resistance to any hostile force that might attack us on shore, yet they are insufficient to induce that perfect sense of security which I believe is essential to the prosperity and progress of this colony in a peculiar degree to which no other colony affords a parallel.

According to the official Blue Book for 1854, the military presence consisted of posts at Victoria, Stanley and Sai Wan. There were other military works at Kellett's Island, now inland and home of the Royal Hong Kong Yacht Club, the nine-gun Wellington Battery on the seafront, slightly to the east of the town, the six-gun Murray Battery and a dismounted four-gun battery at West Point. The returns of guards furnished by troops, dated May 20 1854, show that relatively few were fit for duty (see Table 1.1).

Table 1.1 Troops Fit for Duty on 20 May 1854

	Sgts	Cpls	Drummers	Ptes
59th Regiment	18	18	7	263
Royal Artillery	—	10	1	28
Gun Lascars	2	8	1	66
Royal Sappers	3	5	—	16

Caine said in his despatch that work was going on to improve the batteries. He said that at West Point work was in hand to mount eleven 32-pounders in one battery; there was to be another battery immediately below with two eight-inch howitzers; a battery of three 32-pounders was to go in on Kellett Island; 12 guns were to be placed on board the *Hercules* military hospital ship. 'This could merely assist a couple of Men of War in crippling an invasive force,' he wrote. 'But it is much to be doubted whether unaided they could prevent the total destruction of the town by an enemy's fleet.'

As a final indication of the danger, Caine added a further note to his despatch:

Since writing the above I have received the accompanying report from the Superintendent of Police of an attack made near Macao on four war junks by a fleet of, as the deponent says, 53 piratical vessels. The number is probably an exaggeration, but of the attack there seems to be little doubt.

In a further communication Caine again stressed the danger of unsavoury elements of the local population causing trouble:

The danger to be apprehended is that during an attack by an enemy or a gang of pirates, these vagabonds might form themselves into bands for the purpose of plunder, to be joined perhaps by others from this vicinity, and then immense loss of property and life might ensue if through the troops or Police being otherwise engaged there be no reserve force to stop their progress; nor must it be forgotten with what facility the Chinese houses in some parts of the town may be fired by incendiaries to increase the confusion, and consequent facility of plunder. The existence of a reserve such as would be formed by a Colonial Volunteer Corps might stop such proceedings at the outset or prevent them altogether; it might tender effective aid in other ways to the troops by making them free to devote their undivided attention to their more immediate duties; and the safety of the place would be thus materially increased. The Commander of the troops has undertaken to equip and drill such a corps whenever it may be formed. To guard against immediate danger doubtless a body of paid men might without any great difficulty be raised; but a reserve such as that proposed I do not see any other method of procuring than the usual one of a sort of local militia or Volunteer Corps.

In June the previous year, the Governor, Sir George Bonham, had written to London expressing his worries about the situation in no uncertain terms. He pointed out in a despatch of 29 June, that the naval strength in Hong Kong was quite insufficient to meet any problems that could arise and requested that three companies of the Ceylon Rifles, under orders for India, should remain: 'I am of the opinion that the absence of the three rifle companies from Ceylon for a limited period, will not be of much consequence to the government of that island, while their services are particularly required at the present moment in the colony.'

It was pointed out in one report that at a farewell parade for a senior officer, the total number of troops that could be mustered amounted to only 400. The *Friend of China* newspaper said that a consultation had been held between the Governor and the senior naval and military officers to discuss defence:

The Hercules hulk will be moored across the harbour, it is said, and the ten 10-inch guns now in arsenal placed on board her with a company of the 59th who will be trained fully in the necessary exercises. Red-hot shot, well delivered, will be ample defence against the Russian squadron that may assail us we take it; but there must be a better look out on this side too if the reported virtues of Russian gold are to be guarded against. After writing this we heard that another battery would displace some Chinese graves at West Point. Stonecutters Island is the place for a battery.

There was a pressing need for more troops to defend Hong Kong and a variety of schemes was considered, but, as ever, cost had the upper hand.

The state of the regular troops, few in number and weakened by sickness and disease, continued to cause concern. In one month alone, 73 soldiers went down with fever and dysentery. Beri-beri, previously unknown in Hong Kong was found among Indian troops. A commentator said:

A handful of sickly land forces, such as we have had in Hong Kong for ten years past, are of no use, except to the grogshops and the gravediggers, while they tend to keep up the delusion that Hong Kong is not a commercial settlement, but a military station where civilians are permitted to live under an absolute government.

It was against this background of war with Russia and turmoil in China that discussions were held with the Officer Commanding the Garrison, Colonel Griffin. The situation was considered further at a special meeting attended by seven prominent citizens and it was decided to raise a Volunteer Corps and an Auxiliary Police. A circular was issued to the European community on 30 May 1854, inviting volunteers.

The seven at the special meeting were: Mr D. Jardine, Mr Williamson Dent, Mr Antrobus, Mr Livingstone, Mr Holliday, Mr Edgar, and Mr Still.

Although there were only a little over 300 European and American men eligible to volunteer, that did not mean that all was sweetness and light in the civilian community. The town was rent with factions and many were the disputes, libel actions and upsets. Perhaps the two greatest cliques were the Jardine and Dent camps. These two houses had long struggled for supremacy in the China trade and many people in the town allied themselves formally or informally with one or the other. It is interesting that a Jardine and a Dent attended the May 29 meeting.

Bridges said that he briefed the meeting on the present state of the available defence forces, then he and Colonel Griffin retired. The seven great men discussed the matter and decided, 'It is highly desirable that a Corps of Volunteers should be raised and that to support the paid auxiliary force a special rate of three per cent be at once levied on the police assessment and be renewed at the expiration of three months if necessary.'

The first public meeting, held on Friday, 2 June, was not, as Caine noted, a success. Eighty people attended and many were opposed to the idea of a volunteer force, seeing it as nothing more than conscription. At the second meeting, called for the following day, Hillier explained that the purpose was not to raise a force to fight the Russians but to protect life and property locally. A number of the leading figures in the community attended this meeting and the idea of a Volunteer Corps was adopted in principle.

Though feelings were running high in Hong Kong, the Governor and the Rear Admiral, away at sea in search of Russians, had a more general view of affairs. The former wrote a letter dated, 'At sea. HMS *Winchester*. 26 May, 1854.'

In the letter, Bowring said that he had read the despatches giving details of public feeling and had discussed them with Sir James Stirling:

Who has had the goodness to consult with me as to the best disposal of his Naval Forces, with a view to the *general* security of British interests over the vast field committed to his jurisdiction and with such inadequate means to supply the many claims for protection which are presented to his notice, and after all deliberation I have come to the conclusion that the arrangements made by His Excellency are on the whole the best that could have been adopted and the most likely to provide for the permanent safety of the property and persons of Her Majesty's subjects in these regions.

Though there was no lack of expressions of patriotism and support for the fight against the enemy, there were many who had a rather jaundiced view of setting up a volunteer, as opposed to a militia, force. The *China Mail* of 1 June was in favour of the latter: 'Consisting of every British subject able to bear arms, between the ages of 16 and 60. Then work would have been shared by all. But what happened? A circular was sent round ... by a policeman who knows nothing of Hong Kong or its residents.' The 'policeman' description was a dig at Caine and the report claimed that only 40 men signed the circular:

Though by this time it might have been expected to have borne the signatures of every Englishman on the island. The individual excuses are said to be of the most frivolous description and so further confirms us in the opinion that, in default of a public meeting, the government would have done much better to have taken the matter in its own hands.

None the less, volunteers quickly came forward and the 'Ninety-nine', to whose memory a toast is drunk at formal occasions to this day, were enrolled.

Caine accepted the colonelcy of the Volunteers. He had had a long career in the army and in colonial service in Hong Kong where he was regarded as a tough and able administrator. It was said that few of the Chinese inhabitants could ever name the Governor of the day, but that all knew Caine.

Caine had served in a variety of posts and had made many enemies. Caine's first appointment in the colony, on 30 April 1841, was as Magistrate with wide powers. Soon afterwards he became Superintendent of the Jail. He remained as Magistrate and, in 1843, was appointed to the Legislative Council — although this was not properly constituted until 1844.

Believing in action as much as words, Caine would personally patrol the streets with another individual whose name appears in the genesis of the Volunteers; his assistant, former ship's mate, C.B. Hillier. Both men were firm believers in the virtues of corporal punishment. When not occupied with his official duties, Caine also involved himself in the profitable business of land speculation. He later became Colonial Secretary, with Hillier succeeding him as Chief Magistrate.

In the first fifteen years of Hong Kong's history, the Governor had also been the Superintendent of Trade in China generally. In 1854, it was decided to split the two roles and Caine became Lieutenant Governor, nominally in charge of the government of Hong Kong, with Sir John Bowring as Superintendent of Trade and Plenipotentiary. However, Bowring also retained the title of Governor of Hong Kong. The arrangement was a messy one, and disputes between the two men resulted. Eventually, Bowring became Governor with full power for the administration of the colony. Caine retired in 1859.

The original 'Ninety-Nine':

A. Adman	G. Duddell	John McVeity
W.H. Alexander	H.J. Edwards	John McLaughlin
J.M. Armstrong	Jameson Ellis	James Michell
R.C. Antrobus	H.M. Gibb	E.R. Michell
Samuel Appleton	Peter Giles	Alexander Michie
John Ashton	Robert Gordon	W. Moresby
Luiz Barros	A. Grandpre	Y.J. Murrow
A. Berenhart	James Haddow	R. Neil
W.F. Bevan	E.H. Hance	George Norris
F.H. Block	G. Harper	E. Oppert
J.F. Bouges	C.B. Hillier	G. Overbeck
N. Boulle	H.J. Hoey	F.S. Pedder
W.A. Bowra	William Hoolmany	Edward Pereira
J.M. Brimelow	F.S. Huffum	Edward Reimers
G. Brodersen	H.H. Hunt	R. Reinaecker
J.A. Brooks	J. Hyndman	Hugh Reinhardt
James Brown	Thomas Irwin	John Ricket
George Cameron	S. Invanowich	William Ross
R.H. Carvalho	John Lamont	H.V. Sage
William Chapman	T.A. Lane	S.O. Schmidt
J. Chomley	D. Lapraik	Richard Scott
E. Cohen	F.W. Lawrence	W.W. Shaw
P. Cohen	J. Lemon	T.M. Simson
C. Collins	G. Logan	Charles Smith
J. Collins	G.F. Maclean	J. Smithers
R.H. Crackenthorp	Charles Markwick	Thomas Spence
W. Davis	R. Markwick	J.W. Stanhope
John Denis	P. Marques	T. Stewart
W. Dent	H. Marsh	Robert Strachan
David Dick	J. Marshall	M.H. Sutton
Thomas Dick	D.K. Mason	Joseph Thornton
A.S. Dixson	N.R. Masson	H. Winniberg
F. Duddell	F.A. McQueen	James Young

The names of the 99 men who constituted the first volunteers in Hong Kong have been enshrined in the regiment's memory.

In 1854, the number of European males in the colony stood at just over 300, so the figure of 99 volunteers, placed in that context, shows the very strong level of support which the new body attracted at its outset.

The researches of the Revd Carl T. Smith throw light upon the original 99. The names come from the commercial community — shopkeepers, tavern owners, auctioneers, newspapermen and traders. But there are few names of the Taipans, or heads of major trading houses, in the list, though the family and friends of Dent and Company are in evidence. Dent was the great rival to Jardine and that is probably the reason that none of the 99 were connected with the latter firm.

The first two Captains to be elected were Robert Crawford Antrobus and John Ricket. Antrobus was a trader, having been admitted as a partner of the firm of Lindsay and Company in 1852. He came from a family well established in the China trade and one of the earliest of the large tea traders. He was the son of Sir Edmund Antrobus, the second baronet, and appears to have arrived in Hong Kong in about 1850. His later career was spent in Shanghai, where he served on the Municipal Council and carried on Lindsay's business there. He died in 1911, in London at the ripe old age of 80.

The reports of June 1854 have it that the second Captain to be elected was 'John Richett'. However, no such name appears in the list of the 99 and it is therefore probable that this was a misspelling of John Ricket.

Ricket was listed as early as 1831 as having been in Macau and he came to Hong Kong in about 1847 to work as a marine surveyor. In 1858, he became Government Marine Surveyor and he resigned in 1860 to return with his family to England, where he died in 1878, aged 77.

The two Lieutenants elected were W.F. Bevan and T.A. Lane. William Frazer Bevan was involved in the colony's early newspapers and with the firm of W.T. Gemmell and Company. In 1853, he was involved with the *Hong Kong Register* and the following year seems to have retained this involvement while also acting as clerk to the Chief Justice. He was the editor of the *Register* in 1858, the year in which he died at the age of 39.

Thomas Ash Lane is remembered today in the name of one of Hong Kong's leading retail stores — Lane Crawford. Lane was a clerk and shopkeeper rather than one of the mighty Taipans. In 1843, he was working with the Post Office but the following year he went into business with a partner as commission and general

agents. The partner, A.H. Fryer, dropped out the following year
and he carried on as Lane and Company. He continued in business
until 1850 when the partnership Lane Crawford and Company
was set up with Ninian Crawford. Though the business flourishes
today, Lane did not live long to enjoy its fruits, dying in 1869, in
the United Kingdom, at the age of 44.

At the head of the Dent and Company men in the list of the 99,
stood W. Dent. This could have been either Wilkinson Dent or
William Dent. The latter was the youngest and, therefore, more
probably the Volunteer. William Dent was admitted as a partner in
the family firm almost at the same time as he joined the Volunteers. Little else is known about him. Wilkinson Dent was listed as
a merchant in Canton in 1836 and became a partner in Dent and
Company in 1845.

There were plenty of other Dent men amongst the Volunteers.
Edward Reimers was employed by the company when he joined
up. He resigned as Consul of the Free Hanseatic City of Hamburg
in 1856, an honorary appointment which he may also have held in
1854. Francis Chomley was a partner in Dent and Company for
many years and, when John Dent resigned from the Legislative
Council in 1861, Chomley was appointed in his place.

G. Overbeck — Baron George, or Gustav, Von Overbaeck —
gave distinguished consular service to the Austrian and Prussian
governments, as well as working for Dents. His title came in
reward for his assistance in gaining exhibits from the East for the
Vienna exhibition of 1873. Overbeck was the ancestor of several of
today's prominent Eurasian families in Hong Kong. He appears to
have served with Dents from the early 1850s until its troubles in
1866 and he acted as Liquidator's Agent for the firm. He was
closely involved, with Alfred Dent, in the setting up of British
North Borneo, though he had to cease his connection because of
his nationality.

The name listed as Edward Pereita is probably a mistake for
Edward Pereira, another Dent man. He came from an old Macau
family and was listed as one of the firm's clerks at Canton in 1835.
He became a partner in 1846.

Pio Marques was working as a clerk for Dents when he enrolled
in the Volunteers and he later served as a clerk in the Colonial
Secretary's Office and as British consular agent in Macau, where
he died of diarrhoea in 1871, at the age of 48.

The 99 liked a drink along with their soldiering — if the

number of publicans and tavern keepers in their number is anything to go by.

John McLaughlin kept the Albion Hotel. Richard Neil was his
partner until November 1856. James Wentworth Brimelow was
involved with the Hong Kong Inn, near the Lower Market, though
he was also involved in wholesale wines and spirits, a ship
chandler's business, a soda water manufactury, and a number of
other ventures.

Frenchman, Joseph Napoleon Boulle, was also a tavern keeper
involved in a range of other businesses, such as baking bread,
selling coffee and general trading. In 1845, he was advertising ice
cream in a range of flavours for sale to the ladies and gentlemen of
Hong Kong.

The name listed as 'John McVeity' was probably the Irishman,
John McVeety, who was involved at various stages with the
Nemesis and Union Taverns. The Pilot Boat Tavern, the Old
House At Home and the Liverpool Arms were all projects of Joze
Felippe Borges. James Young, meanwhile, offered drinks at the
Seaman's Return Tavern, the American Eagle and The Land We
Live In.

George Cameron ran the El Dorado Tavern and, when he died
in 1859, left it jointly to a friend and to the Chinese woman with
whom he had lived for the previous seven years. James Michell
ran the National Hotel tavern and boarding house in Queen's
Road.

William Vincent Sage was probably the man listed as H.V. Sage.
He ran the British Queen Tavern and provided boarding accommodation for sailors. He too, when he died, left his estate to his
female Chinese companion and a young girl who may have been
their offspring.

Henry Edward Hoey was involved with the Fortune Of War
Tavern and with the Victoria Hotel and its associated billiard
rooms. Henry Winniberg was Polish, but he ran the popular
British Hotel, billiard rooms, and dealt in wines, beer and spirits.

Presumably many of the fellow volunteers of these early Hong
Kong tavern keepers were also their friends and customers.
Schoolmaster, Joseph Thornton, must have known his way
around the town's pubs as he eventually had to be dismissed for
what were described as 'irregular habits'. Another schoolmaster,
James Henry Stanhope, had no such problems, operating a school
in Wellington Street before becoming, in 1854, a clerk in the

Registrar's office. He also published a short-lived newspaper called *The Spectator*.

Frederick William Lawrence was a businessman linked to a variety of firms, mostly involving Americans, which suggests that he himself was American. One of those with whom he was at one stage involved, through the company of Drinker and Co., was fellow volunteer John Martin Armstrong.

Douglas Lapraik was an influential and popular businessman in the early history of Hong Kong. Basically a watch and chronometer maker, he became involved in a variety of ventures, including the founding of the shipping firm of Lapraik and Company which principally served Amoy and Formosa. When he died in England in 1870, his Hong Kong estate was valued at the huge sum, for the time, of $350,000. The ornate Lapraik Castle, now part of University Hall, still stands in Pokfulam. William Davis was one of his clerks.

Another notable businessman was John Lamont. He began life as a ship's carpenter, but built up a large fortune with shipyards at East Point and later at Aberdeen — where the huge New Hope Granite Dock was constructed, together with all the necessary ancillary services and equipment. Samuel Appleton worked with him as a shipwright and clerk.

The name Gibb was famous on the China coast and there were several members of the family in Hong Kong when the Volunteers were formed in 1854. The man listed as H.M. Gibb could have been Hugh Bold Gibb, who became a partner in Gibb, Livingstone and Company the following year. He was described as a 'model representative of an English merchant and English gentleman.' Jameson Elles, rather than Ellis, also worked for Gibb Livingstone, though he subsequently went into business on his own and went bankrupt at Amoy. H.H. Hunt was probably William Henry Hunt, another Gibb Livingstone man.

Certainly a merchant, though not, perhaps, quite such a gentleman as Gibb, was George Duddell, who had a finger in an enormous range of commercial pies. He arrived in Hong Kong in 1844 and was soon in business dabbling in opium and auctioneering. He had a sideline in horse trading and, commented one newspaper: 'Mr Duddell is an old and conspicuous sinner in regard to furious driving and riding.' That does not seem to have counted against him, for on the death of another of the first Volunteers, Charles Markwick, he took over in 1857 as government auctioneer. His enterprise was unrestricted by the appointment, and he continued, in addition to running auctions, to operate a bakery, a ship supply business and even to become involved in the supply of tombstones. More than one commentator recorded Duddell's 'love of gain.' He is commemorated today in Duddell Street, Central.

Frederick Duddell was George's brother and he too was active in the young colony's commercial life, as an auctioneer and storekeeper and opening an hotel in Macau. His wife ran a millinery and haberdashery shop in Queen's Road. George Logan was a hair cutter and perfume supplier. Robert Gordon worked as a clerk and later may have been manager or steward of the Hong Kong Club.

Charles Markwick was first noted as being in business in Canton in 1837, trading, auctioneering and running passage boats. He appears to have come to Hong Kong soon after the founding of the colony, and is recorded as being an auctioneer with his own rooms. He became Government Auctioneer and in 1857 was strangled in his bed, probably by his own servant. Richard Markwick (Junior) was Charles' brother and he too was an auctioneer before he joined the Chinese Imperial Maritime Customs where he had a long and distinguished career.

Given that Hong Kong was a port above all else, it is not surprising that many of the names on the list of the 99 are connected with shipping, ship-building and ship supply. David Dick was a shipwright and blacksmith, carrying on a shipsmithing and farrier business in a forge at the back of the auction mart in Queen's Road.

William Ross was another shipwright, with a yard in Spring Gardens, Wanchai. George Harper had his shipwright's premises near the present Theatre Lane in Central.

Frederick S. Pedder was the son of Lieutenant William Pedder, the Harbourmaster, and he spent some time in the Harbourmaster's Office and as a civil servant before going into business. Edmund Rufus Michell was another man involved with the Harbourmaster's Office where he served as a clerk under Captain Pedder and worked his way up to become Harbourmaster and Marine Magistrate. William Henry Sutton, listed in the 99 as M.H. Sutton, was a sailmaker.

From its earliest days, Hong Kong has had a flourishing and vigorous press and several of the first Volunteers (such as Bevan, mentioned earlier) were connected with newspapers and book-binding.

There were two men called Lemon in the mid-1850s, which makes identification of the name listed as J. Lemon difficult, as both John and James were bookbinders. However, in 1855, John Lemon disposed of his business to Tomas Spence who soon after-wards disposed of it to his Chinese assistant.

Robert Strachan published the *Hong Kong Register* newspaper from 1849–60 and, although he was nominally editor, he was mainly concerned with the business aspects of its affairs. The newspaper was an ascerbic critic of the government and a fierce rival of the *China Mail*.

Merchant Yorrick Jone Murrow founded and edited the *Daily Press*. Though this involved him in a hectic series of disputes, and even jail for libel, he was also interested in numerous other ac-tivities — including the coolie trade, which he eventually op-posed and campaigned against. Murrow had been charged with abduction and slavery, and fined in connection with the coolie trade. It is interesting to note, in view of the absence of Jardines men from the 99, that Murrow had a particular grudge against that firm.

Henry Ferne Edwards was a commission merchant and, for a short period, managed the affairs of the *Friend of China* newspaper. Andrew Scott Dixson came to Hong Kong to work for Shortrede and acted as foreman, general manager and assistant editor of the *China Mail*. At the same time, on his own account, he published *Dixson's Hong Kong Recorder*. He eventually took over the firm of Shortrede. He was a crusading editor who fought for the rights of the Chinese population.

Another old firm, which failed in the mid-1860s, was Lindsay and Company. In 1854, Alexander Michie was listed as a clerk with the firm and he was a partner when it failed. He was a pioneer in visiting Cheefoo and was a member of the first expedi-tion to the Upper Yangtze when the gorges were first passed. Later he became a newspaper editor in Tientsin and wrote a book deal-ing forcibly with the opium and missionary questions.

Hugh Reinhardt was also involved with Lindsay and Com-pany. In 1851, he was listed as a clerk. However, later he went into government service, becoming a clerk in the Surveyor General's Office and Colonial Treasurer's Office. He acted as Auditor General. John Ashton was another Lindsay man, starting with the firm in 1852 and going into business on his own account after its failure.

The legal fraternity was also well represented in the 99. James Brown was a solicitor and Notary Public. William Hastings Alexander held a variety of appointments, including Deputy Registrar, Registrar, and Clerk of Court of the Supreme Court as well as acting Colonial Secretary for a period. Norman Ramsay Masson was also employed at the Supreme Court and served as Deputy Registrar and acting Registrar. John Smithers was a clerk, usher and bailiff at the Supreme Court. W. Moresby was a solicitor and Notary Public.

Also closely associated with the law were the magistrates and police officers of the young colony. Charles Batten Hillier has already been mentioned. He arrived with the first settlers and, in 1843, was gazetted as an assistant magistrate. He went on to hold the positions of Assistant Chief Magistrate, Chief Magistrate, Coroner and several other offices. According to a newspaper report, he came to China in his teens on board a merchant ship and gained employment with a commercial firm which soon failed. It was then that he went into the law. Eventually he was appointed British Consul in Bangkok and he died in Siam, now Thailand, in 1856.

Frederick Sowley Huffam, or Huffum, was a clerk with Drinker and Co. when he joined the Volunteers, but he later worked with the courts and became Deputy Registrar of the Supreme Court, eventually completing 23 years of government service.

Stefan Ivanovitch, or Yvanovich, was a European Usher in the Chief Magistrate's Office. He came from a Macau family, but the name suggests a Russian origin. Alexandre Grandpre also came from a Macau family and in 1845 was listed as a clerk in Hong Kong. At the time he joined the Volunteers he was a clerk in the Colonial Secretary's office, but in 1856 he became Acting Superintendent of Police. He continued his association with the police from then on. Something of a stir was caused in 1856 when his wish to marry in the Roman Catholic church was turned down on the grounds that he was a Freemason. He was married in St John's Cathedral instead.

James Collins was another Volunteer involved in law enforcement, serving as Magistracy clerk and gaoler. Charles Collins also served with the Magistracy, though it is not known whether the two men were related.

Other Volunteers included W.W. Shaw, a clerk; Thomas Dick, a court interpreter who later became Commissioner of Customs at Ichang; George Norris, clerk, auctioneer and shopkeeper; Charles Frederick Otto Broderson, clerk and later partner in the firm of Wm. Pustau and Co; Edward and Phillip Cohen who both worked with the Jewish firm of Philips, Moore and Co; Frederick Horsen Block who worked with the Danish firm of Burd, Lange and Co; Ernest Oppert, who worked with Meyer, Scheffer and Co; Richard Harvey Crackenthorp, Chief Clerk at the Post Office and, for a time, Acting Post Master; William S. Chapman was working in the Harbour Master's and Marine Magistrate's Office when he became a Volunteer though he later became Post Master General; Charles Smith, undertaker and sexton; James Marshall, clerk with Holliday, Wise and Co; Luiz Barros who was involved with the P and O Steam Navigation Co; David King Mason was a clerk with the same company; Robert Reinaeker was a civil servant who worked with the Colonial Treasury as accountant and book-keeper; Joao Hyndman was a clerk with the Superintendent of Trade in 1854; Henry Marsh was a shopkeeper, milliner, saddler and mercer; James Alfred Brooks was another auctioneer and general businessman; There were two F. McQueens in Hong Kong in 1854, one a clerk with Lyall, Still and Co. and the other a ship's captain; Ricardo Homen Carvalho was secretary of the Hong Kong Club.

There are more names on the list of the 99 but for some no records exist, and for others, it is not possible to make definite identifications.

The original 99 were joined by others keen to volunteer their services and the strength of the force soon stood at 127, of whom 92 were British, 16 Portuguese, and the remainder of European nationalities.

Training started in a burst of enthusiasm with meetings almost every night and a variety of equipment that included converted flintlock muskets and old bayonets without scabbards, provided from army stores.

The disputatious nature of the Hong Kong community is recorded in the letter columns of local newspapers where correspondents aired their views on various matters relating to the Volunteers.

'One of the Enrolled Volunteers' objected to a statement by Caine that the colony was in a defenceless state. Some might agree, he said, and:

It may be they are right in thus arguing; but, one of the old school as I profess to be, I can but say that I think the precedent of such a notice a dangerous one, and one which should not have been resorted to until all other means had failed ... It would have been quite time enough to guard against "the defencelessness" when the Colonists indicated their belief they were indeed in such a predicament; in which belief, I beg to assure you, I do not rest.

Others waxed poetic:

The Hong Kong Volunteers

What is that gallant band we met,
With musket and with bayonet,
All marching through the rain and wet?
    The Volunteers.

Night after night, devoted men,
Leaving their pleasure or their pen,
Their welkin make to ring again.
    These Volunteers.

With 'Shoulder arms', 'about', 'present',
'Present by way of compliment',
'At ease' — left knee a little bent
    These Volunteers

Me thinks there gleams from every eye,
In speech erst heard in Italy,
'Tis sweet pro patria mori.'
    O Volunteers.

Ye lazy loons, of spirit poor,
Who loll and criticise; I'm sure
No wonder 'tis ye can't endure
    The Volunteers

While you lie snugly in your beds
Others may labour in your steads
Avaunt. Hide your diminished heads
    Non-Volunteers

The ladies e'en at once decide
T'eschew their walk or ride, or drive
And send their lords with honest pride
    As Volunteers

Horde of degenerates, beware,
'None but the brave deserves the fair',
Then come; your proper burden bear
    As Volunteers

Another observer viewed a parade of the Volunteers held on 12 August. The weather was very hot and, not surprisingly perhaps, only a third of the corps turned out. The commentator said it had been reported that Colonel Caine had said he was satisfied at the progress made in drill and that their firing was very soldier-like. Such progress had been made that it would henceforth be necessary only to meet once a week, on Saturday evening.

A supposed conversation then followed between Mrs Harris and Mrs Gamp. These were two comic gossipers invented by Charles Dickens in his novel 'Martin Chuzzlewitt' and great favourites with the public at the time.

Mrs Harris: Dear Me, Sara! If that isn't the Hon. Lieut. Governor, a-inspecting of the Hong Kong volunteers — what a pity it is that, owing to the weather — or its not being generally known that the Hon Lieut. Governor would be on the ground, only twenty three of the corps have turned out.

Mrs Gamp: Hush! There's the Hon. Lieut. Guv'nor a-going to address the 'Dear Gentlemen' of the corps. Now, Do you hear that? 'Beautiful evolution — satisfaction at progress in drill — firing very Soldier like — colony under great obligations — promptitude in coming forward to repel the Rooshans — services in defence — drilled so well once a week will do now — every Saturday!

Mrs Harris: La! Sara, what a bee hut te full speech — how proud the Volunteers must be of such an address! Isn't that Lieut. Buggins? La! Let us ask him to come and have a cup of tea, and write a paragraph for the Register. Well, I didn't think they'd have mustered so strong as twenty three, there was only fifteen on the ground last time — but I suppose the extra number know'd the Colonel was a-coming!

The Volunteers were far from satisfied with the state of the parade ground, which was roughly at the site of the present-day Hilton Hotel. One complained:

On Tuesday evening last, when hurrying to the Artillery ground, the drum having already beat to quarters, I was making as usual for the old footpath, when judge my terror and surprise to find myself suddenly up to my neck (nearly) in water, and looking up, perceived a perfect lake extending all around. Being an 'old soldier' (though I may say a young man), my first thoughts were for my ammunition — which Cromwell recommended should always be kept dry, — and this with difficulty I succeeded in preserving before extricating myself.

Several other Volunteers came up just then, who in their anxiety to get across (evidently they were no sailors), proposed we should make a raft of our muskets. This was however overruled, it having been argued they would not float; on which some started on the long voyage round by Murray battery, while others, still more daring, (myself amongst the number), attempted the North-west passage; and I am happy to say we all fortunately succeeded in reaching the Old Commisariat — just as drill finished — without any serious accident.

From the unaccountable absence of Colonel Griffin and all his junior officers that evening, we were afraid some casualty had happened to some of them in their attempts to cross the lake, and which might have resulted in an inquest; but as several green spots were (by the aid of a powerful glass) observed in various parts of the lake, it is to be hoped they succeeded in reaching dry land.

On first arriving at our destination, we thought of making application to our brother Volunteer, Mr Hillier, lately appointed an Executive Councilor; but he appeared so intent on the duty that he was engaged in, that we hesitated to disturb him, lest he might mistake us for Russians — and make a charge upon us. However, as he is said to be a reformer of colonial abuses, it is to be hoped in his Legislative capacity he will 'bring in an Ordinance' either for the establishment of a ferry across the marsh in question, or for its drainage, otherwise it may find him employment as joint Coroner.

Despite this and other protests, nothing seems to have been done about the parade ground that summer.

While the Volunteers were drilling and the fleet was searching for the Russians, the opposite shore to Hong Kong Island was in turmoil. A band, associated with the Tai Pings had seized Kowloon City. The attack went in between seven and eight o'clock, one morning in the middle of August 1854, with thrusts being made simultaneously at the North and West gates and a fort falling soon afterwards.

Caine reported in a despatch of 21 August that it seemed that the attackers were nearly all Hakka, most of whom were stonecutters from Hong Kong and nearby, and all of whom were associated with the Triads. Advance warning of the attack had been given and most of the Imperial officials had withdrawn. The garrison commandant and one other remained as the attack went in but eventually 'both saved their lives by flight'. Caine noted, 'The object of the insurgents appears to be merely plunder; they do not belong either to the rebels at Nanking or to those about Canton.'

Twelve of the attackers were said to have been killed in the attack, while three of the Imperial defenders were killed and 15 wounded. The inhabitants of the city were told that if they did not assist the garrison, they and their property would be protected but, in fact, the place was thoroughly looted: 'Pigs, poultry and even dogs were seized for food.' Caine said he had had advance warning of the attack and had stepped up police and military guards: 'Here in Victoria all was quiet and peaceable.' In early September, he reported that the insurgents had quarrelled amongst themselves and had withdrawn, with the city being back in Imperial hands.

By the latter part of 1854, enthusiasm for the Volunteers was already beginning to fade as the Russian threat came to be less of a concern. An auxiliary police force had a short-lived existence, 76 men being recruited in June only to be disbanded the following month. Not long afterwards the Volunteers were also disbanded.

Worries over manning the defences of Hong Kong did not entirely abate though, and in 1855 there was a plan to raise two extra battalions (500 men each) of the Royal Malta Fencibles, one for service in Malta and the other in Hong Kong. Fencible troops were normally liable to serve only in their home posting. However, this plan would have seen volunteers receive special incentives and pay.

The *China Mail* was most unimpressed: 'A corps of Maltese will be worse than useless as soldiers, except in proving that it is not military but naval protection that we require, or rather the protection of armed vessels independent of the navy.'

Nothing came of the plan.

It was significant that the civilian soldiers of 1854 were raised as Volunteers and not, as some suggested should be the case, as militia. The important point being that Volunteers are just that — while a militia implies the involvement of all able-bodied men with an element of compulsion. The Hong Kong Volunteers of 1854 preceded by five years the great volunteer movement of 1859 in Britain.

A probable influence on public opinion in Hong Kong leading

to the decision to set up a volunteer force was the establishment, and blooding in battle, of a similar corps in Shanghai earlier in 1854.

Shanghai, long an important settlement near the mouth of the Yangtze had been officially opened as a treaty port in 1843. By the mid-1850s the turmoil of the surrounding area was causing grave concern to the traders in their settlement on the banks of the Huangapu River. Like Hong Kong, the foreign community was very small. With the exception of the missionaries and the Parsee merchants, nearly all worked for trading firms.

A small ad hoc volunteer force had been formed as early as 1851, when residents had organized themselves to withstand 'the aggressiveness of certain Fokienese.' The Cantonese and Fukienese sailors and tradesmen who had established themselves at Shanghai were a turbulent crowd, and in frequent conflict with the Imperial officials there. It seems that there was friction with foreigners which came to a head at the Fives Court, where the gentlemen would gather to play the public school handball game. However, the trouble, as it affected the foreigners, blew over and the force disbanded.

The problems did not go away so far as the Imperial authorities were concerned and eventually, on 7 September 1853, a rising occurred and the Chinese city, to the south of the foreign settlement fell to the rebels. Quickly afterwards several nearby cities also fell, though the link between the rebels around Shanghai and the Tai Pings was not clearly established.

The disturbed state of the surrounding country in 1853, however, led to a meeting on 8 April at which the first steps were taken towards setting up a formal volunteer force in Shanghai. This meeting created the framework for a company of volunteers, but there was little enthusiasm to go further. Three days later a committee was set up comprising local dignitaries. The committee talked with consular and naval officials. The Americans then appointed their own committee and, on 12 April, there was a general meeting which representatives of the three consular powers — Britain, the United States and France — attended. From this meeting came the first Shanghai Volunteer Corps.

Captain Tronson, of the Second Bengal Fusiliers, was appointed commander and drill began. An initial supply of arms and ammunition was provided and, at the end of the year the rifle in use was replaced with a better weapon and bayonets were replaced by swords — perhaps in anticipation of the need for close-quarter combat.

In October, Imperial forces laid siege to the Chinese city at Shanghai. The government forces were attended by an unruly collection of camp followers and there were frequent incidents involving foreigners. The Imperial explanation was always that the authorities had no control over the people responsible. The scene was set for the 'Battle of Muddy Flat', which, in April the following year, blooded the new Volunteer force.

The year 1854 saw a third Volunteer force formed — in Singapore.

Again, the turmoil in China caused the birth of the Volunteers. As early as 1846, suggestions of forming a volunteer unit had been made during riots by Chinese. A further outbreak of rioting in 1854 lasted 10 or 12 days when certain Chinese from Fukien objected to joining in a fund-raising effort to assist rebels from Chiu Chow who had been driven out of Amoy.

Like Hong Kong, the outbreak of the Crimean War focused attention on matters of defence and this, combined with the internal disturbances, led to a public meeting on Saturday 8 July, at which it was decided to form a volunteer unit — the Singapore Rifle Corps. Thirty-two men put their names on the roll, but this figure soon grew to 61.

Despite all the worry in 1854 in the colony, Hong Kong remained relatively calm and, after all, business came first. Thus, by 1855, the Volunteers had faded quietly away.

2

The Growing Threat

THE second appearance of a volunteer movement in Hong Kong came in 1862. However, the fact that there was no volunteer force between 1854 and that year did not mean that all continued quiet in the colony.

The events which were to lead to the Second China War started only a year or so after the first Volunteers had turned their attentions back to their civilian jobs. It is important to note that Canton, although included as one of the five ports to be opened to trade under the agreement which ended the First China War had not allowed foreigners to enter the city. Such rights of entry had been promised in 1849, but not yet acted upon because the citizens were so anti-foreigner, the Chinese officials said. This rankled in Hong Kong and in the other treaty ports and was one of the reasons for the adoption of a hard line in the troubles to come.

In October 1856, Chinese officials searching for pirates boarded a lorcha named the *Arrow* at Canton. A lorcha was a curious mixture of a Western-type hull and Chinese sails. The *Arrow* had a Chinese owner, resident in Hong Kong, and a Chinese crew. It had been registered in the colony, thus acquiring British protection — though it subsequently turned out that this registration had lapsed. In the confusion of the search, it was claimed that the British flag was hauled down. The British Consul at Canton, Harry Parkes, and Sir John Bowring, British Plenipotentiary as well as Governor of Hong Kong, responded, demanding an apology.

When no apology was forthcoming, Canton was bombarded by a Royal Navy ship moored in the river. Eventually, following skirmishes, the British landed and, on 29 October marched through the city to the yamen, or office, of the Governor of Kwangtung. Incensed, the people of Canton attacked the 'factories', long the centre of foreign trade, and burnt them to the ground on 14 and 15 December.

The overbearing attitude of Bowring and Parkes came in for severe criticism at home, with Gladstone leading the attack. The government lost a vital vote and a general election resulted. Palmerston made much of the importance of protecting British honour and interests overseas and was returned to power. Public opinion in Hong Kong was firmly behind the adoption of a hard line.

Lord Elgin was sent to lead an expedition to China to seek redress. He was to demand reparations, that the provisions of the treaties be observed, diplomatic presence at Peking and the opening of further cities to foreign trade. The French, with their own grievances, decided to join the expedition.

Elgin and his force arrived in Hong Kong in July 1857, only to find that the Indian mutiny had broken out. This caused a delay in operations. In December, however, Canton was stormed and the city remained under allied administration for the next three years.

Negotiations took place at Tientsin and this resulted in the 1858 Treaty of Tientsin, which contained provisions on the right of a British minister to reside in Peking, rights of foreign travel in China, the opening up of new ports on the Yangtze River and the payment of an indemnity. The treaty, it was agreed, would be ratified a year later and British troops withdrew from the north of China.

However, the story was far from over. Frederick Bruce, Elgin's brother became British Envoy Extraordinary and Minister Plenipotentiary. He arrived in China in May 1859, to ratify the treaty, only to find that the Chinese were unwilling to allow him to travel to Peking, insisting rather that the matter should be dealt with at Shanghai. An angry Bruce quickly set off with troops and ships for Peking. Rejecting a request on his arrival at the Pei-ho river to take a circuitous route he tried to force a way past the obstructions in the water. The ships became stranded and stuck on mud banks, on 25 June 1859, the Taku forts had sitting targets before them and they opened up — causing 434 casualties, sinking four ships and badly damaging another two. Among those seriously wounded was the British admiral.

Bruce was censured for being so headstrong, but the British were determined to ratify the treaty at Peking. Lord Elgin was recalled to lead a second expedition to China, and again, the French sent a considerable force. Elgin, with 41 warships, 143 transports and 11,000 soldiers pushed north. Soon he was in Peking where, in reprisal for the capture and deaths of allied personnel carrying a flag of truce, and in a bid to affect the Emperor directly, he burnt the Summer Palace.

The Convention of Peking of 1860 established firmly the British right to a diplomatic presence in the capital, increased the indemnity and opened up Tientsin. Importantly for Hong Kong, the Kowloon Peninsula was ceded to Britain. Also ceded was Stonecutters Island on which defences were erected. The island was to remain an important military area for a century and a half and was to become well-known to Volunteers in years to come.

In Hong Kong, the events in China were followed with intense and understandable interest. As the major staging post for the expeditionary force, the colony was full of soldiers and the harbour full of ships. It was in 1858 that the military suggested that the Kowloon peninsula be taken for defensive reasons. Bowring supported this. Pointing south across the narrow stretch of water to the city of Hong Kong, Kowloon had long been viewed with covetous eyes by those looking for expansion and it was regularly visited by sportsmen and hunters.

After Bruce's setback at the Taku forts, the forces gathered for the final attack on Peking had camped at Kowloon and several illustrations depict the tents spread across the peninsula.

As ever, great concern remained in the small foreign ocommunity in Hong Kong about the potential for trouble in the Chinese community. Just a few weeks after the attack on Canton and the burning down of the foreign factories in response, the *Friend of China* newspaper expressed worries about the potential for chaos. An attempt had been made to kill Europeans by poisoning bread, the police were weak in number and criticised as ineffective. Dire threats were issuing from the authorities at Canton.

What would happen, the paper asked, if an order came from Canton to servants in Hong Kong to poison their employers — backed up by threats against families in China. 'How many of our servants do you think would have enough nerve to disobey the proclamations coming as they always do with "tremble and obey".' The paper called for a pass system to be instituted in order to drive out bad characters. If any were found after the introduction of such a scheme, 'Make an example for the rest. A few hangings in the cross roads would soon give encouragement to the well disposed, and strike terror into the hearts of those who designate us barbarians.' Many letters to the press reflected this sense of fear and worry.

In the United Kingdom, the seeds of the great Volunteer movement were starting to grow and so it was natural that this, combined with the worry about local conditions, should lead to the possibility of the re-establishment of a Volunteer force being raised. Sir John Bowring, concerned at the weakening of the garrison in Hong Kong by operations against Canton suggested that the Volunteers be revived, 'but every attempt to effect this object has proved an utter failure.'

Another attempt to get the civilians back into uniform was made in 1859 when news reached Hong Kong of the disaster at the Taku forts, but Caine who, though soon to retire, was temporarily in charge of the government, was against a revival of the force of which he had been Colonel. His attitude was that the police had been strengthened enough to handle any trouble. If it turned out that they could not, only then would he think about raising a volunteer force.

It was not until 1862 that the idea of volunteering became popular again. In Britain at about this time, relations with France had rapidly deteriorated to such an extent that influential opposition to volunteer forces had weakened. Public meetings had been held and there was strong support in the counties for setting up such forces. *The Times* commented:

There can only be one true defence of a nation like ours — a large and permanent Volunteer Force, supported by the spirit and patriotism of our younger men, and gradually indoctrinating the country with military knowledge. We are the only people in the world who do not have such a force. We want men of ordinary occupation, trained by a certain amount of skill, to support the regular force either in the field or in the fortress.

Eventually, officialdom came to appreciate this view and arrangements were made to lay down guidance and regulations for the new volunteer forces. By February 1859, there was already an 'unofficial' enrollment of more than 60,000 volunteers and a year later there were 130,000.

Hong Kong newspapers carried column after column of 'News From Home' and, therefore, note was taken of these developments.

The Colonial Office was keen to see this renewed Volunteer enthusiasm spread to the colonies and, in 1860, there was press discussion of the possibility of setting up a new Hong Kong force. However, this came to nothing.

As is so often the case, it took the enthusiasm of an individual to get the project under way. Captain Frederick Brine was a Royal Engineers officer with a personal enthusiasm for volunteer forces. It was he who revived the volunteer spirit in Shanghai in 1861. He was also to be involved in the formation of Volunteer units in Hankow and Yokohama.

In 1862 he arrived in Hong Kong and the volunteer movement had someone to fan the flames of enthusiasm. A public meeting was held at the Supreme Court on March 1 at which the enthusiastic audience agreed that a volunteer force should be set up.

A short time later the Governor, Sir Hercules Robinson, was penning a despatch to the Secretary of State for the Colonies, attached to which was Ordinance Number Two of 1862 authorising the enrolment of such a force.

This Ordinance was submitted by me to the Legislative Council in consequence of my receiving a representation signed by upwards of 100 British residents here expressing their desire to form themselves into a Corps for the protection of the Colony and requesting me to legalize the movement.

The Volunteers have since the passing of the Ordinance determined to form themselves into an Artillery Corps, and I am happy to be able to report that they are devoting themselves with zeal and assiduity to drill.

The ordinance was significant, for it was to form the basis, a decade later, for the establishment of a volunteer tradition in Hong Kong which was to then continue unbroken. The ordinance, dated 17 March 1862, stated:

No. 2 of 1862

An Ordinance to authorize the Enrollment of a Volunteer Force.
17th March, 1862.

Be it enacted by His Excellency the Governor of Hongkong, with the Advice of the Legislative Council thereof, as follows:

1. Such and so many of the Inhabitants of Hongkong as shall volunteer and offer themselves, and as His Excellency the Governor shall approve of, shall be permitted to form themselves into a Corps for the Protection of the Colony of Hongkong, and such Corps shall be called the 'HONGKONG VOLUNTEERS' and shall continue so formed during the Pleasure of His Excellency the Governor; such Volunteers shall be

instructed in the Use of the rifle and the Management of Artillery, and be subject to drill accordingly.

2. The Governor shall appoint such Commissioned Officers as to him shall seem proper for such Corps.

3. The Commanding Officer of the Corps shall appoint the necessary non-Commissioned officers.

4. The Commanding Officer of the Corps shall, as soon as he conveniently can do so, frame such Rules as he may deem proper for regulating the Period of Enrollment, Arms, Dress, Acoutrements, and Equipment, of the said Corps and of the Members thereof, which Rules may be enforced by reasonable Fines and Penalties for Breach thereof; and he shall from Time to Time alter and vary such Rules and Penalties as to him shall seem fit.

5. All such Rules and Alterations of Rules shall be submitted from Time to Time to His Excellency the Governor, and shall not have any Force until confirmed by him; and all such Rules as shall be so made or altered, and as shall be so confirmed, shall have the same Force for the Regulation of the Members of the said Corps as if the same Rules so confirmed had been inserted in, and had formed part of this Ordinance.

6. All Fines inflicted under or by virtue of any Rule when so confirmed as aforesaid, shall be recoverable and be enforced before and by a Police Magistrate in like Manner as Fines imposed by such Magistrate are now recoverable and enforceable respectively.

7. After the Promulgation of such Rules as aforesaid, the Commanding Officer shall admit Volunteers from Time to Time and enroll them as Members of the Corps.

8. Every Volunteer being a Christian upon being admitted shall subscribe his Name on the Roll of the said Corps, and shall take before a Justice of the Peace an Oath according to the Form following:–
I A.B. do promise and swear that I will be faithful and bear true Allegiance to Her Majesty Queen Victoria, and that I will faithfully serve in the 'Volunteer Force' during the Term of my Enrollment: So help me God.

And every Volunteer not being a Christian shall make a Declaration according to the Form following:–
I A.B. do solemnly, sincerely, and truly declare that I will be faithful and bear true Allegiance to Her Majesty Queen Victoria, and that I will faithfully serve in the 'Volunteer Force', during the Term of my Enrollment.

L. Almada E. Castro
Clerk of Councils.

An address presented to the Governor, Sir Hercules Robinson, on his departure on leave in July 1862, and looking forward to his return, listed the members of the new body. The officers were:

Fred. Brine, Captain and Commandant
Wm. Kane, Captain
R.B. Baker, Lieutenant
Jno. Dodd, Lieutenant and Adjutant
J. Frazer, Lieutenant (Absent in Shanghai)

Brine was appointed as Commandant while the other officers were elected by members of the Corps.

Provision of arms and equipment caused problems. The Volunteers had decided to equip themselves at their own expense but were not sure as to what would suit best. In the meantime, 120 stands of arms were lent from military stores to allow training to continue, and a basement room in Murray Barracks which had been condemned, was made available as an armoury.

For some reason, the Brigadier General, who was then out of Hong Kong, was incensed at this and demanded that the arms be returned to store and the use of the room withdrawn. The Governor was puzzled, as were other military officers. He said that the arms had already been issued to the Volunteers and that they were not be be withdrawn pending a decision from London, as to do so would at once put an end to the Volunteer movement in the colony.

The Brigadier General, in Shanghai, was unimpressed and was of the view that every weapon in the colony would be required by regular troops in the coming summer. A brave Lieutenant Colonel Moody, RE, commanding the garrison in Hong Kong, wrote back to Shanghai seeking clarification. Obviously, he was unimpressed by a precedent which had been quoted at him: 'I would also submit for the information of the Brigadier that a decision formed at one time may have to be revised from later circumstances.' He went on: 'At the present time, when the garrison of Hong Kong has been so much reduced, it is a questionable policy not to offer every facility to a Volunteer movement that has received the support of H.M. Government at home, and in the colonies.'

Eventually, word came through from London that the Volunteers should be assisted. The Brigadier, Stavely, received a rap over the knuckles from the War Office: 'You would have done better in the circumstances had you waited the arrival of the reference made to the Secretary of State for his sanction of the proceeding instead of then pre-emptively directing the immediate return of the articles.'

The Rules and Regulations of the Volunteers laid down the structure of the new body. The title was to be 'The Hongkong Volunteers' with the motto 'Caelum Non Animum Muto' — 'I have changed my skies but not my spirit.' Provision was made for a class of Volunteer to be known as Honorary Members. These gentlemen, on payment, in advance, of an annual subscription of $25, were to have the use of the rifle butts and targets and be eligible to take part in competitions and other activities. The working Volunteers were to be 'Effectives'. The entrance fee for Effectives was set at $5 with an annual subscription of $5 for officers, $2 for staff sergeants and $1 for the rank and file.

No member could be rated as Effective unless he attended, properly armed and accoutred, on the muster or exercises of the corps an aggregate of 24 days a year and was certified as having passed his drill.

Any individual wishing to join the Volunteers after 1 June 1862, had to be proposed by an Effective member and would only be admitted on the approval of the commanding officer.

A schedule of fines was set down:

For discharging a rifle accidentally, $1.

For pointing the same, loaded or not loaded, at any person except in the discharge of his duty, $5.

For being found with a loaded rifle and in uniform, and when not on duty or at target practices, $5.

For firing a rifle in uniform, after the corps has been dismissed parade, $1.

For firing during practice from a point not ordered as a practice station, $1.

For non-attendance at parade or drill, when summoned by the Commanding Officer, within 10 minutes of the time appointed, unless satisfactory cause of absence be shown, $1.

For making improper use of the sword bayonet, $1.

For talking in the ranks, for each offence 50 cents.

Volunteers could discharge themselves after 14 days' notice, providing a state of war did not exist. An annual general meeting of the Corps was to be held in the first week of March each year for the purpose of transacting the non-military business of the Volunteers. The property of the corps was legally vested in the Commanding Officer, but a committee to aid him in the management of the finances and other civil business was to be appointed. This committee was to consist of the Captain, Officers, and seven other Effective members who would be elected by ballot.

These regulations were signed by Frederick Brine and confirmed by the Governor, Sir Hercules Robinson.

The Volunteers initially consisted of a battery of artillery. A 'Return of Artillery Corps', dated 24 June 1862, showed the date of formation as 7 April. There were 123 officers and men, three horses, and no field artillery guns, though training may have been going on at the fixed defences of the various forts. The Volunteers were training four days a week. It was noted that the unit was, 'In want of an Artillery drill instructor and a light rifled field battery.' In December 1862 a band was formed.

In 1863, a rifle corps was added. In February 1863, the government sanctioned, provided there were at least 75 effective members of the corps, an annual outlay of 195 pounds.

The first formal appearance in public of the Volunteers came on 16 February 1863, when the colours were presented by Mrs W.T. Mercer. The wife of the commandant presented a silver bugle to the corps and Bishop Smith, Bishop of Hong Kong, acted as honorary chaplain. A successful dinner followed at St Andrew's School, presided over by Mr Mercer.

Interestingly, at about the same time, foreign residents of Canton were said also to have taken up volunteering and formed a rifle company which seemed to have been attached in some way to the Hong Kong Volunteers. The strength of the corps was said to be 267 all ranks, with the Canton detachment providing 91 of this total.

Though enthusiasm among the volunteers themselves was high, it seems that few of the business houses of the colony looked with much enthusiasm on seeing their staff go off to military duties.

In April 1863, a rifle competition was organized and there was a big parade in celebration of the Queen's birthday the following month.

In 1864, the Volunteers received an invitation from the Governor of Macau to visit the Portuguese colony. This invitation was quickly taken up and, such was its significance as evidence of the friendship between the two colonies, that a full report appeared in the *Illustrated London News*.

The Volunteers landed on 19 November, bringing with them a field battery of three-pounders. Major Brine and the other officers stepped ashore and were received with every honour. With the band in front they then marched to the Governor's Palace to salute him, receiving in return a salute from the San Franciso Fort.

In the evening a social gathering with the Portuguese residents took place on the parade ground and the hotel in which the Volunteers were staying was brilliantly illuminated. The next morning, there was a church service at the Protestant Chapel, officiated by the Honorary Chaplain of the Corps, the Revd T. Stringer. In the afternoon there was a lavish dinner in a pavilion erected on the parade ground and presided over by the Governor, Brigadier J.R. Coelho do Amaral. He proposed the health of the Hong Kong volunteers and this was returned by Major Brine.

The pavilion was a large rectangular structure, hung with flowers and surmounted with flags, complete with a banner extolling the Volunteers. Many other toasts followed and in the evening there was an impressive display of fireworks.

Back in Hong Kong, rivalry in rifle competitions was keen and training continued. In 1864, the Governor presented a cup to the Corps to be competed for each year. However, the first winner, H.J.H. Tripp, apparently took it back to the United Kingdom on departure from the colony. It was returned in 1931 but was lost during the Japanese occupation.

In December 1864, the Volunteers were called out for the first time. Despite all the long-expressed misgivings about the potential for trouble amongst the Chinese community, it was, in fact, rioting involving Europeans which caused the call out.

The doings of governors, generals and businessmen, often receive the most attention, but in the early 1860s there was a major problem involving the often unacknowledged European working class in Hong Kong. In the tough business of shipping, owners were, and are, always looking to reduce costs and thus undercut the rates of their rivals. In the 1860s, companies started to employ Malay seamen who were far cheaper than their European counterparts. In days without any social welfare that meant that several hundred western sailors found themselves beached without any means of support. Understandably, tensions ran high.

On 12 September 1864, there was a terrible fight when European sailors attacked a boarding house in Hollywood Road which was occupied by Malays. A number of deaths resulted, including three Europeans. Off-duty soldiers of the 99th Regiment and some policemen joined in the disturbance and more deaths resulted. With the police themselves involved in the fighting, a third force was needed to restore order. Instructions were given on 15 September that the 99th should move out to a quickly erected camp at Kowloon. The Volunteers were called out to mount guards over the camp and a week later they were ordered to patrol the streets to calm public opinion.

The Volunteers were involved at this time in an incident which gives a fascinating insight into how the social distinctions were maintained in a small community thousands of miles away from home.

As one wag has pointed out, 'The important thing about a British club is not who you let in but who you keep out.' That was certainly the case so far as the Hong Kong Club was concerned in 1864. The club was then situated in Queen's Road, between Wyndham Street and D'Aguilar Street, offering accommodation, food and drink to such as were fit to receive it.

On 14 September, the Volunteers fell out in front of the club, hot and tired after duty in the riots. Some Volunteers were members of the club and so, quite naturally, invited their friends who were not, inside for a drink. Well, any right-thinking Englishman would know that this was quite beyond the pale. The outraged club members were horrified to see dusty non-members inside the hallowed halls and hooted them out of the club. 'There ensued an extraordinary amount of animosities which for a long time after this incident lacerated social life within and without the club.' Perhaps this incident had something to do with a falling off of enthusiasm for Volunteering which set in soon afterwards.

The colony had plenty to worry about at that time. Sir Hercules Robinson had left in early 1865 and, in the interim, the administration was in the hands of W.T. Mercer, the Colonial Secretary. Mercer was a man bitter at having missed out on his own governorship and the new Governor, Sir Richard Graves Macdonnell, found an almost chaotic situation confronting him on his arrival in Hong Kong in March 1866. There were problems with pirates, with the police, with public health and sanitation, with water supply and with general administration.

A significant recession had started both in the United Kingdom and in Hong Kong. The great commercial house of Dent and Company, so significant in the first Volunteers, was heading towards a disastrous end. Banks began to fail and government revenue dried up as land sales practically stopped. Against this background it is not surprising that the Volunteer spirit began to weaken.

In January 1865, the man who had done so much to get the Volunteers going again, Major Brine, left. He was replaced by Major Scott, of the 22nd Regiment. For one reason or another the new commandant did not inspire such enthusiasm as his predecessor and attendances began to fall off. Major Scott soon moved on.

On Saturday 26 May, official notification appeared in the *Government Gazette* of the winding up of the Hong Kong Volunteer Corps with effect from 31 May. The notice said the Governor had accepted the resignation of commissions from Captain and Acting Commandant, H. Cohen, Captain and Adjutant H.J.H Tripp, Lieutenant T.G. Linstead and Second Lieutenant F.I. Hazeland.

Tribute was paid to 'the zeal and patriotic spirit' by which the Volunteers were animated, and it was said that the community was under a special obligation 'to those gentlemen and to all who in similar manner expended their time, exertions and money for objects so essentially public'. No doubt, should they be needed the Volunteers would come forward again if 'any real and urgent necessity were to arise for defending, by force of arms, the rights of the Crown, or maintaining the supremacy of the law in this colony ... The Volunteers would doubtless in such emergency come to the front again more numerous and efficient than ever'.

The Shanghai Volunteer Corps was encountering its own problems and was wound up the following year, although its rifle club lived on.

3

To Assist the Regular Forces

THE third appearance of Volunteers in Hong Kong again had fears of Russian expansion at its root. In April 1877, Russia declared war on Turkey and succeeded in advancing almost as far as Constantinople. The resulting Treaty of San Stefano, of March 1878, saw the Turks accept the creation of a large Bulgarian state which, in reality, would have become a Russian vassal and an extension of its interests in the political and strategic cauldron of the Balkans. Britain, together with Austria-Hungary, was opposed to this and an international congress was held in Berlin in June 1878 at which Russia was persuaded to accept a smaller Bulgarian state.

While Hong Kong had acquired the Kowloon peninsula and Stonecutters Island through the 1860 settlement of the Second China War, Russia too had gained Chinese territory. The Russians had long been pushing into Chinese areas in Turkestan in the west and the Amur region in the east. In 1858, the Russians had intimidated the local Chinese commander into giving them territory on the north of the Amur and Sungari rivers and joint possession of the land up to the sea east of the Ussuri river. All three rivers were open only to Russian and Chinese vessels. However, the court at Peking, refused to ratify this agreement.

When, in 1860, the Ch'ing court was prostrated by the allied invaders at Peking, the Russians stepped in to the role of mediator between the two sides. Once the British and French had departed the Russians quickly demanded their reward and a Supplementary Treaty of Peking, signed in November 1860, gave Russia the ratification of the 1858 treaty — and included a vital area east of the Ussuri river to the sea. Important benefits were also gained in the west and, under 'most favoured nation' clauses, Russia reaped all the benefits of the British and French agreements with China.

The Russians quickly began to survey their new territory and the decision was made to develop a port and base known as 'Rule The East', or Vladivostok.

The port quickly became an important ice-free centre for the Russian navy and in 1872 it became the main naval base in the Pacific, taking over the role from Nikolayevsk-na-Amure nearly 800 miles to the north. By 1878 an article in the *Straits Times* pointed out that the only possible source of attack on British possessions would be Vladivostok.

The increased Russian presence in Asian waters was already cause for concern in the late 1860s and early 1870s in relation to protecting British interests, including Hong Kong. The war between Russia and Turkey, and Britain's worry about its outcome, naturally revived fears about the protection of the colony.

The strength of the garrison was summed up thus in April 1877:

At the close of last year there were at Hong Kong 107 of the Royal Artillery, 20 Royal Engineers, 935 infantry of the line, 66 of the Colonial Corps, and 18 of the Army Hospital Corps, making a total of 1,146. This year it is proposed that there be a garrison battery of Royal Artillery of 109 of all ranks, three Royal Engineers, a battalion of infantry of 916 men, two companies of Lascars of 176, and 18 of the Army Hospital Corps, making a total of 1,222.

The need to build up a strong British base in Asia was considered in an address to the Royal Colonial Institute delivered in 1873 by a Captain J.C.R. Columb. He was concerned that the colonies were widely scattered and difficult to guard against surprise attack. Worrying about the Russian threat, he advocated that 'A great Imperial dockyard' be established in the east. Some in Hong Kong hoped that any such base would be established in the colony.

Domestically, there was much concern at what came to be called a 'blockade' of Hong Kong trade by Chinese Customs. The Chinese claimed that they were losing valuable revenue due to smuggling by vessels registered in Hong Kong and revenue cruisers were operating near the colony's waters. In November 1867, a junk carrying opium was seized. Hong Kong merchants were also taking an expanding portion of the coastal trade. In 1868, marine and land customs stations were set up around Hong Kong and all vessels were subject to stop and search. This enraged public opinion in the colony — ever eager to preserve maximum freedom to produce maximum profit.

There was constant friction and irritation over the question and, in 1876, an Anglo-Chinese Commission was set up to consider the matter further. However, this soon became bogged down and the 'blockade' went on.

Against the background of fear of war with Russia and the customs ring around Hong Kong, the idea of setting up a corps of Volunteers came to the fore again.

The project was closely followed in the pages of the *Hong Kong Daily Press*. The suggestion that privateers, operating under Russian authority, might appear around Hong Kong was raised, though one correspondent thought this unlikely: 'In the former war with Russia, which took place before the Declaration of Paris and when privateering was not identical with pirating, not a single privateer appeared on the sea. If privateers did not appear in 1855, how can they in 1878?'

On 4 May 1878, an official announcement, signed by the Acting Colonial Secretary, J.M. Price, appeared in the *Daily Press*:

Volunteer Artillery Corps
Colonial Secretary's Office, Hongkong, 3rd May, 1878.

Sir, as an adjunct to the general force required for the batteries in course of organisation, I am desired by the Governor to make known through the medium of your columns, His Excellency's desire to accept the services of any of the inhabitants of Hongkong, who may be disposed to volunteer for the defence of the Colony under the previous Ordinance Number 2 of 1862 Section VIII.

Though still hopefull that the questions engaging the Imperial Government may find peaceful solution, and that it may yet be possible to avert from the mercantile community of Hongkong the self-sacrifices attendant upon military duty, the Governor deems it of no less moment that, following the example of the mother country and sister colonies, we should be prepared for any contingency that may arise.

To those who may respond to this appeal His Excellency desires me to state that the equipment of the proposed artillery corps will be defrayed by the Colonial Government, and as it is only reasonable that the intending volunteer can know beforehand what proportion of his time will be required, I am to add that he will be expected to go through a preliminary course of instruction at Wellington battery, under Royal Artillery officers, for at least two hours a day, one hour in the morning and another in the evening, until his proficiency shall admit of his being told off for duty at the particular battery to which he will be permanently assigned.

At the latter place his service will continue to be required on such days

of the week as the Military Authorities may decide, due regard being had
that the hours selected shall interfere as little as possible with his business
avocations.

A register is open at the office of the under-signed for the reception of
the names of those who may desire to enroll themselves in the corps,

J.M. Price
Acting Colonial Secretary

One wit was unimpressed by the display of martial enthusiasm
and commented:

I hear that the new Corps of Volunteers about to be raised under the
auspices of H.E. The Governor Hennessy is to be called the "Islanders." I
hear also, upon the best authority, that H.E. has raised a Brigade of
Volunteers for the laudable purpose of planting cones all over the island
and that its official name is the 'Fir Brigade.'

Prominent businessman Granville Sharp wrote in a rather more
positive vein:

The construction of the batteries and the conveyance of big guns to them
during the last few weeks has proved a source of ever increasing interest
to all classes of the community. Feelings of apprehension have been
forestalled by these timely preparations, and a sense of calm determination and quiet confidence is generally entertained. A firm belief is almost
universal among us that if Britain is, most unwillingly, compelled to draw
the sword for defence of British interests, she will, by the good help of
God, as in former times, be brought through victorious. Great sacrifice of
life and treasure may, however, be involved; and it would seem right that
we should seriously contemplate our individual duties as citizens at this
time. We may indeed be thankful that Russia has not succeeded in
preventing by her duplicity the operations of our country in any contingencies which may arise. Whilst she has been persistently crying for
peace, peace, we have for many months past been making ready for war.

Whilst, however, the naval and military authorities are thus actively
engaged, it would surely be as well that civilians should do what they
can. It is now some weeks since the governor proposed forming a Portuguese Volunteer Corps. Certainly a most excellent idea. It was not,
however, His Excellency's intention to entirely depend on them. We must
have also a British Volunteer Corps, and with contingents from our Indian
fellow subjects, and others, we might speedily raise a body of men, of all
ages, equal in number to the 74th regiment, with the Artillery and gun
lascars. However, many of the young men in the Colony are already
performing rifle practice; there is also a remnant of the old Volunteer
Corps and besides a considerable number have been drilled at home;

almost all are either young or in the prime of life, and it is to be hoped that those who are distinguished by gray hair have not lost their pluck. There is no doubt that our police force, accustomed as they are to drill would be capable of efficient service. They would be supplemented by a great number of Chinese, who would join heart and soul in the defence of their lives and property.

It is quite superfluous to enter into details as to the reasons for justification for such a movement. It should be enough for us that the Home Government has voted 6,000,000 pounds for preparatory measures; and that our own authorities are busily engaged in defensive operations.

I believe that if an assurance were given that no drill or parade would be required in the sun, there would be no lack of Volunteers in Hong Kong.

This brought a sour response from one signing himself 'Dispart' about Sharp:

What the object of the letter is I fail to see, except that he desires to air his name in your columns on the occasion of what may be called a crisis ... He goes on to tell us a lot we knew before, and winds up by saying 'I believe that if an assurance were given that no drill or parade would be required in the sun, there would be no lack of volunteers in Hong Kong.' Dear me! He, at all events, can remain at home and preserve his complexion.

The letter also expressed reservations about the invitation to men to join the proposed volunteer corps and called for a circular to be sent to the heads of the principal firms in order to encourage them to release their staff: 'Will employers as a rule agree to dispense with the services of their clerks and assistants to mount guard or man a battery, as the case may be, without being consulted in the matter?' Furthermore, 'Britishers are a minority in this place, and, always excepting men in the Government Service, three-fourths of those one meets in the streets at any hour of the day have no more interest in England than in Patagonia.'

A few days later this correspondent was back in print again castigating the government:

Do they intend to have a rifle corps, an artillery corps or only the latter? Do they intend members of the corps to be drilled morning and night, no matter at how much inconvenience to themselves, or will they allow members a little option?

... As to whether there should be a rifle and an artillery corps there can be two opinions — The Europeans for artillery and the Portugese for light infantry; the latter being peculiarly fitted by their litheness and activity for the rifles, and the former by their strength and stamina for the heavy work of artillerymen; and I may add that this is the opinion of one of the most experienced officers of artillery.

The least that should be required should be six drills a week with a fine of a dollar for every drill missed, he said, and drill sergeants should be ready to drill one batch of men at 5 am and another at 6 am.

The actual set-up of the corps was explained by the Acting Colonial Secretary:

The object in view in the formation of the corps is to impart to as many as possible sufficient military instruction to enable them to assist the regular forces in time of war or danger of attack.

For this purpose the volunteers would be expected to go through the following course of instruction.

Each member to be drilled at least once a day, either morning or evening as he may elect, for one hour in squad drill as laid down in the field exercise book, copies of which are being printed for distribution. Squads to be formed under drill instructors from regular troops.

Members will be moved progressively from squad to squad according to proficiency, and to arrive at the first squad as soon as possible should be an object of ambition of all.

After qualifying in this preliminary infantry drill, members will be instructed in gun drill, but no member will be eligible for the latter unless he shall have passed the first squad.

The first squad after completing its preliminary infantry drill will be placed under tuition of Royal Artillery non-commissioned officers under the supervision of the Officer Commanding Royal Artillery, in such numbers as he may be prepared to receive, and they will be instructed in drill of the different descriptions of guns in the command.

These artillery drills will take place daily, morning and evening, at the same hours as the preliminary drills. Members to select either the morning or evening drills as may suit their convenience.

The uniform of the corps will be supplied by the Colonial Government, and will consist of a loose fitting smock of dark blue serge with scarlet collar and cuffs, white shoulder cords, and white metal buttons. White trowsers in summer, and in winter blue serge trowsers with narrow red stripe. White pith solar helmet and pugree during the summer months, and in the winter round blue forage cap with white band. A white waist belt for ammunition pouch when necessary.

The corps will be issued with Schneider rifles and bayonets, and members will be taught the manual of firing exercises by the military drill instructors, as far as may be found practicable without undue interference with their gun drills. The manual and firing rifle drill though of importance subordinate to the artillery one, will be essential in the event of close quarters.

The Commandant and Officers will be appointed by His Excellency the Governor, and will, with the concurrence of the Officer Commanding the Forces, to be from among the regular military officers of the station.

Non-commissioned officers will be appointed by the commandant. The drill instructors will, with the concurrence of the Officer Commanding the Forces, be selected from amongst the most competent regular military non commissioned officers on the station.

The corps will be formed into companies or batteries; each company or battery to be lettered A,B,C,D, etc., according to the number of volunteers, and to have a certain number of officers and non commissioned officers.

Hours and place of parade will be duly notified to the corps. The office or orderly room will be opened at the Government Office (on the ground floor opposite the Colonial Treasury) where all the business of the corps will be transacted and all returns kept connected with its equipment and movements.

The preliminary squad drill will take place on the ground formerly the Parade Ground of the old Volunteer Corps, situated opposite the Government office. The subsequent artillery drills will take place in Wellington or Murray Batteries as the military authorities may decide.

When the Volunteer Companies shall have mastered their gun drills, they will be expected to continue them periodically by way of practice at the different batteries to which the Military Authorities may hereafter assign them.

In the event of war the corps will be placed under the orders of the Officer Commanding the Forces, to assist the regular troops in manning the guns, in guarding the fortifications, and in all artillery duties connected therewith.

The following are the batteries to which the Volunteers are liable to be detailed on duty:–

1. Belcher's Bay Battery, situated above the Western slaughter house.
2. West Point Battery, immediately above the Roman Catholic Reformatory.
3. Bonham Road Battery, above and near the Berlin Mission House.
4. Wellington Barracks Battery.
5. North Point Battery, on the road to Shaukiwan.
6. Kowloon Dock Battery, Kowloon.
7. Tsim Sha Tsui Battery, Kowloon, near the Officers' Quarters, Military Cantonments, Stonecutters Island Battery.

Until the office of the corps is opened, any further particulars which

intending volunteers may require will be furnished to them at the
Colonial Secretary's office.

Although the morning or evening drills are compulsory it is earnestly
hoped that the volunteers will make a point of attaining proficiency in
their new military duties as soon as conveniently possible by attending, if
not both, at least one drill a day.

Still the wits continued with their complaints, one Volunteer
went along to the uniform contractor in Queen's Road East, as
instructed, to collect his outfit:

Imagine my surprise on making myself known to that individual, he
quietly told me that no trowsers were allowed by the Government of this
Colony and only a blue smock, pith hat, and small cap. Perhaps through
your columns you will kindly inform me and for the benefit of the
gentlemen who have signed their names whether we are to go to drill
trowserless, or perhaps, like the gallant pipers of H.M. 74th Highlanders,
with kilts, or am I to find my own inexpressibles? So that I may be ready
at any moment to receive my elementary education in the art of war fare?

Another Volunteer responded, in effect telling the man not to be
stupid and deploring such petty quibbles: 'The statement about
the trousers is quite innacurate. He will be provided with trousers
all in good time if he can only rake up a pair or two from his own
wardrobe to use until the tailor has time to complete his extensive
order for helmets and tunics.'

Misgivings were expressed about the decision to consult the
heads of business houses seeking their support for the setting up
of the corps — the worry being that staff could feel pressured to
sign up. 'It seems to me that this application to the bosses savours
somewhat more of the press gang than is necessary in Hong
Kong,' complained one man, adding, 'The circular doesn't state
whether or not the bosses themselves are expected to join the
practicing the goosestep.'

Another resident agreed:

I cannot refrain from saying that I never, in the course of a few years
experience in the East, saw any popular movement started in such a
miserable manner as the proposed Hong Kong Volunteer Artillery force.
The whole affair from the outset has been, as far as we, the humble
outsider can judge, a muddle; one would have given those in power the
credit of knowing 'how to do it'; but it is evident that the training of the
Circumlocution Offices is too perfect and somebody is completely au fait
'how not to do it.'

Writing, as I said before, as a humble outsider, it seems there has been no method, no system in the matter. The result is that what should have been a most popular and enthusiastic movement, if started with the least degree of rationality or plan, promises, from what I have heard to prove a very great fiasco.

He called for a public meeting to be held at which volunteers could come forward rather than asking them to sign up at the government offices. 'Give us an organisation worthy of the name, and started in a more workmanlike way, and I don't hesitate to say that the muster role of the Volunteer force would be raised from its present meagre total to something worthy of the movement.'

All this squabbling irritated the editors of the *Daily Press* who commented in an editorial:

The authorities have gone about the formation of the corps in a quite businesslike manner. They may have made some trifling mistakes at first, but they have shown no indisposition to receive suggestions, and have evinced a laudable desire to heed the convenience of those wishing to join the corps. The result of their efforts so far has not been discouraging. On Saturday afternoon no less than one hundred and seven gentlemen were enrolled and sworn in at the City Hall as Artillery and Rifle Volunteers. The former corps has proved by far the most popular, no less than ninety six of the whole number of Volunteers having joined it. Artillery are more needed for the defence of the island than riflemen, but we hope to see the ranks of the latter reinforced. So far, but few Portuguese have enrolled, and the Rifle Corps will no doubt be generally recruited from that branch of the community.

The editorial called for the arguing to cease: 'We take it that the Volunteers have joined from motives of patriotism and loyalty only, and hence there ought to be no paltry jealousies, no petty quibbles among them.'

After the first swearing in ceremony there was supposed to be a parade but this was cancelled — leading to a protest from a Volunteer called A. Scott:

Of course we were much disappointed, and felt our spirits more damped than would have been the case had our clothes been wringing wet and the parade had taken place. In such critical times as these, and when war, from latest accounts, seems imminent, I can not help feeling and expressing myself as a volunteer that not a few will regret that the parade did not take place as we should mizzle altogether in a shower of bullets.

The rain must have stopped, for the parade, although not in uniform, took place on the afternoon of May 22:

Nearly all members were present. They were divided into five squads, number one squad consisting of men who have drilled before either as volunteers or soldiers. They were given their respective squad numbers and taught how to stand. Drills will now be held every day from 6.30 to 7.30 am and from 5.30 to 6.30 pm.

Despite the cynics, others came forward to join the new Volunteers and the first uniformed parade took place on 4 June. By the middle of the month practice was taking place on the guns: 'A squad of Volunteer Artillery were exercised for the first time on gun drill yesterday evening at the Royal Artillery battery. The corps is generally making fair progress in drill,' it was reported on 14 June.

Despite the original announcement, The Volunteers elected their own officers:

Circulars have been issued to the members of the Hong Kong Volunteer Artillery Corps requesting them in accordance with paragraph ll of the rules, to send to the Commandant by Saturday next the names of four members of the Corps whom they would choose to be appointed officers — two Captains and two Lieutenants.

A. Coxon became Commandant, with W. Danby as a Lieutenant.

In June it was reported that Enfield rifles, converted to Schneider, being used by the Volunteers would be replaced by carbines. Artillery consisted of seven-pounder, muzzle-loading cannon.

The gunners wore a loose fitting dark blue serge smock, with scarlet collar and cuffs, white shoulder cords and white metal buttons. They had blue serge trousers with narrow red stripe, and wore a round blue forage cap with white band. In summer they wore a white drill smock with white trousers, and a white solar pith helmet with pugree. The Rifle Corps wore a scarlet serge smock with blue facings and a round dark blue forage cap with chin strap in winter. Their smock had a shoulder strap with HKR (Hong Kong Rifles). In summer their uniform was similar to the gunners. All members wore a white waist belt and ammunition pouches.

Training was frequent:

From 1st July until further orders parades will take place morning and evenings three times a week namely on Tuesdays, Wednesdays and

Thursdays. On such days it is required that each Member will attend at least one drill. On Wednesday afternoons all are requested to attend for company and squad drill with rifles and bayonets, white uniform, forage caps to be worn unless otherwise ordered. On Tuesdays and Thursdays Gun Drill and Squad Drill as usual, but Members desirous of attending drill daily, as at present, can do so by giving their names to the Senior Drill Instructor.

Imperial emotions were strong at the celebrations of the Queen's birthday in 1878 and the Volunteers were as enthusiastic as anyone.

Monday, the 27th of May, being the day officially fixed for the celebration of the Queen's birthday, the Royal Standard was flown from Government House, Head Quarter House, the Naval Yard, and other Government establishments. All the men-of-war in harbour dressed ship and a great number of the merchant steamers and sailing vessels did the same. A feu-de-joie was fired by the troops in the morning and at noon Royal salutes were fired from the Victor Emanuel and the shore battery. At six o'clock a solemn Te Deum was sung in honour of Her Majesty, at the Roman Catholic Cathedral, at which His Excellency the Governor and Mrs Hennessy were present, as well as the Foreign Consuls, and a number of Military and Naval Officers. In the evening a ball was given at Government House, which was largely attended.

At the supper table, having called upon his guests to fill a bumper, his Excellency said he was only giving expression to the loyal feeling of the whole community in asking them to drink with enthusiasm the health of Her Majesty the Queen (applause) now in her fifty-ninth year. She was unrivalled by any Sovereign in the world in a knowledge of public affairs, in the difficult art of government, in a single-minded devotion to the true interests of her Empire, and in the heartfelt love of her millions of subjects (loud applause). This would be a memorable year in her reign, for a national emergency having arisen she had called out her Reserves, and from the shores of England to this remote part of Empire, the Queen's forces were being arrayed.

For the first time the native troops of India had gone to the Mediter-ranean. The Queen's popular and gallant cousin, the Duke of Cambridge, was going to review those troops in the South of Europe, and he (Mr Hennessy) believed that it would be the first time also that any Com-mander-in-Chief had left England on such a duty. Even in this distant Colony, they had seen Her Majesty's Forces already at work. The British Navy was today maintaining in the China Sea its old and famous reputa-tion. The Squadron was on the alert, and the Naval Arsenal of Hong Kong was furnishing rifled cannon from its reserves, and manufacturing tor-pedoes for the defence of the Island. The recent torpedo experiments in the Lyeemoon Pass showed what deadly instruments of impregnable defence the Hong Kong Naval Arsenal could rapidly produce.

The historic 74th Highlanders, whom they had the fortune to have in garrison this year, had, within the last few weeks, been performing somewhat unusual military duty, that of dragging twelve-ton guns to the batteries so admirably improvised in various parts of the Harbour. In those batteries our local Volunteers would have the honour of cooperating with the regular forces in working the guns if the necessity should arise. Therefore he felt he would be only doing justice to the universal sentiment of the Colony in taking this opportunity, in the Queen's name and on behalf of her subjects here, to thank the Navy, Army and Volunteers in this part of the Empire (applause). If the necessity should rise, they had full confidence in those sailors and soldiers, (loud applause). Recent revelations respecting the Crimean war enabled us also to appreciate the fact that the interests and efficiency of those forces were sedulously guarded by their Royal Mistress, and we know that the ultimate success of that war was due in no small degree to the administrative skill and indefatigable labours of Queen Victoria. In wishing her a long reign, and drinking her health, they were drinking to the best guarantee of national safety and success (loud applause).

The toast was drunk with full honours to the strains of 'God Save the Queen' by the band of the 74th Regiment.

Enthusiasm began to wane, however, as the immediate war scare passed and keenness to drill daily fell away. Press reports kept a watch on the continuing practices, however, such as the story of 23 January 1880:

The Artillery Volunteers were to have had a moonlit drill last night, but only a dozen men assembled and as the weather was rather threatening they were dismissed. The arrangement that the Royal Artillery should go out to Stanley today for their annual target practice has been altered, and they will not leave for some days. We understand the alteration was made in consideration of the Volunteers, the field guns having been placed at their disposal for moonlight drills for a short time.

Although enthusiasm for volunteering might be on the wane, the concern in Hong Kong about the possible intentions of the Russians in Asian waters did not decrease. In January 1880, the *Hong Kong Daily Press* said that the present fleet consisted of one double-screw iron frigate, three wooden corvettes 'of no great power', 18 small sloops and gun vessels, a despatch vessel and a receiving ship.

The small vessels are all of a class now almost obsolete and quite incapable of making any show against modern heavily armed gun boats such as Russia is said to be sending out for the reinforcement of the Pacific Squadron.

There are 20 open ports in China, seven in Japan. The ports of the Philippines, Hong Kong, the Straits Settlements, Siam, Labuan, Sarawak and Borneo, all to be looked after by a fleet of 23 vessels, none of which, save the flag ship, could hope to successfully contend with one of the new Russian corvettes.

Cautious welcome was given to a recent announcement that the British squadron in the China Sea was to be strengthened by the sending out of the *Comus*, 'a gun boat of a very superior class to those here at present' and of a vessel called the *Wyvern*. The *Comus* was a steel corvette, displacing 2,380 tons with an armament of four six-inch breech-loading guns, eight 64-pounder muzzle-loading rifled guns, two light guns, eight machine guns and two torpedo carriages. She was brand new in 1878.

The *Wyvern* was built especially for operations in shallow rivers — so, inevitably, it ended up in the deep, typhoon-prone waters of Hong Kong. This odd ship had two turrets fore and aft and a freeboard of only six feet. She was built for the Confederate Navy and launched in 1863. To get round Britain's neutrality in the American Civil War, the ship and a sister ship were to be sold first to Egypt. However, the British government stepped in and the two ships were then sold to the Royal Navy. They received the heaviest armament then afloat in the Royal Navy, four nine-inch guns, two in each turret. They were bad sailors, rolling heavily and steering poorly.

The *Daily Press* could not have been aware of this when it wrote that the Wyvern was 'More especially intended for the defence of the harbour and Colony of Hong Kong, though of course it will be valuable for service wherever necessary and it will doubtless make cruises to the different ports of China and Japan.'

However, a report a month later said that the *Army and Navy Gazette* had reported that a number of ships were to be withdrawn from China Command and the result would be that there would be fewer, rather than more, vessels available.

The war scare had largely passed by 1881, however. Disputes had occurred within the Volunteers and in 1880 Captain Coxon and Lieutenant Danby resigned, to be replaced by lawyer Captain J.J. Francis and Lt J. McCallum. The former presented a cup, the Francis cup, which was competed for until the Second World War.

With the passing of the war scare, as usual, the Volunteers began to decline. The eccentric Irish governor, Sir John Pope-Hennessy, fell out with the Garrison Commander, General Donovan, and, in 1880, the two men even organised rival dinner parties on the Queen's birthday. Equipment borrowed by the Volunteers from the military had to be returned and this had an inevitable effect on morale.

By 1881 the Volunteers were in a sorry state and hardly lived up to their new motto: 'Nulli Secundus In Oriente', or 'Second To None In The Orient.'

4

An End and a Re-establishment

THE 1880s were a decade of great importance in the history of the defence of Hong Kong. It was during this period that many of the sizeable forts, batteries and other defences, the remains of which can be seen around the colony today, were started.

For the Volunteers, however, things were not going well in the early part of the decade. The immediate fear of war with Russia had passed and, as had happened before, it had proved difficult to maintain enthusiasm in the absence of an immediately perceived threat.

Some of the annoyances were petty: 'Yesterday the Hong Kong Artillery Volunteers went to Stanley for their second target practice' it was reported on 11 February 1880. 'Through some mismanagement some of the Volunteers who have been regular attenders were deprived, some of one and others of two rounds each, in consequence of the ammunition running short, whilst members who have only recently joined had their three rounds.'

There were also personality clashes which resulted in the resignation of the Commandant, Coxon. In February 1882, the arms and equipment used by the Volunteers were withdrawn and from that date the corps 'ceased to exist except in name.'

The corps was finally disbanded in November 1882. However, as will be seen, this was not the disaster it might at first appear.

In December 1882, the Officer Administering the Government, Marsh, had written to the Secretary of State for the Colonies, the Earl of Kimberly, saying that the suggestion of reviving the volunteers had been put forward. He noted that the surrender of the arms to the military authorities had caused a considerable falling off in morale. However, he had expressed the willingness of the government to give every encouragement to the volunteer movement. He had been supported in this by the General who had agreed to lend a Royal Artillery officer to command the Volunteers and to provide carbines and training on the guns of the forts.

After careful consideration I came to the conclusion that the only way in which such a Volunteer Corps could be successfully organized was to commence by disbanding the old corps; and finding that the Executive Council as well as some of the Volunteers agreed with me on this point, a notice was issued disbanding the corps, and at the same time another notice invited all those who were willing to join a new corps to come forward and subscribe their names. A public meeting was then held, a copy of the proceedings of which I have the honour to enclose, and it was there resolved that a Volunteer corps consisting of two Companies of Artillery should be formed in Hong Kong again, and that no person should be eligible for the Corps unless he had been passed by the Surgeon as fit for service, a very necessary condition which had not existed in the old Corps.

With the consent of the Major General Commanding I then appointed Major Moore Lane, R.A., to be Commandant of the Corps. It was a special desire of the Corps that they should be commanded by an officer of the Royal Artillery.

Marsh noted that provision of money would be included in the Estimates and that the Volunteers had been given the old drill shed that was used by the previous volunteer formation in 1865. He included a request for carbines, accoutrements and mountain guns and suggested that these be handed over to the civil authorities to avoid problems such as had arisen with the military recently. 'I may add that the Volunteers especially requested that they may be supplied with arms of the modern pattern, and if this request may not be complied with, I do not think it will be of any use to send any others.'

Marsh said that a bill for the enrolment of a Volunteer Force had been read for the first time in the Legislative Council. This was substantially the same as the 1862 Ordinance.

Though Marsh was enthusiastic, London was rather more lukewarm — as reflected by the scrawls on the file bearing illegible signatures:

I doubt the practical advantage of a Volunteer Corps in Hong Kong, I doubt its longevity unless stimulated by wars or war scares in Europe or China; but it may be undesirable to throw cold water upon it.

I agree. There were very good reasons as everybody knows why the Volunteers revived so energetically in Hong Kong and other colonies in or about 1878; if the recruits who then joined had really desired to make the corps permanent they should have been able by keeping and pulling together to have prevented the collapse in 1881. I believe the War Office insists upon the return of its arms and accoutrements when the corps has fallen below a certain standard. I accordingly distrust the movement, and dislike the cost it will impose on the public.

Others were not so cynical:

I think it is desirable to encourage any movement of the kind in Hong Kong because there is always a possibility there that an organised force may be of value in dealing with Chinese or other difficulty, and also because it is not easy for young men to find occupation and exertion on the island.

It will not do to seem to discourage such movements though they may not appear very helpful.

The public meeting referred to was held on 16 November 1882 at the City Hall with 100 to 150 persons, mostly young men, in attendance. At the meeting the Colonial Secretary, F. Stewart, paid tribute to the evident enthusiasm displayed and read a series of statements by Marsh:

- The government would pay the expense of winter and summer uniform, and ammunition.
- The corps would be one of volunteer artillery with the question of forming a rifle corps left for later consideration.
- Moore Lane, RA, to be the Commandant.
- The General to lend some arms and accoutrements while application was made to the Secretary of State for 150 stands to be the property of the civil government.
- The guns in the Murray battery and one of the harbour force to be made use of for training on certain days.
- Efforts were being made to get the old drill shed back.
- A surgeon was to be appointed.

The meeting heard that it was planned that the corps should consist of two batteries. The officer strength would be one major, commanding, one major, second in command, and, for each battery, one captain and two lieutenants. Each battery would also have one honorary sergeant and one quartermaster. While the guns in the batteries were available, the question of acquiring field and mountain guns would be postponed. These statements were received by the meeting with much loud enthusiasm.

Mr Francis, the late commandant of the disbanded Volunteers, rose to address the meeting, saying that all present knew how the men of Hong Kong had rushed to join in the troubled year of 1878 and that 160 or 170 had attended each parade.

When the emergency passed over the attendance of course fell away; but still some 80 or 90 men held together and attended drill with fair regularity. Then an attempt was made by Capt. Coxon, at that time the Commandant, to put the corps on a better footing, and he made propositions and submitted them to the Government. Those propositions were approved at a public meeting in the Council Chamber by His Excellency the Governor and it was promised the corps that all suggestions then made, and all that was asked for with a view to improving the position of the corps would be granted.

They were very well aware, however, that nothing of the sort was done and not one of the promises then made to them was fulfilled, and not only were they left as they had been, but they were put into a much worse position, and before the end of the year they had returned to store all their arms and accoutrements. Left without arms and accoutrements, there were naturally no parades of the Volunteers and neither he (Mr Francis) nor Mr Grant thought it right to call the men together for drill under such circumstances. The corps remained in abeyance, but it still remained in existence, and some 50 or 60 men kept their names on the list, and were ready and anxious to do all they could to revive the corps, and numerous suggestions were made to him and Mr Grant for that purpose. But it was not until recently that anything could be done, and when the Egyptian War broke out, it seemed to be a fitting opportunity of doing so, and he communicated with His Excellency the Administrator as to whether the Government desired to see the movement revived. His Excellency expressed his willingness that this should be done, and desired that the corps should be put upon a sound basis.

At His Excellency's suggestion they consulted together, and laid before him their desires and propositions — the same as were put forward by Captain Coxon on a previous occasion, and practically the same as had now been accepted by His Excellency. As they had heard, those suggestions were submitted to Major Moore-Lane, the Commandant, and they were approved by His Excellency the Administrator, and, he believed, the Executive Council. He (Mr Francis) wished to point out that it was not the fault of the officers, non-commissioned officers and men that it had been found advisable to disband the old corps and to start a new one, and he had been assured by his Excellency the Administrator, in answer to a dispatch, that it was not because in his opinion that any blame attached to the officers, non-commissioned officers and men of the old corps that this had been done, but because it was deemed advisable to take this step in the interest of the new movement.

Mr Francis went on to say that he was on record as saying that he regretted the decision to disband and that he did not think it would be helpful to the new movement. 'It would be looked upon as a reproach to the officers, non-commissioned officers and men who had held together for the past three years in the face of every discouragement.'

However, the Colonial Secretary was quickly on his feet protesting that no slight was intended and calling on all present to join the new Volunteers: 'a most excellent movement.' The packed room agreed and a committee was unanimously elected to draw up rules and regulations with Major Moore-Lane.

The 1882 Ordinance and its Rules and Regulations, published in the *Government Gazette* on 16 December were basically similar to the 1862 Ordinance. Recruits had to be physically fit for duties as gunners and attend three drills a week during the drill season. They became 'effective' only after having passed squad and company drill and one type of gun drill at the end of the season. Honorary membership was retained with annual subscriptions reduced to $5 due to government subsidies. All forms of levy were abolished. Honorary members could wear uniform and take part in shooting matches of the corps though they were not liable to military duty. This strange class of Volunteer was not formally abolished until 1893.

The establishment of a battery was laid down as shown in Table 4.1.

Table 4.1 Number of Troops in a Gun Battery under the 1882 Ordinance

Captain	1
Lieutenants	2
Sergeants (one to act as Battery Sergeant Major and QM Sergeant)	4
Corporals	4
Gunners	36
Trumpeter	1
Total:	48

The Commandant was to be a regular military officer appointed by the Governor and the Second In Command was to be a major, to be appointed by the Governor from among the Volunteer officers. They were themselves to be appointed by the Governor with the Commandant having responsibility for N.C.O. promotions.

Effective members failing to attend the proper number of drills were liable to fines and expulsion.

Uniform was similar to that of the former Corps. The blue trousers now had a broad red strip, the same as the Royal Artillery. Officers provided their own clothing and equipment which was the same as for the Royal Artillery, but with silver instead of gold lace. A simple mess dress was introduced.

The Volunteers were now armed with Martini-Henry carbines and sword bayonets. This carbine was a shortened-barrel version of the famous Martini-Henry rifle and it had been issued for the use of the regular cavalry in the 1870s to replace the obsolete muzzle-loading rifled muskets. The Volunteers received their carbines after they had been discarded by the Household Cavalry. They had a ferocious recoil and Volunteer E.B. Wettenhall recalled they 'Kicked like the devil when fired.' He acquired a bruised shoulder and chest after firing on a range in Kowloon.

The Volunteers were issued with cartridges in paper packets of 10 rounds. In battle order, each man carried four packets in leather ammunition pouches on his belt and 10 loose rounds in a small canvas pouch. Each effective member was provided with 90 rounds per year. Ammunition in excess of this had to be paid for by the corps or individual.

The bayonet was the sword bayonet for the Martini-Henry with an 18.5 inch blade. The officers carried the cavalry sword, pattern 1853, which was 36 inches long, with a straight blade, and carried in a steel scabbard.

The battery was equipped with seven-pounder, rifled muzzle-loading guns. These guns were designed as mountain guns and weighed 200 lbs, being three feet two inches long. They were later superseded by a 'screw-gun' version with a steel, rifled muzzle-loading barrel and breech in two portions which were screwed together.

The Volunteers had a heavy drill schedule. During the drill season, from the start of October to the end of March, there were three morning drills each week, from 6.30 to 7.30 am, and three evening drills, from 5.15 pm to 6.30 pm. A Volunteer had to attend three each week. In addition, they had to attend at least 12 Commanding Officers' parades. At the end of 1886, the Corps' strength stood at 191.

The new Governor, Sir George Bowen, arrived in Hong Kong in March 1883 and, in a report of 30 May, he informed London that two batteries of Volunteer Artillery had been formed: 'Chiefly among the Officers of the Government, and the junior members and clerks of the banks, and principal European mercantile firms.'

These batteries had taken part in the parade of the garrison on the Queen's birthday the previous week, when they fired salutes and drew compliments from the Major General Commanding for their 'soldier-like bearing.' Bowen said the Volunteers were important as the garrison was small, with not more than 800 effective regular troops.

The Governor noted that he had always supported Volunteer movements in the various colonies in which he had served: 'It provides a feeling of comradeship among men of all different religious groups, social class, and political parties; and is eminently calculated to foster a general spirit of national patriotism and loyalty.'

In July, Bowen stated that one of the main problems to be faced in Hong Kong was that the land defences had hitherto been almost entirely neglected.

There was the ever-present fear of Russian expansion but there was now an added factor to contend with — French ambitions in what is now Vietnam. These resulted in war with China in 1884–85.

Given fears over England's ancient enemy, the appearance of a powerful French naval squadron in the harbour, in July 1883, did nothing to reassure the people worried about security. The main British squadron was away in northern waters and there were only three small ships for immediate service in the harbour. 'Under these circumstances, some unfounded and exaggerated alarm has been expressed in some quarters here,' Bowen informed London.

It is, however, satisfactory to learn that Her Majesty's Government have decided on despatching to this station at least one more ironclad — making two in all with the 'Audacious,' the flag-ship of Admiral Willes. It is manifestly inexpedient that the English squadron on this important station, where the English trade and general interests are of such great value, should remain inferior in ironclads to the French and Russian squadrons.

It is to be hoped, moreover, as I have already remarked in my despatch of May 12th ult., that the War Office in England will at last decide on carrying into early execution some one of the several plans that have been under consideration of late years for the defence of Hong Kong. It is notorious that the existing fortifications could not long resist an attack from a strong naval and military force, provided with the powerful artillery of the present day. And it will be recollected (as I have already observed elsewhere) that Hong Kong is distant by only seven or eight days' steaming from Vladivostock, the chief port, arsenal and naval and military station of Russia in the Pacific.

Bowen noted the continuing moves towards war between France and China, and he visited Canton in January 1884, where he saw the preparations being made. In a letter of March that year he detailed his efforts to improve matters:

I am supposed by the most competent judges to be 'doing the state some service here' in many ways; among others, by constantly bringing together on the neutral ground of the Government House the English, French, German, Italian, Russian, Dutch, American, Spanish, and Chinese admirals, ministers, viceroys, and other high officers, when they visit the port of Hong Kong, and by thus keeping them all in good humour with England, and to some extent with each other.

Soon afterwards he reiterated his fears about the defenceless state of the colony:

I am constantly urging on the Home Government that our position here is somewhat humiliating, for the French have four ironclads in China, whereas we have only one (the 'Audacious'); and Hong Kong is an open town, with a garrison of only 900 English soldiers, and could be taken any day by a coup de main. Just now, in case of war, the French could sweep our ships from these seas, and bring 5,000 men in three days from Tong Kong to seize Hong Kong. The British property here in shops, houses, stores, specie in the banks, etc, is valued at twenty millions sterling, without reckoning the naval and military arsenals, barracks etc. What a temptation to an enterprising enemy! The English defenceless, although they have paid for more than twenty years a military contribution of 20,000 pounds a year, or half a million sterling in all. If this money had been spent on fortifications, Hong Kong might have been as safe as Gibraltar. However, the Colony has now, at my insistence, agreed to raise a loan for the erection of the necessary forts, on the condition that the Home Government will arm them with heavy guns.

It is interesting to note that the Admiral Commanding the China Station, Sir W. Dowell, was a midshipman on the vessel which originally hoisted the British flag on Hong Kong.

As the Volunteers drilled, China fought, unsuccessfully, French aggression in Vietnam during the years 1884–5. The ever-present unease about Russian intentions was increased by the Russian occupation, in 1885, of Port Hamilton in Korea. There was considerable unrest in Hong Kong in 1884 with the cargo boatmen refusing to work on French ships and a strike eventually resulted which involved rioting and violence.

The Volunteers were training regularly. On 21 February 1885, they fired a practice and competition on the 6.6 inch howitzers at Belcher's Battery. Contests involving 64-pounders had taken place a short time previously, on the first day of the Lunar New Year. A competition to be fired with the nine-inch guns on Stonecutters Island was to follow and all three contests operated under the same rules. Fifteen points were scored for a hit, or three yards either side, at range distance; ten points for shots in that line within 40 yards beyond the target; eight points for shots three yards on either side of this space within 40 yards; any shot falling short of the target was disqualified. The range was 1,400 yards and anyone taking over a minute to lay the gun was disqualified.

The nine-inch competition followed: 'As the ammunition fired away from this heavy ordnance is expensive, only seven rounds were allowed and this narrowed down the number to compete.'

There were some problems:

The shooting was not up to that of previous competitions, three of the shots being short, two over the 40 yards allowed beyond the target, thus leaving only two within the rectangle of 40 yards by 12. This may be accounted for to some extent by the fact that the competitors were not allowed to put up the sight until after they had commenced to lay, which is not usual, and as there are four different sets of marks upon them, it takes a man who is unused to the sight some time to get the correct one, and this hurries the laying. Projectiles fired were Palliser shell and shot, common shell and shrapnel. For the Palliser projectiles a charge of 50 lbs of powder was used, and for the others 32 lbs. The range was 1,850 yards.

A week later there was a major garrison exercise which involved the Volunteers. The various forts in Hong Kong and Kowloon were manned by detachments of infantry and artillery.

The troops marched off from the Garrison Parade Ground at 9.30 am and proceeded to their allotted posts, where they were shortly afterwards visited by His Excellency the Lieut-General Commanding, accompanied by his staff. The different detachments returned to barracks in the afternoon.

During the day there was a good deal of firing practice from the big guns at the forts. In the afternoon a skirmishing party of the Buffs marched up to the Volunteer Headquarters and they were joined by the Volunteers who had mustered between 50 and 60 strong. The Buffs party marched ahead, followed by the Volunteers, who had manned four seven pounders. There were more than enough to have marched the whole six guns, but as the men had to draw the guns up to the Pokfulam Road, past Belcher's Point, it was deemed advisable to over man them, so as to have extra strength for the work. The party were to operate against an imaginary landing force, and on arrival at the point selected, some officers of the Buffs sent their men out on the hill side in skirmishing order, and the seven pounders were got in position on the road to command a bend further on.

After a little preliminary drill, the men fell out, to await the arrival of Lieut-General Sargent, who was then completing his round of visits and inspection. His Excellency the Governor arrived shortly before the General, and witnessed the operations. The Buffs party were supplied with blank ammunition, and the Volunteers with five blank charges per gun were drawn up in a separate squad. The firing commenced as soon as General Sargent was present, and then the party marched back to town. On arrival at headquarters Major Tripp addressed the corps. He said he was glad to see so good a muster, and informed them that General Sargent had expressed himself very much satisfied with the way the Volunteers had handled their guns. A considerable number of people followed the force down and witnessed the operations.

The Volunteers were delighted to be mentioned in General Orders a few days later: 'The Volunteer Artillery turned out in the most soldierlike manner and handled their guns very well; they, with their escort of "The Buffs", took up a position on the Pok-Foo-Lum Road to prevent the advance of an enemy from the south'.

A newspaper added the comment:

This will doubtless be highly satisfactory to members of the corps, and to all who take an interest in that body. It shows that at the time the detractors of the Volunteer movement say the thing will not stand that the corps is endowed with its greatest life and vitality. This is precisely what has been found elsewhere.

With defence a prime concern in Hong Kong, the late 1880s became a 'golden age' in the construction of fortifications. Work started on sizeable forts and batteries at Lyemun at the eastern entrance to the harbour, at High West in the west, and on Stonecutters Island. The remains of many of these impressive projects can still be seen today — though they are often wrongly thought to date from the years prior to the Second World War.

Bowen wrote to London in March:

I am co-operating zealously with the Admiral and General Commanding our sea and land forces in placing Hong Kong in a condition of defence. Admiral Sir W. Dowell has given orders for the concentration of his entire squadron in this harbour, and at other points whence it could, in the event of war being declared, strike most speedily and effectively at the Russian ships in these seas, and, if possible, aim a blow at Vladivostock, the chief Russian arsenal in the Pacific, which is distant by steam only eight or ten days from Hong Kong.

Moreover, the 'Wivern' and 'Tweed' reserve ships have been put in commission for the defence of this harbour, while torpedoes and sub-marine mines are being made ready, and will be materially assisted by the flotilla of steam-launches belonging to the Colonial Government, which I have directed to be armed and equipped for that purpose. On land, the new forts which are being erected at the expense of the Colony are being pushed forward as fast as possible; while among other measures of precaution, steps have been taken for victualling the garrison for several months. on the 14th instant, the General Commanding ordered all the batteries to be fully manned, so that every officer and soldier may know his proper post in case of hostile attack.

The Governor personally inspected the preparations and, though he did not know it, saw the place where later Volunteers were to fight a vital engagement in 1941 — Wong Nei Chong Gap.

A body of regular infantry, accompanied by the Volunteer Artillery with their light mountain guns, was also exercised in holding the pass by which an enemy landing on the south side of this island would march on the city of Victoria. I went out with this latter force myself, and have every reason to be satisfied with the discipline, efficiency and spirit of our Volunteers.

The man who followed Bowen as Governor was Sir William Des Voeux, with Marsh administering again for most of the period between the former's departure in December 1885 and the latter's arrival in October 1887. Des Voeux, like his predecessor found many problems, including defence, to be faced.

Des Voeux was ahead of his time in rejecting the European view that Chinese were unsuitable as soldiers due to some inherent trait. Writing in 1903 he said:

The good riding of the Chinese attached to the racing stables has caused me often lately to wonder whether Hong Kong and Wei-hai-wai might not be utilised as recruiting grounds for mounted infantry, which next to artillery seems to be the force most required in modern warfare. Though those offering for service would never probably have been on horseback, the same may be said of most of the recruits who join our cavalry regiments, and I am inclined to think that the Chinese would quickly learn to ride equally well.

Hitherto, Chinese soldiers have gained a reputation for cowardice, because they have usually run away when faced by European troops. But knowing the remarkable courage with which individual Chinese commonly face death, I have always been of the opinion that this reputation was undeserved, and that if led by English officers they would make exceptionally good soldiers, as being able to withstand hardships, insanitary conditions, and insufficiency of food, which would cause most European troops to succumb.

The experience of the British officers in command of the Chinese regiment at Wei-hai-wei has, I believe, tended to confirm this view, and I feel sure that what in the past has seemed to be cowardice, was in fact due to the example of officers who, as belonging to a profession which in China is regarded with contempt, had no feeling of honour, this being, I imagine, quite as important a factor as natural courage in the maintenance of a bold front to the enemy.

Defence continued to be a prime concern throughout Des Voeux's tenure and this culminated in a massive row over the size of the military contribution — which, in 1890, was doubled to 40,000 pounds a year. London had indicated that the garrison would be increased to more than a thousand men at the same time. The Legislative Council seized upon this and in March agreed the increase on the understanding that this would come about and that the cash would not be required until then. Unfortunately, the size of the garrison actually slightly diminished by the time, in December, that London was pressing for the money. The Legislative Council was outraged and Des Voeux had to resort to some fancy footwork to see that the extra 20,000 pounds was paid. Des Voeux was savaged by council members. Although he had sympathy with the Hong Kong view that the extra money should be related to extra troops he had no option but to use the official majority to force approval.

The Volunteers were starting to assume, in the late 1880s, their modern shape. In 1889, a Machine Gun Corps, partly mounted and armed with Maxim guns presented by leading members of the community was formed in addition to the artillery companies. In 1885, under Bowen, a Hong Kong Auxiliary Flotilla, consisting of volunteers from the Water Police and yachtsmen had been formed with the Harbour Master as Commandant. Tension remained high in the early 1890s and every effort was made to increase the number of Volunteers. This led, surprisingly, to yet another paper disbandment.

5

The Active 1890s

THE 1890s were to be a decade of tremendous activity for the Volunteers. It might, at first, seem odd that an important event in 1893 was the disbandment of the corps. However, it was immediately re-formed and placed on a new legal basis.

The reason for the change was that concern had arisen that, as it was then constituted, the Volunteers were not under the supervision of the military authorities as they were in England — though, of course, liaison was close. Neither were they subject to the Army Act.

That situation was remedied by Ordinance Number Six of 1893 which provided for the establishment of a 'Volunteer Force.' Interestingly, there was also provision for a special unit of 'Coast Defence Volunteers' to assist in 'the service of the sub-marine mine defences or in any measures involving the employment of steamers, launches, boats or other vessels.' This unit was only to be formed if the outbreak of war was likely. If no war broke out, then the period of service was to be six months, if war did occur then they were in for the duration. For practical purposes the coast defence force would operate on the same basis as the main Volunteer body although they would be deemed to be on actual military service from the date of enrolment. As it happened, this force was never formed.

The ordinance stated that the officers of the Volunteer Corps would be commissioned by the Governor. Conditions were laid down under which any Volunteer could resign, except on actual military service, by giving 14 days' notice and surrendering his arms and kit.

It was clearly stated that in operations the regular forces would be in control:

Whenever any volunteers are on actual military service or are undergoing

drill excercise or inspection together with Her Majesty's regular forces or
are voluntarily doing duty together with such forces, they and their
officers shall, subject to regulations under this Ordinance, be under the
command of the officers of Her Majesty's regular forces so nevertheless
that the volunteers shall, when the circumstances of the service admit, be
led by their own officers under such command.

The paragraphs relating to actual military service were specific:

In case of great national emergency or in case of actual or apprehended
invasion of or attack on the Colony the Governor may by Proclamation
call out any Volunteer Corps for actual military service.

Every officer and volunteer belonging to every corps so called out
shall be bound to assemble at such place and perform such service as may
be directed by the Governor.

Every such officer and volunteer from the time of his corps being so
called out shall for the purposes of this Ordinance be deemed on actual
military service. If any such officer or volunteer not incapacitated by
infirmity for service refuses or neglects so to assemble he shall be deemed
a deserter.

The period of service would be decided by the Governor but no
volunteer would be liable to service outside the colony, except in
the case of the coast defence volunteers who could be employed in
the waters around Hong Kong. While on actual service, volunteers would receive the same pay and allowances as regulars and
in case of hardship their families would be entitled to relief. There
would be a pension entitlement in case of death or injury. All the
above applied only in the case of actual military service.

The first part of general disciplinary paragraphs applied in
normal times. However, the second part clearly stated:

With respect to the discipline of officers and volunteers when they are on
actual military service or are undergoing drill, exercise, training or inspection together with or are voluntarily doing any duty together with
Her Majesty's regular forces or any part thereof the following provisions
shall take effect:

The provisions of the Imperial Act Forty-four and Forty-five of Victoria
Chapter Fifty-eight and of any other Imperial Act for the time being
amending the same shall so far as the same are applicable and consistent
with the provisions of this Ordinance apply to all officers and volunteers
with the following modifications only:–

A. That no officer or volunteer shall for any offence against such Act
or Acts be subject to the penalty of death.

B. That no sentence of a Court Martial for the trial of an officer or volunteer shall be carried into execution unless confirmed by the Governor.

Other parts of the ordinance dealt with the property of the corps and other administrative matters.

The oath was laid down, with an alternative declaration also provided should a volunteer object to taking an oath. The oath ran:

I A.B. do sincerely promise and swear that I will be faithful and bear true allegiance to Her Majesty Queen Victoria and that I will faithfully serve Her Majesty for the defence of the Colony of Hongkong against all Her enemies and oppressors whatsoever according to the conditions of my service.

In 1894, it was reported that there were 92 members of the corps, of whom 61 had qualified as Efficient. The Garrison Officer Commanding (G.O.C.), Major General Digby Barker, commented, 'In view of the short time the new corps has been in existence in its present form, and the difficulties they have had to contend with, the Inspecting Officer's report may be considered fairly satisfactory. It points to some shortcomings which, I trust, will be rectified in the coming year.'

The Acting Commandant, F. Jerrard, had called for the services of a first rate army N.C.O. to be provided as Quartermaster and for a C.O.'s clerk to look after the ammunition stores and equipment. He also asked for an official government notification to heads of government departments and to private businesses saying that the government favoured the movement and hoping they would support it.

The organization consisted of a Field Battery and a Machine Gun Company. There were six officers and 30 N.C.O.s and men classified as effective in the former, and six officers and 19 effectives in the latter. There were no marksmen, 23 first class shots, 17 second class shots and 20 third class. Both units were found to be 'in a fair state of efficiency as regards drill and turnout.'

The Field Battery fired 51 rounds against a practice attack on the vital Tai Tam Reservoir on New Year's Day, 1894, using its seven-pound, rifled muzzle-loading guns. They were in action again on 13 January, beating off a simulated boat landing in a southern bay. On 6 February, the Volunteers fired 64-pounders from South Shore Battery on Stonecutters Island.

The story of the Volunteers in the second half of the 1890s is covered by a series of annual reports which were laid before the Legislative Council each year and which provide much information on the corps. Perhaps the most significant item of information in the report for the 1894–5 year is the inclusion of an item, 'Five Chinese Medical Students', in the report on the Inspection State of the Corps.

No names are given but the presence of these Chinese students is almost certainly due to the enthusiastic participation in the life of the corps of Dr James Cantlie, then at the Hong Kong University medical school. Cantlie was a seminal figure, both in medical history and in British and Hong Kong Volunteer history.

James Cantlie joined the London Scottish Volunteers as Assistant Surgeon in 1882 when the War Office was becoming increasingly concerned about the lack of trained volunteer medical personnel. The regular army had its medical department but the Volunteer formations had their own surgeons and stretcher bearers who would fall in from their regular positions when required.

Cantlie started to give lectures on first aid to the London Scottish stretcher bearers. At about the same time, a Lieutenant Andrew Mclure, of the same regiment, called a meeting of volunteer surgeons to discuss improvements. He was eventually given an office in Whitehall and started to organise the Volunteer Ambulance Department.

Some Volunteer medical men, however, remained sceptical, perhaps worried about incursions on their patches. Cantlie, on the other hand, was enthusiastic and he saw also that medical students ought to receive instruction in stretcher bearing and other duties as part of their training. He started classes for students at the Charing Cross Hospital. He also helped lay the foundations of the Volunteer Medical Association which later developed into the Volunteer Medical Staff Corps. This was gazetted on April 1, 1885, and it became an established part of the British volunteers on the creation of the Territorial Army in 1907, when it became the Royal Army Medical Corps (T.F.). Cantlie put a tremendous amount of time into the corps and without his founding enthusiasm it is unlikely that it would have flourished.

In 1887, Cantlie decided to work in Hong Kong and he was soon involved in drawing up plans for a College of Medicine for Chinese. One of the first students was Sun Yat-sen, the founder of modern China.

Cantlie threw himself into his work, lecturing, demonstrating and administering. Given his earlier dedication to volunteering in England, it is not surprising that he was soon involved with the Volunteers in Hong Kong. As can be seen from the 1895 report Cantlie, who was then Surgeon Captain, had five of his medical students in the corps with him.

It may be speculated that the man revered in China today as the father of the modern nation, Dr Sun Yat-sen, may have been a Volunteer, as well as a medical student during his training in Hong Kong. Unfortunately, no records have yet been found to prove it.

But in July 1892, Cantlie spoke at a dinner which followed the presentation of the diplomas to the first students to receive their diplomas from the College of Medicine for the Chinese. He noted the reserve forces were in a state of transition, continuing:

But I may say that the students of the College of Medicine are a great feature of the Reserve Forces of Hong Kong, and I always plead guilty to having 'rushed' his excellency Sir William Des Voeux and General Barker, in as much as I managed to get the students of the College of Medicine marched past with the British regiment here on the occasion of the Jubilee of this colony.

People said: 'What are those Chinamen doing here?' And we said, 'They are students of the College of Medicine.' I have no doubt that telegrammes were sent to the Russian Government notifying that the Chinese were taking part in the celebration of the Jubilee, and I have no doubt that the Russian agent and Russian fleet, which was here at the time, took supreme notice of it as being evidence of the sympathy between England and China.

Sun Yat-sen was present at this dinner at the Mount Austin Hotel on the Peak where he received the Medicine, Midwifery and Hygiene and Public Health prizes. In replying to the toast 'The Licentiates', of which he was one, he thanked those present and expressed a wish that the College would be successful: 'Not only for ourselves but for all in Hong Kong.'

Later, Dr Cantlie was to play a vital role in rescuing Dr Sun from imprisonment in the Chinese Legation in London. Given the close personal friendship of the two men it may be valid to speculate, at least, that the latter might have been one of the medical student volunteers.

The year 1894 saw significant developments in Asia which

caused concern in Hong Kong. Japan was encroaching on China's legitimate interests in Korea which was a tributary to China. Also anxious to protect its interests was Russia which, in 1885, had taken the ice-free port of Lazareff on the northeastern coast of Korea. Britain took Port Hamilton, at the southern tip of the country.

In 1894, a rebellion broke out in Korea and this in turn led to the outbreak of war between Japan and China. The former had been industrializing quickly and achieved a decisive naval victory in a battle off the Yalu river in the Yellow Sea, on 17 September. In five hours fighting, China lost four ships and more than a thousand officers and men while the Japanese lost only one ship. The remainder of the Chinese fleet withdrew to Port Arthur and then moved across to the Shantung naval base at Wei Hai Wei, not yet in the possession of the British. The Japanese then took the base by landward assault, having used the same tactic successfully a couple of months earlier against Darien and Port Arthur.

It has been said that those who ignore the lessons of history are doomed to repeat them. These attacks took place nearly 50 years before the Japanese assault on Singapore.

The Treaty of Shimonsekei, which was signed in April 1895, greatly increased Japanese influence in China. One result was the cession by China of Taiwan, the Pescadores and the Liaotung Peninsula. This, of course, caused great concern to other powers, and a week after the treaty had been signed, France, Germany and Russia warned Japan that the agreement threatened the existence of peace in the region. Japan considered carefully and then agreed to drop its claim on Liaotung in return for an extra indemnity. Russia had its eyes on the ice-free ports of Darien and Port Arthur on the peninsula, but it seemed to China as if it at last had an ally against Japan. After due negotiation a secret alliance between Russia and China resulted.

Great jockeying continued, with other foreign powers continuing to pressure China for concessions. Down in Hong Kong developments to the north were watched with an understandably wary eye.

The Volunteers were settling down after their reorganization. The only regulars in the year to 16 April 1895, were the Acting Commandant, Major Arthur R. Pemberton, of the First Battalion Rifle Brigade, Captain L.A.C. Gordon, of the Royal Artillery (as Adjutant), and the Quarter Master Sergeant G.W. Watling.

Pemberton had taken over command from Lieutenant Colonel Jerrard on 1 February 1895, and he had considerable experience with Volunteer units in England.

The Volunteer officers of the Field Battery were Captain J. McCallum, Lieutenants H.E. Denson, W. Machell and A. Chapman. James Cantlie was the Surgeon-Captain. There were 47 non-commissioned officers and men.

Captain W.H.E. Murray commanded the Machine Gun Company and E. Osborne and C.M. Adamson were Lieutenants. J.A. Lowson was the Surgeon-Lieutenant. There were 27 non-commissioned officers and men. Murray was an A.D.C. to the Lieutenant General, G. Digby Barker, who commented that it was Murray who had organized and commanded the company from its commencement: 'Which mainly by his untiring exertions, great tact and popularity has been brought to its present state of efficiency.'

The Acting Commandant, Major Pemberton, reported that all the volunteers listed had completed more than the 30 drills required, but that some had done more under some heads and less under others than they should have according to schedule. The figures only included men qualified as Efficients, so there would have been in the corps, additional recruits and others who had not reached this stage. The overall corps numbered 112.

The musketry returns give an interesting insight into the training level. Of the Machine Gun Company, 46 men fired, with 11 classed as marksmen, 22 as first class, 13 second class and 11 third class. Of the Field Battery 73 fired, with no marksmen, 44 first class, 10 second class and 19 third class.

The Field Battery was engaged in four major practice exercises, together with normal routine training. The first annual camp of instruction was held at Stonecutters Island in January, 1895.

On 17 November 1894, the Volunteers operated their seven-pounder rifled muzzle-loading guns in a practice firing against boats attempting to land near a battery at North Point. Twenty-six rounds were fired. On 19 January 1895, the seven-pounders were in action against a simulated boat landing at Sandy Bay, Pokfulam, at the west of Hong Kong Island, during mobilization of the garrison and 25 rounds were fired. A week later, on 26 January, 64-pounders were used against a barrel target anchored off the South Shore Battery at Stonecutters Island and 72 rounds were fired. This battery is just west of the present Lido swimming pool area on the island and is well preserved. Finally, on 16 March, the seven-pounders were in action again in an exercise involving an attempted boat landing at Kowloon East Bay, with 33 rounds fired.

The Maxims of the Machine Gun company were used on 3 November 1894, when 1,211 rounds were fired in practice against a simulated troop landing at Sai Wan Bay, at the east of the island. On 17 January 1895, a thousand rounds were fired at a simulated landing at Deep Water Bay, on the south of the island, during mobilization of the garrison. A further 924 rounds were fired two days later during the same mobilization at Sandy Bay, where the Field Battery was also in action with its guns.

In his report on the year, the Commandant said that he was pleased with the support he had received from the officers and non-commissioned officers who had attended regularly at parades and who were largely to thank for increased efficiency. He noted an increase in strength over the year of 17 in the Field Battery and seven in the Machine Gun Company.

On uniform, he recommended that khaki and blue puttees be substituted for the summer clothing at present worn by the Field Battery. He suggested that the machine gunners replace the pipe-clayed buff accoutrements they then wore with brown leather belts.

The climate of Hong Kong meant that the drill season was not sufficiently elastic, reported Major Pemberton. Despite the enthusiasm, it was difficult to obtain good musters at parades held after 1 April and he suggested the season should open on 1 October and close on 31 March.

I feel certain that this alteration would enable members to attend the requisite number of drills with less inconvenience to themselves and their employers than is the case at present. In England the drill season is during the summer months, and the minimum duration is four months.

The rest of the Headquarters Building of the corps had finally been handed over and would be furnished as a recreation room which: 'Will eventually prove very beneficial to the Corps generally.'

Lieutenant General G. Digby Barker, in his covering report, said that both branches of the corps were now in an efficient state: 'The turn-out of the men and their drill was most satisfactory. The Officers know their drill fairly well and are zealous in the performance of their duties. The guns, small arms and equipment are well kept up, the Maxim guns looking particularly serviceable.'

Formerly, labourers had been hired to move the field guns, but Barker reported that ponies had now been substituted with complete success. The appointment of an experienced Quarter Master Sergeant had added to efficiency.

The General remarked:

The handing over by the Government to the Corps of the complete building in which its Headquarters is situated — thus enabling members to feel that the Corps has a home of its own, with space for all its requirements social as well as official — has largely tended to place the Corps on that permanent footing which was so much required.

He backed Pemberton's's suggestions on uniform: 'I quite endorse the Commandant's recommendation for khakee clothing and brown belts and slings to be substituted for the present white drill clothing and buff belts and slings of the Field Battery.' However, he had his reservations on Pemberton's views on the drill season: 'I should advise a longer test of the present system which was adopted after much consideration as being the best adapted to the peculiar local circumstances, and the elasticity of which — as provided for in existing regulations — seems to have been hardly availed of to the full extent.'

Despite the efficiency of the Volunteers, concern about the defences of Hong Kong continued in the local community. In April 1895, the colonial government sent to London a copy of an editorial headed 'Are We Safe?' The languid comment scrawled on the file read, 'The Hong Kong Telegraph is not a paper of repute. I doubt whether notice need be taken of it.'

The point raised by the paper was that the land beyond Kowloon and waters around the colony remained outside British control.

The Home Government proposes to spend a very considerable sum of money in improving the Naval establishments in Hong Kong and the construction of docks is spoken of as one of the special works likely to be taken in hand at an early date. Well and good so far, but where are these docks to be constructed so that they shall be out of range of the enemy's guns in time of war? How can they be reasonably protected from capture and destruction by an enterprising enemy and how are they to be defended? The whole range of hills on the mainland on the northern side of the harbour is Chinese territory. The water ways leading to it are half Chinese — to the mid-channel — and in case of war, let us say by way of illustration, with Japan, would be neutral waters and Japanese men of war might sail in under the guns of Ly-ee-mun forts and 'fetch up' where we have repeatedly seen the Chinese fleet anchor, opposite Chinese Kowloon within a couple of miles of Hung Hom Docks and within gunshot of every part of the harbour and yet all the time in Chinese waters and, theoretically at least, entitled to lie there unmolested.

The defences of the Lyemun channel could be quickly overwhelmed by attack from the north, said the paper, noting:

The entire south side of the island is undefended and within easy distance lies Lamma with deep bays and sheltered harbours under the protection of which hostile ships might assemble within sight of our stations and from which descent might be made on our shores before the presence of the enemy could be notified in town and men sent out to oppose a landing.

This explains the Volunteer exercises at Deep Bay and at Pokfulam, where the field pieces and Maxim guns were used to contest simulated enemy landings.

As far as modern artillery is concerned, how many spots are there in Hong Kong waters which are out of range of hostile fire from commanding positions on Chinese territory — hostile territory in the event of war with China, neutral territory if we were at loggerheads with any other power, but neutral territory which no enemy would under existing circumstances hesitate to utilize against us. China is unable, and will for many years to come, be unable to cause her neutrality to be respected.

The leader writer said that, in the event of war with a great naval power such as France, Russia, Germany, the United States or Japan, Lamma and the mainland to the north of Kowloon would be essential to the defence of Hong Kong.

Would it not be as well, before large sums of money are spent in making docks and increasing the naval establishments to meet the uncertain contingencies of war, to consider carefully whether Hong Kong with its present boundaries, in time of war, be a safe place for ships to dock and repair and, if not, whether it would not be as well — while we may and can — to take or obtain possession of such more extended boundaries as would ensure us against all risk and which we would most certainly take possession in case of war on the plea of absolute necessity of self defence?

In conclusion he wrote, 'The time has now come for us to think seriously of extending our boundaries a little more widely, or make up our minds to forfeit our claim to the title "Malta and Gibraltar of the East".'

Though not deigning to take much notice of mere scribblers, the civil and military authorities both in Hong Kong and London were giving serious consideration to the defensive needs of the colony and the G.O.C. distributed copies of a new, secret defence scheme in September 1895.

The annual inspection report for the year ending in April 1896, of the G.O.C., saw Major General W. Black comment:

The turn out of the men was satisfactory, their seven-pounder guns, Maxims, arms and equipment are well kept up and appear to be in serviceable condition. The officers and men know their drill sufficiently well for practical purposes, and from personal observation at tactical exercises and field firing, I know that the Field Battery shoots well, and believe that the Maxim Gun Corps usually makes good practice. The adoption of khaki clothing and brown belts gives a serviceable appearance to the Corps.

The keenness of the Volunteers to do their own heavy work, however, drew reservations from the G.O.C.:

That the members prefer drawing the guns instead of employing coolie draught shows a good spirit, but I consider it would be wise to accustom Chinamen to drag and carry the guns over the rugged hill sides, and I approve of the Commandant's intention to use coolie draught more frequently in future in operations at a distance from head quarters.

Black was also concerned at the fact that strength had only increased slightly and that muster at the annual inspection parade was poor, 'But I have great faith in the loyal spirit of the British residents of Hong Kong, and feel sure that if the colony were to require their services they would rally to the Volunteers in great numbers.'

The Acting Commandant, Major Pemberton, reported that the return for the corps showed an establishment of 238 officers, N.C.O.s and men. The actual strength was 125, leaving a shortfall of 113.

Major Pemberton commented that there was an increase of 13 over the previous year in the actual strength figure and that the corps had never been up to this figure of 125 before. Allowing for resignations, a total of 37 new members had joined, 'Thus shewing that Volunteering in Hong Kong is not on the wane.'

The change to khaki drill and putties in the Field Battery for summer wear, instead of white clothing, had been welcomed. The

corps was armed with Martini-Henry carbines and revolver practice for the officers and staff sergeants had been fired for the first
time.

A 10-day camp had been held in October 1895 at Stonecutters
Island at which outpost duties, guards, and reconnoitering were
practised along with the usual drills. It had not been possible to
use the naval range there as it was under reconstruction.

The Field Battery again fired from Stonecutters Island at targets
at sea and practiced repulsing landings at Sandy Bay. The Machine
Gun Company also put in target practice at Stonecutters, and
defended against landings at North Point Battery.

One Volunteer who joined up in 1897 was E. Abraham, who
was then 17 years of age. After completing initial training he was
posted in 1898 to the Field Battery as a gunner. More than four
decades later he was to serve again as a Volunteer — as a member
of the 'Hughes Group' of the Hong Kong Volunteer Defence
Corps, consisting of elderly men. 'We wore khaki uniform with
Indian Army topees in summer and blue-cloth uniforms and pill-
box caps in winter,' he recalled. 'On and off I served 17 years in the
Volunteers. When conditions were peaceful I resigned and when
there was likely to be trouble I rejoined.'

Another man who joined up in 1897 was Mr Lionel Lammert
and he and Mr Abraham were present at a wreath laying
ceremony and parade during the Volunteer centenary celebrations
in 1954.

A third 1897 Volunteer was Mr E.B. Wetenhall who remembered
the division of the corps into artillery and machine gun units:

I belonged to the latter. We had Maxim guns which jammed continually
the barrels sometimes becoming red hot. We were armed also with Carbines, discarded Household Cavalry weapons, Martini Henrys, which
kicked like the devil. I remember my bruized shoulder and chest after
firing on the Kowloon Police Range.

Our Commandant was Sir John Carrington, the then Chief Justice, for
whom we had the greatest respect. He was a very keen amateur soldier.
The only officers I remember were Captain Sanders, of the Hong Kong
Bank, and Lieutenant Maitland, an insurance broker.

The outstanding event I remember was the part played by the Volunteers in the Victorian Jubilee celebrations in 1897 when we marched
dragging our guns to Happy Valley and there took part in the Military
Parade with the regulars and had a place in the line which fired a feu de
joie.

I also remember going into camp on Stonecutters Island and an inspection by General Black, the then C. in C. Hong Kong forces. I think we nearly shot him and his staff through a mistaken order or an order being mistaken (action front for action rear) ...

I am afraid we weren't very efficient but we made up for it by enthusiasm.

Major General Black, G.O.C., was not, it seems, worried by his experience at Volunteer camp, for in his annual report on the corps he commented that the guns were well kept and serviceable and that the men handled them exceedingly well, both on the uneven parade ground and the steep hillsides.

He added:

From personal observation I know that the shooting of the Field Battery and Maxim Gun Company is satisfactory, and that all ranks take a considerable interest in it; but I have observed that time is often wasted and much ammunition expended in endeavours to 'find the range'; this ought to be remedied by the use of range-finders at all practices at targets.

The former Acting Commandant, Major Pemberton, had resigned command in October 1896, on the departure of his regiment from the colony. The new Commandant, Major Sir John Carrington, who was also the Chief Justice, was able to report that the total strength had risen to 159 of all ranks, the highest since the 1893 reorganization: 'The number of the Field Battery is now 107, compared with an establishment of 80 as fixed by the Regulations of the Corps. On the other hand, the number of the 'A' Machine Gun Company is only 47, as compared with an establishment of 51 as fixed by the Regulations.'

He hoped to be able to make a start on forming a second machine gun company adding that the corps had 12 Maxims — enough for three companies. 'It is, I believe,' wrote Carrington in a prophetic phrase, 'the opinion of competent officers that machine gun fire will be found of considerable value in repelling a hostile attack on the colony.'

Routine training, drills and practices had been carried out and had been well attended. Annual camp was held over a nine-day period in October 1896, on Stonecutters Island and this time the Volunteers, mainly recruits, were able to use the naval range there. Competitions added spice to practice. On 2 February 1897, six detachments manned 64-pounder guns at Stonecutters Island, using plugged shell. They fired at a target moored at sea between the battery and Green Island which was 2,175 yards away and excellent results were obtained.

On 23 March, the Field Battery and the Machine Gun Company were both involved in competitions from a position near Wong Nei Chong Gap from which the gunners fired, using ordinary and shrapnel shell, at a target on the shore of Deep Water Bay, while the machine gunners fired at targets in a ravine.

The Martini-Henry Carbines were now, however, showing signs of considerable wear and tear, and it was pointed out that the question of replacing them with newer and more efficient weapons would soon have to be considered. The report of the G.O.C. for 1897–8 accepted that the carbines were past their best and said that recommendation had already been made to the colony's government that the corps be re-armed with a more modern weapon.

The vexed question of using labourers to draw the guns had not gone away and Carrington had to state again how the Volunteers 'display a strong repugnance to allowing this work to be done by coolies.' He added that the corps' finances would not, in any case, permit their employ and that there was always a large pool of available labour to draw on if required. 'I am, however, informed that coolie draught for the guns has always proved slow and generally unsatisfactory.'

The hoped-for establishment of a second machine gun company had not come to pass, partly because new Regulations for the corps were be drafted, but, more importantly: 'Because the local government has repeatedly and emphatically expressed its desire that no expenditure should take place in excess of the sum voted for the Volunteers,' reported Major Carrington.

Music had come to the corps, for during the year 1897–8 a drum and fife band had been formed from 22 enrolled members of the corps and one unenrolled boy signaller. The sound of the fifes and drums was much appreciated.

The genesis of the Volunteer engineer units came in that year too, when consideration was given to setting up a small company of engineers. A final decision was still awaited.

The Honorary Colonel of the Corps, Sir W. Robinson, relinquished his position as Governor during the year and vacated his Volunteer appointment in February 1898. Another important personal connection came to an end with Captain J. McCallum, Field Battery Captain, resigning in January the same year to return to

Scotland. He had been associated with the Volunteers in Hong Kong since May 1878 — however, on his return home he was to join a battery of volunteer artillery.

The usual Stonecutters Island camp took place in the autumn and there were competitions and exercises throughout the year. The Commandant's report also contained the usual tributes to the enthusiasm of various people. 'I am especially glad to be able to say,' said Carrington, 'that talking in the ranks on parade is much less frequent than it used to be, and I am in hopes that this unsoldierlike practice will soon disappear altogether.'

Another long overdue disappearance was that of the Martini-Henri Carbines belonging to the corps. These had been examined by the army's Ordnance Department and all except four had been condemned as unfit for service. The Hong Kong and British governments were engaged in discussions on replacements. Uniform was again being studied and a committee of officers had been set up to look at simplification and reduction in cost.

As the end of the century drew ever closer there was an upsurge of activity within the Volunteer Corps.

This was partly due to the dissatisfaction of the G.O.C., Major General W.J. Gascoigne, who, although pleased with his annual inspection, commented:

previous to the inspection I had given several opportunities to the Corps to turn out at their own hour, to act in conjunction with the Regular Troops, and I confess that I was disappointed at finding that comparatively small numbers availed themselves of the opportunity presented to them.

I think that perhaps there had sprung up a feeling that the services of the Hong Kong Volunteers were not as highly appreciated as I, at any rate, do rate, and appreciate the importance of their services in this colony.

In view of this, Gascoigne took the opportunity of Major Sir John Carrington's absence on leave to place Colonel Mainwaring, Commanding the Second Battalion Royal Welch Fusiliers, in temporary command. This was a significant move as the Volunteers were to be involved in the disturbances relating to the takeover of the New Territories.

The problems had been appreciated some time previously for, in 1898, the then G.O.C., Black, had set up a committee to consider all aspects of the organization of the corps. The committee's deliberations mainly concerned financial matters, calling attention to the need for better funding and the placing of the Volunteer movement in this regard on a par with practice in the United Kingdom. There were special problems in Hong Kong, such as: 'The class of men recruited renders it impossible to require them to wear cast off clothing, as done in the Police Force with Chinese and Indians.'

The Governor forwarded the report to London where enthusiasm was strictly limited. A scrawled note on the file containing his despatch commented, 'There is no end to the Governor's financial proposals — all involving increases of expenditure.'

Nevertheless, new Regulations for the Hong Kong Volunteer Corps were made by the Governor In Council on 2 May 1899. 'The object of the Corps is to aid the Regular Troops in the defence of the Colony against foreign attack and to assist the Government in the repression of local disturbances.' The Corps was to consist of six units and a band (see Table 5.1).

Table 5.1 The Formation of the Volunteers under the 1899 Regulations

A. A battery of light field artillery
B. Three machinegun companies
C. An engineer company
D. An infantry company
E. A band

Volunteers had to be British subjects between 18 and 50 and physically fit and no man could be admitted without two proposers and the approval of the officer commanding his unit and the Corps Commandant. 'The names of a person proposed and his proposers shall be posted at Headquarters for not less than five days before the person proposed is admitted as a member of the Corps.'

The drill season was to run from 1 October to 31 March each year, with an annual inspection by the General Officer Commanding at the end. A camp of instruction would take place, together with drills, practices, parades and classes. Military law was to apply on active service, though Volunteers had to be informed if they were to become liable and to have an opportunity to withdraw from such service.

The financial arrangements were probably the most important part of the new regulations. The government was to pay to the

Commandant an annual capitation fee of 25 dollars for each member borne on the muster roll on 1 January or enrolled between that date and the following 1 October.

An efficiency grant of 25 dollars was also to be paid by the government for each officer and each volunteer certified to be efficient. To be so rated, the individual had to be present at the annual inspection, unless sick or on special leave. Over the year he had to have attended a minimum number of drills of not less than one hour's duration. These drills varied with the unit — a trained Volunteer of the Field Battery in his third and subsequent year of service had to complete squad, company, musketry and inspection drills and gun drills and practice, for a total of 15 drills; an Infantry Company recruit would have to complete a total of 30 squad, company, inspection and musketry drills.

A proficiency grant of 20 dollars was to be paid annually for each member of ranks above and including that of Sergeant certified by the Commandant as 'proficient.'

An allowance of two dollars per day per head was to be paid for camps of between three and eight days. An annual transport grant of 1,000 dollars was to be paid. A grant of 10 dollars per head was to be paid for each efficient member of the Reserve.

If, within six months of joining, a volunteer or member of the reserve for whom the capitation grant had been paid left the corps without good reason, the corps would have to repay the government a proportionate part of the grant.

If, without good reason, a volunteer or reservist failed to obtain a certificate of efficiency, and so cost the Corps money by not qualifying for the efficiency grant, he would be liable to make good the loss.

From the fund formed by these grants, the Commandant was to meet the cost of supply of uniform to Volunteers, supply of practice ammunition additional to that supplied by the government, the payment of instructors, the hire of transport, the custody, care and repair of arms and equipment, the custody of stores, the upkeep of rifle ranges, and all other expenses required to keep the Corps efficient and not otherwise provided for.

The establishment of the corps was:

• Staff — six;
• Field Battery — four officers, eight sergeants, two trumpeters and 96 rank and file;

- Machine Gun Companies (divided between the three companies) — nine officers, 15 sergeants, three trumpeters and 96 rank and file;
- Infantry Company — three officers, two sergeants and 52 rank and file;
- Engineer Company — one officer, two sergeants and 27 rank and file;
- Band — one Sergeant-Drummer, two Corporals and 21 musicians.
- Total establishment — 350 of all ranks.

Colonel Mainwaring's report for the year 1898–9 was dated 17 April 1899; one day after the Volunteers had been hurriedly called out. The report gives an excellent idea of the organization and readiness of the Volunteers at this crucial point.

The corps still comprised a Field Battery, armed with its seven-pound, rifled muzzle-loading guns, and a Machine Gun Company. Efforts were continuing to encourage enough men to come forward for the second and third companies to be formed. The fife and drum band was doing well, and valuable instruction had been received from the Sergeant Drummer Instructors of the King's Own Royal Lancaster Regiment and the Second Battalion of the Royal Welch Fusiliers. The bands of those regiments had also been lent to add a stirring note to more formal occasions. The Engineer Company was about to be formed.

Squad, carbine, company and gun drills and practices had been carried out throughout the winter training season. Camp had taken place on Stonecutters as usual, with good attendance: 'The camp was well attended and much appreciated by all. The camp year by year seems more popular and to it much of the efficiency of the corps is attributed.'

The seven-pounder guns were coming to the end of their life but they had been used in practices against landings, enemy advances and at the range. Orders had been given for the 64-pounder guns to be dismantled so no practices took place with those weapons. Approval had been given to re-arm the corps with new .303 carbines and the possibility of replacing the .45 barrels of the Maxims with .303 barrels was being looked at.

The corps strength stood at 181 of all ranks, again the highest total since the 1893 reorganization.

The question of the coolie draught arose again: 'Coolie draught was tried once more during the past season in conveying guns, targets, etc., to Repulse Bay on 10th February last, but much time was lost and it cost more than conveyance by water.' However, the corps was soon to have rather more to worry about than the question of who should move its guns. Following completion of the negotiations on the New Territories, lease arrangements had been made for the British to take over administration. However, while this had been reluctantly conceded by China, many of the inhabitants of the New Territories and surrounding areas were incensed.

In early 1899, a number of incidents and skirmishes occurred, mainly around Tai Po. Mat sheds erected there by the British were burned, and forces gathered on hills to the north. On 15 April, a company of the Hong Kong Regiment set out for Tai Po and ran into about 1,200 Chinese with an entrenched battery of artillery which opened fire. The Indians of the Hong Kong Regiment (not to be confused with the Volunteer force) managed to sweep away the opposition and the Union Flag was hoisted as planned on 16 April.

That evening the Volunteers were called out. Reports had been received of shots being fired in the Pat Heung area and there was worry over a possible attack by rowdies on Yaumatei and Kowloon from the direction of Castle Peak.

The Volunteers were told to report for duty at very short notice and, as 16 April was a Sunday, they were scattered all over town. The call to arms came at about 10pm and there was a scramble to get ready. H.M.S. *Fame* had sailed across to Kowloon Bay where she lay in a position commanding the road to Kowloon City while her searchlights, and those of the defences of Kowloon, and, presumably, Stonecutters Island, illuminated the approach from Lai Chi Kok. The ship was a 350-ton destroyer completed less than two years previously. Another warship was stationed in Yaumatei Bay.

The Volunteers, with three Maxim guns, marched down to Pedder's Wharf, where they were cheered by a large group that had assembled as they embarked for Kowloon. Some of the men presented an unmilitary and somewhat ludicrous appearance, which was accounted for by the fact that they were in different places throughout the Colony when the call to arms was given. Most of them were in uniform, but a few wore evening clothes, and the most amusing combination was a morning coat, light trousers and khaki helmet and belt, in which one enthusiastic member presented himself at headquarters.

Lieut-Colonel Mainwaring of the Royal Welch Fusiliers, took command, and several of his officers and about half a company of his men turned out to assist in the defence of Yaumati. The three guns were posted in commanding positions. The members of the Field Battery were thrown out as pickets, with instructions to challenge and shoot anyone not answering. The Fusiliers were broken up into detachments acting as supports for the machine guns. Each man carried about 30 rounds of ball ammunition, and in addition to belts with 1,000 rounds ready for action at each gun, reserve ammunition to the extent of several thousand rounds was held in the rear.

A vigilant look out was maintained but no enemy appeared. The troops marched back to the Police Station, and embarking at Yaumati returned to Hong Kong about 6.30 this morning.

There were upwards of 100 men present, individual members turning up at Yaumati as late as 3 a.m. They deserve to be commended for the promptitude with which they obeyed the summons to duty and the only regret is that Major Sir John Carrington was not in the Colony to participate in the operations."

One of the Maxims was set up by a water pumping station covering the main Kowloon Road, while the other two were placed in Mongkok Road. Two civilians with bicycles volunteered to act as scouts for the force.

Later, on 17 April, at 3.45 pm, Lady Blake, wife of the Governor, Sir Henry Blake, hoisted the British flag at Kowloon City. An interpreter read an address from the Governor informing them that the territory 'Was now British and the people British subjects, dwelling on the benign character of British rule, and wishing the people prosperity and happiness.' Copies of the address were distributed and these were 'eagerly seized' while listening children received silver coins.

The Volunteers were not slow to seize on the prestige that their adventure had brought them and a press advertisement appeared:

40 RECRUITS required for 'C' Machine Gun Company, HONGKONG VOLUNTEER CORPS.

Application, accompanied by Medical Certificate (which can be obtained from Surgeon-Captain Lowson or Stedman) to be made in writing to

THE ADJUTANT
H.K. Volunteer Corps
Volunteer Headquarters
Hong Kong, 19th April, 1899.

This drew the editorial comment:

The Adjutant of The Volunteer Corps is taking advantage of the trouble in connection with our new territory to endeavour to get recruits. He is wise as it has been ever and ever again proved that there is nothing like a chance of active work for inducing young men to flock to the standard. The Volunteer force in England was originated owing to a scare of invasion from France, and the Shanghai Volunteer Corps, which had become moribund was revived with vigour at the time of the Tientsin massacre.

The advertisement was backed up two days later by a public letter, headed, 'A Patriotic Appeal' from Colonel Mainwaring, Captain Arthur Chapman and Captain E.D. Sanders:

It appears to us that amongst the British population of Hong Kong, greater interest ought to be taken in the Volunteers movement, a movement which deserves the support of every man capable of carrying arms, in as much as it strengthens that military force which is the safeguard to our commercial, political and religious privileges throughout the Empire.

Circumstances have shown us quite recently, that it is not alone the European Powers, seeking territory in the Far East, whom we have to provide against, but that there is an ever present danger nearer at hand. To the heads of firms and employers of labour we therefore say: 'Grant your employees every privilege compatible with the carrying on of your business, so that they may be Volunteers in real earnest, and not just in name only.' To the young men of Hong Kong we are sure that we have only to recall the fact that they are subjects of the Queen, to induce them to come forward at once and join that organisation which helps to preserve the integrity of their hearths and homes and to promote the peace and prosperity of the community.

To all we say: Remember that the time may come when of necessity your services may be required.

Is it not better, then, that all men should possess that knowledge of arms which will render them efficient defenders of their families and their Empire?

We confidently call on the young men of Hong Kong to join the Hong Kong Volunteer Corps and so obtain that knowledge of arms forthwith.

GOD SAVE THE QUEEN EMPRESS

The Volunteers were called out again a month later, on 16 May, to assist in the actual occupation of Kowloon City:

It was about eleven o'clock in the morning when the Volunteers got word to assemble at Headquarters at one o'clock. The order was obeyed with alacrity, considerably over a hundred putting in an appearance. A couple of seven-pounders and two machine guns were got out, the rest of the members of the corps acting as infantry.

At two o'clock, under the command of Captains Chapman and Sanders, they marched down to the Commissariat Pier, taking with them an ambulance squad in charge of Bombardier Nobbs and accompanied by Surgeon-Captain Lowson. At the pier several launches and a junk were waiting, and the Volunteers got aboard, together with about 150 men of the Welch Fusiliers, a few Royal Engineers, and about half-a-dozen Chinese appeared, the last-named taking with them a flagstaff for erection in the new acquisition. Though the descent on Kowloon City had been kept very quiet, the inhabitants seemed to have got wind of it, for as the launches neared the landing place opposite the Police Station (latterly the Customs House) it was seen that the beach was crowded and that people were also congregated on some of the adjoining hills. On landing the troops formed up on the square in front of the Police station and when the guns had been got ready the march was begun, some men being left to guard the pier. These naturally had a somewhat dull time of it, and when their comrades returned and gave a glowing account of the outing they had had the men who had been told to stay behind grumbled at their fate in not being allowed to go forward.

The march into Kowloon City was made by two or three routes, the troops being split up. The Fusiliers, with Colonel Mainwaring (in command) Major Prendergast, Captain Superintendent May, and other officers went first, and as no one had any idea what sort of reception would be accorded the troops a sharp look-out was kept as the narrow stinking lanes were passed through and the corners were turned. No obstacle was, however, experienced. The natives, evidently much impressed by the display, mostly kept indoors, leaving the whole of the streets to the troops. The latter were not sorry when they reached the paddy fields, as the open sewers which ran down the centre of the streets were filled with stagnant dirty filthy water which gave out an odour which caused not a few of the not over-fastidious Tommies to apply their handkerchiefs to their nostrils. On reaching the walled city the troops found the gates open as usual and hardly a soul was to be seen. Colonel Mainwaring hunted out the Mandarin, and told him what he had come to do. The Mandarin listened to what he had to say and then practically told him he could do what he wished, as he was powerless in the face of such a force. He seemed anxious, however, to be left alone and to be seen as little as possible during the proceedings, and his wish was respected, no attempt being made to make a show of him.

The next thing to be done was to collect all the arms in the place. A couple of magazines, each in charge of a solitary old man, were visited. The doors were broken down and the contents piled up in an open space.

And a miscellaneous assortment of articles there was too! There were a few decent rifles, but the majority were of an antediluvian character, and not only were they old, but they were thickly covered with rust. Several gingals were unearthed and some cannon similar to those captured beyond Taipohu [Tai Po Market] recently, together with a number of old rusty pistols. Box after box of ammunition was brought down by the men, who also brought out spears, rusty swords galore, bows and arrows, war flags, and soldiers uniforms. We understand that it is intended to forward all the stuff collected to Canton.

At about five o'clock the troops formed up behind the wall overlooking Kowloon Bay preparatory to the flag hoisting ceremony. The flagstaff had been erected near one of the embrasures. The troops presented arms, a royal salute was fired, and the good old Union Jack, hoisted by Major Prendergast, was soon floating in the breeze.

Up to now hardly any of the inhabitants of the walled city had been visible, and accordingly the soldiers were sent to scour round for them and bring them up to the scratch. This was a work which both the Fusiliers and the Volunteers enjoyed hugely. Some of the natives, who evidently knew that no harm was meant to them came forward willingly enough and seemed to enjoy the fun as much as any one, whilst others who perhaps had not had so much to do with Britishers came forward with fear and trembling, their fears being increased by some of the troops mischievously shaking their heads ominously and drawing their hands across their throats.

All, however, soon recovered confidence, and when told that they could go hung about in a way which showed that any fear of injury which they might have had at one time had left them. There were no signs, however, of any Chinese soldiers. No doubt many of them were dressed as civilians and were among the crowd collected together.

At about six o'clock the Volunteers and some of the Fusiliers started for home, about 100 Fusiliers being left to garrison the city, and the Commissariat Pier was again reached at about seven o'clock.

The trip was immensely enjoyed by all who took part in it. The force was a fairly formidable one — such a force as many of the inhabitants of Kowloon City had never seen before and they could not fail to be impressed by it. Both the Regulars and the Volunteers looked smart and workmanlike and were altogether a body of men who did credit to the flag.

For Scots, at least, the events in the New Territories stirred military instincts and the idea was enthusiastically raised of establishing a Scottish unit in the Volunteers. This gained the immediate backing of the St Andrew's Society which announced: 'They strongly recommend any young and patriotic Scots who are not already Volunteers, to send in their names for a place in the ranks of the "blue bonnets".'

However, the *Daily Press* cautioned:

A cardinal point to be borne in mind is the smallness of the community from which the Corps is to be recruited, which, it may be contended, should lead to the sinking as far as possible of national and class distinctions and differences rather than to their voluntary multiplication. There are not sufficient Irishmen or Welshmen to form special units of their own, and a decision to base the organisation on national distinctions might exclude many, and conceivably lead to the break up of the Corps after the first flush of enthusiasm had subsided. Mr Anderson's appeal is directed only to those Scots who are not already Volunteers, but if a distinctively Scottish unit be formed, it is probable that many, possibly the majority of the Scottish members of the Field Battery and Maxim Gun Company would apply for a transfer, with a corresponding weakening of the units to which they at present belong.

Not enough Scots could be found for a purely Scottish formation, however, and it was decided to allow English, Welsh and Irish to join as well though, of course, it was to retain its Scottish identity. The authorities had given their approval for the company to be an infantry unit of about 50 men and officers.

Further evidence of Volunteer enthusiasm came in a poem penned by one describing himself as 'Son of a Gun'. Up until recent years the Volunteers have had a rich and deep tradition of poetry. This may be somewhat surprising to those with a simplistic view of the military mind, but in the days before film, video and television, much care and wit went into the construction of verses, songs and other diversions. Though unlikely to win the approval of high-brow literary critics the writings of Volunteers have left a valuable and entertaining legacy. During the dark years of the Japanese occupation, songs, concerts, poems and recitations were to give escape from the barbed wire and suffering. The Volunteer poetic tradition is worthy of further study.

The following verses, jingoistic and bombastic though they may be rated today, are an interesting insight into the attitudes of British residents of Hong Kong at the turn of the century. 'Son of a Gun' wrote in 1899:

Defence Not Defiance

Men of Hong Kong you are wanted now,
Your duty's plain as it well may be;

The way you may help, the means and the how,
Is clear for the veriest dullard to see.

We are checked by Chinese in our Hinterland
And the Black Flags wave at our outer gate,
And shall Englishmen calmly stand
To leave the issue alone to fate?

Not so! While men can shoulder a gun,
Can wield a sword or can strike a blow,
We'll prove our manliness every one,
And carry ourselves that the world may know.

We may not be called out for deeds of fame,
We may not be asked even to fire a shot,
But we'll do our duty, and pitiful shame,
On the errant one who says he will not.

Men of Hong Kong you are wanted now,
Rally around and, with rousing cheers,
We'll greet each other, as we know how,
In the Loyal Hong Kong Volunteers.

At the same time as the excitement of the take over of the New
Territories, the long-awaited new Regulations for the Volunteers
were published, stating: 'The object of the Corps is to aid the
Regular Troops in the defence of the Colony against foreign
attack and to assist the Government in the repression of local
disturbances.'

To be eligible as a Volunteer a man had to be a British subject,
between 18 and 50 and physically fit. However, there was still a
difference between eligibility and acceptability, for the rules laid
down:

No person shall be admitted as a member of the Corps except on the
proposal of two members of the unit to which he seeks admission, and
with the approval of the Commanding Officer of the unit and of the
Commandant. The names of the person proposed and his proposers shall
be posted at Headquarters for not less than five days before the person
proposed is admitted as a member of the Corps

The drill season was from the start of October to the end of
March with an annual inspection by the G.O.C. at its completion.
An annual camp of instruction was to be held together with
classes throughout the season.

It was laid down, in line with the Army Act, that, providing they were not on active service, Volunteers could withdraw from any service which would render them liable to military law. Details were given of financial and administrative arrangements.

Members of the Field Battery were issued with one helmet and fittings, white and khaki colour, one cloth field service cap, one artillery pattern suit of cloth frock and trousers as issued to English volunteers, two suits of khaki drill frock and trousers, one cape and two pairs of blue puttees. Members of the machine gun company received a khaki-coloured helmet and fittings, a field service cap, a suit of serge frock and trousers, two suits of khaki drill frock and trousers, a cape and two pairs of khaki puttees. Members of the Engineer Company received the helmet and fittings, white and khaki colour, the cloth field service cap, a suit of Engineer pattern cloth frock and trousers as worn by English volunteers, two suits of khaki drill frock and trousers, a cape and two pairs of khaki puttees.

Naturally, the uniform for officers was more complicated and there was provision in the regulations for an allowance of not more than two-thirds of the total cost, providing this did not amount to the equivalent of more than 20 pounds, to be paid by the government to each officer on first appointment. Half would be paid actually on appointment, and the other half on gaining a certificate of proficiency.

Officers were to provide and keep a helmet and fittings, appropriate to each unit, a cloth field service cap, forage cap, one suit of serge frock and trousers, two suits of khaki drill frock and trousers, one great coat, one cape, two pairs of puttees, one summer mess suit, one pair of lace overalls, a set of badges of rank, buttons and shoulder badges, a sword, three sword knots, a white waist belt and slings, a cross belt and pouch and a set of Sam Browne equipment

The small arms ammunition scale provided for 75 rounds of ball and 10 blanks to be supplied for each efficient. Seventy rounds and the same number of charges for quick-firing or other guns were to be supplied to each battery. For seven-pounder or similar guns, 150 rounds with charges were to be supplied, together with a further 50 charges alone, for instructional purposes. Each effective machine gun was to be given 1,500 rounds of ball ammunition.

And so, the Volunteers entered the twentieth century.

6

The New Century

1900–1914

THE early years of this century were a time of great activity and enthusiasm for Volunteers in Hong Kong. China was in turmoil. The Boxer Rebellion had brought swift retribution from the foreign powers and the Manchu dynasty was in the last phase of its long death rattle which was to culminate in its overthrow in 1911. As ever, events in China were watched with keen interest by the Hong Kong community. There was a genuine desire to see a better system of government emerge in China, combined with the desire to stave off any unwelcome attentions to Hong Kong from other major powers.

The movement known to the west as 'The Boxers' had its origins as an anti-dynastic force. However, its strong anti-foreigner aspects found much sympathy with the Manchu court. The movement swelled, feeding on widespread resentment and Imperial encouragement. The legations at Peking were besieged until relieved on 14 August 1900 by a large international force consisting of British, Russians, Americans, French, Austrians and Italians.

Apparently, at least one Volunteer managed to get involved in the Allied expedition to relieve Peking. E.B. Wettenhall was a Volunteer at the time and he recalled, 'A fellow gunner — one of the Hutton Potts, somehow got into the British contingent which marched to Peking in the Boxer rebellion under the German Count von Waldersee and somehow became possessed of the Imperial Order which had been presented to the Empress of China by the German Emperor and there was a great fuss about this.'

Britain had problems of Empire in South Africa, and such was the patriotic enthusiasm in Hong Kong that the Volunteers offered to send a detachment with four machine guns for service there. The offer was refused.

The report to the Legislative Council for the year ending March 1900 showed a great increase in size, after the years of constant appeal for support from the community, though this was not without its problems as the Volunteers tried to squeeze into inadequate accommodation, and the usual administrative annoyances came to be more irritating. In April 1899, the corps had consisted of a total of 181 officers, N.C.O.s and men, serving with the Field Battery, the single 'A' Machine Gun Company or the Staff. By March 1900, however, the total strength stood at 311 of all ranks. 'B' and 'C' Machine Gun Companies had been formed, together with 'D' Infantry Company — which presumably had a strongly Scottish flavour — 'E' Engineer Company and the Band. This meant that each of the units sanctioned under the Corps Regulations was functioning.

Another important change was that the six obsolete seven-inch rifled muzzle-loading guns had been exchanged for six 2.5 inch rifled muzzle-loaders, pending the acquisition of breech-loading guns of the newest pattern. 'It is earnestly hoped that this vital question of re-armament will soon be dealt with in a satisfactory manner,' said the commandant, Sir John Carrington.

Six of the .45 inch Maxims had been sent to England for conversion to .303 calibre, with the plan being that the other six would be sent as soon as the first half dozen had returned. Martini-Henry carbines had been replaced by Martini-Enfield .303 calibre Artillery carbines. Magazine Lee-Enfield Rifles, Mark I, had been received for use by the infantry and engineer companies. Pattern 88 sword bayonets had been received to replace the old sword bayonets. There were 150 sets of the old Martini-Henry carbines with sword bayonets and 100 of these were given to the police, with the remainder being retained for drill purposes.

Plans were well in hand to equip the new formations with items such as mess tins and capes. Approval had been received for three machine gun companies and one infantry company to wear crimson facings. Annual camp took place under canvas from 20 to 30 October at Stonecutters Island with a good attendance:

Much practical work was performed, including company, carbine and rifle drill, extended order practice, outpost duties, musketry instruction, fire discipline, gun drill, belt filling, lectures and instruction in gun laying and fuze boring. Gun practice took place over sea and land ranges.

The Corps also took part with the Regular Forces in the defence of

Stonecutters Island during the night mobilization. On that occasion the Engineer Company of the Corps assisted the Royal Engineers in working the electric lights on the island.

One man who joined at about the turn of the century was E. Abraham. He recalled, 'From memory I joined up in 1897 as a signaller when I was 17 years of age and was transferred to the Field Battery as a Gunner in 1898. Sir John Carrington, Chief Justice of Hong Kong, was the Commandant and I think Major C.G. Pritchard, R.G.A., was the Adjutant of the Corps at the time.' (In fact, Pritchard did not become Adjutant, and Quartermaster, until the 1900–1 training year). 'We wore khaki uniforms with Indian Army topees in summer and blue-cloth uniforms and pill-box caps in the winter.' Abraham also took part in the occupation of Kowloon City, recalling, 'When we landed at the stone pier in Kowloon City we made straight for the Mandarin's Headquarters but found the place empty and there were no Chinese soldiers to be found anywhere. In those days when a soldier discarded his blue coloured waistcoat he became a civilian.' Abraham had a very long career as a Volunteer — joining the Hughes Group of the Hong Kong Volunteer Defence Corps in 1940. Subsequently he was transferred to the St. John Ambulance Brigade on account of his knowledge of Cantonese. He survived the battle against the Japanese and internment during the Second World War.

There was much public discussion in the early years of the century over Hong Kong's defences and their inadequacy. Residents followed events in the latest Boer War keenly and the suggestion was made that a military railway should be constructed around the south side of the island along which could run trains carrying quick-firing guns ready to repel any attempt at an enemy landing. Although the railway was never built, this concern with the unprotected south was well merited. However, the authorities concentrated their attentions on improving the fixed defences at the harbour entrances and within the harbour.

The *Hong Kong Weekly Press* of 30 June 1900, reported that the Governor had stated that new guns had been put in place at Stonecutters Island and at the Lower Battery at Belcher's Forts. Guns for the Central Battery at Lyemun were on the way. The paper commented:

It goes without saying that these guns should have been supplied years ago. It is too a very patent fact that there should also years ago have been a sufficient garrison to man these forts. There are not enough gunners to work the guns and provide for contingencies and there is nothing like enough infantry to protect the islands, to say nothing of the territory on the mainland.

The paper was also concerned at the old problem relating to Hong Kong's defences — once trouble broke out somewhere else the garrison was stripped of men.

Why is it that emergencies always find the War Office unprepared? The hand to mouth policy of the department is simply disgraceful and utterly inexcusable, because there is no lack of funds ...

It is not generally known, but it is nevertheless a fact, that the military authorities are very busy just at present in improving and extending the fortifications of the island. A number of new guns have been put in position on the forts recently. It does not necessarily follow that these operations have a connection with the state of things up north, but it is hinted that during the tenure of office of the last General Commanding the progress which the War Office desired in this direction was not made. Apparently the new general is paying particular attention to the improvement of the island's defences.

In 1902, however, attentions were diverted from the immediate worries of defence by the visit of a Hong Kong and China military contingent to Britain. A party of 40 Volunteers was included in the group, under the command of Major Chapman, Second-In-Command of the Corps. Also in the group were detachments from the Hong Kong and Singapore Battalion, Royal Garrison Artillery, the Hong Kong Regiment, the Hong Kong Submarine Miners (of whom almost nothing is known), and the First Chinese Regiment (from the newly leased territory of Wei Hai Wei, in Shantung). The full strength of the contingent was 75 officers and men.

After this high-point of Imperial display, disappointment followed for many Volunteers. The all-too-familiar word 'reorganization' was heard once more.

The improvements which had taken place to the fortifications of Hong Kong have already been noted — as has the lack of manpower to service them. There just were not enough regular troops available to man all the guns. Answer — the Volunteers, much to their disgust: most had joined for the soldiering good life and were none too pleased at the prospect of being stuck at remote static coastal artillery positions staring out to sea. The cause of the problem was that during the 1902–3 year, the Volunteer Corps had been re-arranged into Garrison Artillery and Engineers. There were two companies of artillery, split into left and right halves, and an engineer company. Gone were the Field Battery, and A, B, and C Machine Gun Companies, of the previous year. The Engineer Company and the tiny Band survived and joined the new Garrison Artillery companies.

Resignations followed and the 1903 annual report showed a total strength of all ranks of 274 as against 318 the previous year. The G.O.C., Major General Gascoigne, explained:

There has been a falling off in numbers, but this was to be expected owing to the change in the composition of the Corps — a change which was naturally not acceptable to all former members. But I am thoroughly satisfied that the change was a wise one, Garrison Artillery and Engineers being the two units in the Garrison which require strengthening, and in which the assistance of Volunteers, well-trained, is of the highest value. It speaks well for the common sense and loyalty of the Corps generally that this change was so largely accepted, once it was made clear that it was in this respect that their services were most required.

C.G. Pritchard who, in April 1902, had taken over the duties of Commandant with the local rank of Major said:

The change in the constitution of the Corps was brought about owing to an urgent letter from the Officer Commanding Royal Artillery, who pointed out the absolute necessity of more Garrison Artillery in the command, and when it was found that no more Garrison Artillery could be furnished he strongly urged that the Volunteer Corps should be altered accordingly. The matter was put before the members of the Corps, when the majority at once came forward and agreed to the change, and I wish to take this opportunity of saying that I consider great credit is due to all ranks for thus taking the matter up, as it was done against the personal wishes of a large number and entirely because it had been put forward that the Corps would be of greater service in the defence of the Colony.

One unfortunate result of the change was that the cup presented, a short time before, by Gascoigne, for Maxim Gun practice could not be competed for, and the conditions were altered to provide that in future the two 15-pounder breech-loading guns, newly provided by the Royal Artillery, would be used. These guns were kept at headquarters and therefore practice did not entail a weary journey out to the forts.

Annual camp at Stonecutters Island, not surprisingly, saw much work done on the 10-inch and six-inch breech-loading guns at the forts there, together with the three-pounder quick-firing guns. 'The C.R.A. kindly gave a very instructive lecture on Artillery in Coast Defence' — the C.R.A. being the Officer Commanding Royal Artillery. The Engineers practiced their primary role in manning the lights for the coast defences.

Despite the spate of resignations and the grumbling, it seems the Volunteers accepted the change as inevitable.

The C.R.A. inspected the artillery units at Stonecutters West on October 18th. The guns of the fort were completely manned and there were spare detachments at the six-inch breech-loading guns. Each officer and detachment was seen separately by the C.R.A. and given orders by him personally so that the inspection was very thoroughly carried out. The C.R.A. expressed himself very pleased with the drill of all ranks and stated that he considered that after such a short period of drill the progress made had been exceptionally good and that the officers especially seemed to have been well trained and knew their work very well.

Such a good report was not achieved without difficulty, as reported by Major Pritchard, a regular Royal Artillery officer:

The difficulties in the way of training Volunteers here as Garrison Artillery are very great, and considering these and the short time that has elapsed since the change, I consider the progress made has been very good but unless some arrangements can be made for drill guns near the Headquarters the members can never be kept up to the approved strength nor the efficiency be as good as be wished.

Obviously, the 15-pounder breech-loaders were but a poor substitute for the mighty guns of the coast defence forts. Pritchard continued:

At present any drill with heavy guns has to be done at one of the Forts in the District and for one hour's drill the men have to give up two to three hours to allow for proceeding to and fro. This practically limits these drills to Saturday afternoon, and accounts for many of the men resigning as they cannot possibly give up the time.

He went on to say that unless heavy guns were provided for practice, 'It will be practically impossible to keep the present number together.'

The fort lights were, naturally, at the forts, and the same problems of travel encountered by the reluctant garrison gunners applied for the engineer company. Pritchard made a strong appeal for 'a shed to be put up in a central position in Kowloon, and that an engine etc., and an electric search light installation should be placed there for special instruction of the Volunteers to obviate the necessity of all the instruction being given at Belchers and Stonecutters.'

This was noted by the authorities and, in 1905, Pritchard was able to report that 'The Engine Shed with engine and Electric Light installations at Kowloon for the H.K. Volunteer Engineers was completed and handed over to the Corps in September 1904, this has enabled the members of this unit to carry out their drills without the great delay which was formerly unavoidable in proceeding to and from the Forts.' Night mannings at the forts, with the Royal Engineers, took place once a month. No practice coast defence guns were provided, however.

The new Regulations for the Hong Kong Volunteer Corps were published in the *Hong Kong Government Gazette* of 14 November 1902. Composition was laid down as two Garrison Artillery Companies, an Engineer Company and a Band.

The object of the Corps is to aid the Regular Troops in the defence of the Colony against foreign attack and to assist the Government in the repression of local disturbances ...

No person shall be admitted as a member of the Corps except on the proposal of two members of the unit to which he seeks admission, and with the approval of the Commanding Officer of the unit and of the Commandant. The names of the person proposed and his proposers shall be posted at Head Quarters for not less than five days before the person proposed is admitted as a member of the Corps ...

The drill season will extend from the first of October to the 31st of March in each year or a similar period at such other time of the year as may be found more suitable ...

The establishment schedule was laid down with the grand total for all ranks standing at 400.

The 1904–5 year saw an event, not perhaps as operationally significant as the change to a garrison-artillery role, socially extremely important: a Mounted Troop was born. Like their contemporaries around the Empire, the British residents of Hong Kong were fanatically keen on horse racing and and the mounted troop of the Volunteers must have been a logical extension of that. Many Volunteers kept their own ponies, of sturdy Mongolian or Australian stock.

The New Territories now had to be patrolled and there were very few roads but a lot of mountains and remote areas. Thus, Major General V. Hatton, G.O.C., was able to report in 1905: 'The Corps has been strengthened by the establishment of the Mounted branch, which will shortly be fully equipped. I have inspected them and was entirely satisfied with their turn out. They are a most useful addition.' Major Pritchard reported that members of the troop had shown a great keenness in their drills, but that their saddlery and equipment had not yet been supplied. 'I therefore cannot include them amongst the Efficients, although I consider the majority of them should be so classed.' The mounted Volunteers probably also received great encouragement from the then Governor, and Honorary Colonel, Sir Matthew Nathan, who was a former Royal Engineers officer. Anecdotal evidence for this can be drawn from the nickname with which the 29 troopers were dubbed — 'Matthew's Mounted Mugs.'

Another significant development in the 1904–5 training season was the setting up of the Hong Kong Volunteer Reserve Association. This consisted of a manpower reserve to the Volunteers and it quickly climbed to a membership of 154 individuals, all of whom were over 35. 'The members are taking up rifle shooting with great keenness, and they should be of great value as a Reserve Company in case of urgent need,' reported Major Pritchard.

After the disappointment of the change to the artillery and engineer set-up, numbers were climbing again and Volunteers were tending to attend more than the minimum number of drills. One recruit managed to complete 110 drills between September 1904 and March 1905, rather than the minimum number of 30 to qualify as 'Efficient'. An engine shed with engine and electric light installations had been completed for the engineers to practice upon. However, together with the Royal Engineers, they still took part in night mannings at the forts, about once a month. The artillerymen carried out a full programme of drills and practice shoots.

During that year, a new pattern silver dragon badge was introduced for the helmet and field cap.

A feature in the *South China Morning Post* of 1905 gave a brief history of the Volunteers, adding:

Now the Corps is so efficient and well up to date, and with the knowledge that a suitable headquarters is to be provided, where the members can not only gain martial knowledge, but also have a club room provided for them in the form of a reading room and billiard room, every able-bodied man should hasten to enroll his name, either in one of the Artillery Companies, the Engineer Company, or the Band. The Troop is up to strength and so bring up the total number to at least 400. It is true there would be no difficulty in raising more than that number in case of emergency, but why wait for that in the folly of unpreparedness? It should be the proud boast of Hong Kong that its Volunteer Corps is not only efficient and up to date, but is up to strength, with not a few names down for the first vacancy.

Concern was still being felt at the total lack of protection on the south side of the island — particularly for the great dams at Tai Tam which formed the main water supply. One newspaper correspondent wrote,

A gentleman who has made a study of the defences of Hong Kong — that is to say as far as a mere civilian can study them — points out to me the utter inadequacy of the protection provided for the very heart of the island's vitality, Tytam Reservoir. From the direction of Waglan the great retaining wall of the reservoir could be destroyed with a few accurately placed shells and Hong Kong made practically uninhabitable or liable to capitulation.

Much mystery surrounded a big military exercise carried out in February 1905. The *Hong Kong Weekly Press* reported:

The talk of the ninth of February was the capture of Belcher's Fort. It was taken, during the annual mobilisation manoeuvres by the attacking party in the early morning. The torpedo boat steamed into harbour as bold as a red light could make it, and the defenders' searchlights flashed on it in an instant. The enemy, in the meantime, quietly pulled their boats to beach under the cover of the temporarily interrupted darkness and before the military knew where they were, the bluejackets surrounded the heights and demanded surrender.

A week later the newspaper reported that it was extremely difficult to get any information about the mobilization manoeuvres — which was probably just as well as what had already been reported should have been enough to alarm readers. Among the problems was that 'the swiftest means of communication between the sentinels or outposts and the massed troops waiting to be summoned were lacking.' It summed up sombrely, 'Considering how nearly the British government has approached the brink of war in recent times, the condition of our garrison is by no means all that we could wish for.'

Much of the colony's apprehension came from the Russo-Japanese War of 1904–5 and the British Far Eastern Fleet was temporarily reinforced.

The cost of the Hong Kong's defence was naturally continuing to rise. The defence contribution from the colony stood at $508,976 in 1898, but in 1904 it had risen to $1,314,773. The proportion of the total revenue devoted to defence costs had been raised from 17.5 per cent to 20 per cent in 1901. It is worth noting that this was not an arrangement which related to the actual cost of Hong Kong's defence, twenty per cent of total revenue was required.

The following training season, 1905–6 saw continued strong Volunteer growth, with the total strength of the Corps on 31 March 1906, standing at 274. Showing equally strong growth was the Volunteer Reserve Association, which increased by 76 men during the year to achieve a membership of 230 — almost equal to the Corps itself. Major Pritchard reported:

It has become a very popular association. The members have carried out a large amount of rifle practice throughout the year and a very good average has been obtained. The members have the same privilege of obtaining ammunition at reduced cost as the Volunteers, and carry out their practice at the King's Park Range, Kowloon, which is more accessible than the Volunteer Range at Tai Hang. It has also been decided that a range shall be built for their use at the Peak.

The remains of this Peak range can still be seen today. The butts are near the slopes of the sharp High West hill, close to a picnic area at the junction of Harlech, Lugard, and Hatton Roads. Firing took place across the valley from a position on Harlech Road.

All members of the corps were now equipped with the new Short Rifle. Members of the mounted troop made use of the Patterson Rifle-carrying equipment, and swords had recently arrived from England.

H.B.L. Dowbiggin, whose name was to feature in Volunteer activities for decades to come, was a mounted trooper at that time and he recalled:

We were fortunate to have as our CO Charles Henderson Ross, later Taipan of Jardine Matheson and Company here and of Matheson and Company in London. He had served in the South African War and was a fine horseman and polo player, and an excellent range and game shot. In the ranks were a number of Taipans, including two members of the Legislative Council, the Hon W.J. Gresson and the Hon Murray Stewart.

Most of our parades were held on the old polo ground at Causeway Bay or on the sand track at the race course. We were armed with carbines and swords. Invariably we led the march past at the Review of Troops on the King's Birthday Parade. At these we had to be drawn up next to the RA guns which fired salutes. To get our ponies used to this Ross [the Lieutenant in command] practiced us with a very noisy brass-cannon he had used on his houseboat up country in China.

The rest of the Corps did their annual camps at Stonecutters Island — obviously a place unsuited for cavalry of any sort. Ross, with his great knowledge of the New Territories, soon found a suitable camping site for our first annual camp, for a week, over the Christmas holidays in 1906, at Lo Wu. Tentage and equipment were sent round by junks, whilst the Troop rode out the 23 miles to reach it. It should be appreciated that there was no railway and no roads beyond Kowloon, only a footpath as far as Tai Po, and everywhere only the very old and narrow Chinese tracks. During our camps out there, we covered many miles each day on reconnaissance, taking out haversack rations for ourselves and a bag of feed for the ponies.

Not long afterwards, the army took over Lo Wu Camp, and the Mounted Infantry (as the Troop was then designated), and the Scouts Company used Sun Wai (also discovered by C.H. Ross). Later, the army took over Sun Wai camp, and the Volunteers had to hunt about for another site, and settled on one near and east of Fanling Railway Station, which was in every way most convenient for all members of the Corps.

Thus, the Volunteers came to what is today known as Volunteer Slopes, home to many more camps in the future.

Dowbiggin continued:

One interesting event in these early days was the visit of HRH the Duke of Connaught and his daughter, Princess Patricia, to Hong Kong, I think in early 1907. On his landing at Blake Pier, the Mounted Troop acted as escort to him in his eight-coolie chair, and during his stay at Government House, the Mounted Troop provided a small mounted guard of which, for many hours, I was a member.

Dowbiggin said that the knowledge of the New Territories gained by the troop was of great value to each British regiment which came to be stationed in Hong Kong. Two or more mounted Volunteers were attached as guides to each regiment during combined operations.

Typical of the training at the time for the corps as a whole was a field day held on 25 January 1906, Chinese New Year's Day, when, in the morning, half the Volunteers attacked a strong position held by the remainder. In the afternoon the two sides swapped round. 'This was a good opportunity for the Troop and the other Units to work in conjunction, and some good scouting work was done.' The Volunteers also took part in the garrison mobilization exercise and in the usual annual camp at Stonecutters Island.

Constant repetition by the Volunteers of the need for a permanent headquarters had finally paid off, for on 15 December 1906, the opening ceremony took place. The building, roughly on the site of the present Central Government Offices, in Lower Albert Road, was paid for out of Volunteer Corps funds, with the addition of $5,000 from the government. Major Arthur Chapman, who wrote the annual report for the 1906–7 period during the absence of Major Pritchard on leave, commented:

All the roms have been well furnished and the Officers' and Sergeant's Mess Rooms and the Billiard Room have been completely fitted up out of private funds at no cost to the Government. The building has already proved very popular ... I am convinced that this will tend to make volunteering more popular, and trust that the numbers will increase; the separate messes for Officers, Sergeants and rank and file should also improve the discipline of the Corps.

A small cadet corps was started in May 1906, with 12 boys from the Victoria British School who were instructed in squad drill and semaphore signalling. Also in that year, the Mounted Troop started to wear Sam Browne sword belts and leather buckets for carrying their rifles.

The vagaries of history and the devastation of Hong Kong's records by war mean that the last report from this period to have survived in the territory is for the 1907–8 training year. It is worth, therefore, taking a look at it in some detail.

On March 31st, 1907, the total strength of the Corps was 289 and on March 31st, 1908, it was 295.

During the past year 68 members have resigned (three on medical certificates, 27 in the Colony, and 38 on leaving the Colony. Seventy-four new members have been enrolled.

The Hong Kong Volunteer Reserve Association had on March 31st, 1908, a membership of 219, a decrease of 29 during the past 12 months.

Members of the Hong Kong Artillery Volunteers of 1882.

Volunteers on parade towards the end of the training session in April of 1895.

Officers outside Volunteer headquarters in 1895.

Volunteer camps at Stonecutters Island were a regular feature of life in the decades around 1900. Here the 1907 camp is illustrated. The stone buildings date from the original prison which was constructed in the 1860s. The picture looks towards the east, with the Kowloon hills in the background.

Volunteer officers photographed at the 1907 camp. The building behind now houses the headquarters of the Hong Kong Military Service Corps, although at the time of the photograph it appears to have been in use as a powder magazine. Originally, this was the entrance to the prison.

The Volunteers are pictured on parade in 1913, just before the outbreak of the First World War.

Volunteers in action in the mainland hills during the 1914 camp.

Volunteer Reservists posed for a group photograph during the First World War.

The Volunteers on parade at the Cricket Ground, probably for the peace celebrations in 1920. The smoke is from the battery which fired the salute. What is now the Legislative Council building is on the right. The area is now the site of Chater Garden.

A formal dinner of the Volunteers at headquarters in 1924 or 1925. The social life of the corps was always lively.

Almost every chest bristling with medals, Volunteer signallers pose with trophies in the mid-1920s.

Major General C.C. Luard is seen inspecting the H.K.V.D.C. in February 1927.

'Guns fore and aft'. This odd vehicle seems to have been used shortly after the formation of the Armoured Section, members of which are pictured here in the mid-1920s.

Members of the Mounted Infantry, probably in the 1920s, are seen crossing a small bamboo bridge in the New Territories, where 'the China pony goes merrily along'.

Members of the Mounted Infantry on parade in 1926. This section of the Volunteers was then enjoying a boom both militarily and 'as the most practical and cheapest avenue of approach to hacking, hunting, polo, racing and chasing'.

Volunteers on parade — a cartoon from a 1930s yearbook.

Volunteer camp at Fanling in 1932, looking northwards. The plume from a steam train on the Kowloon–Canton Railway can just be made out at top right. The paddy fields have long since disappeared beneath modern developments and roads.

One of the machines used for Volunteer flying training — a D.H. Moth Major two-seater. Built by De Haviland, the aircraft belonged to the Far East Flying Training School, and was registered in Hong Kong on 26 April 1935.

Members of the Air Arm photographed in the mid-1930s.

A Christmas card from the 1930s showing representatives of the Volunteer units outside their headquarters. The group includes Artillery men, Machine Gunners and members of the Scots, Australian, and Armoured Car sections. The card comes from Major (Retd.) Frank M. Lewis, who taught battery gun drill while serving with the Hong Kong and Singapore Royal Artillery.

A Sikh section was formed in the
Corps Signals at the end of 1936,
to join the Muslim section.
This picture is of
Signaller S.S. Chowdhury.

The first battery 'washing the gun' in 1936.

Number Two Armoured Car, front, and Number Three Armoured Car, rear.
Pictured on exercise in the New Territories in 1937.

Mobility was the key feature of the Volunteer motorcyclists. Here they are seen
taking a break from exercises in the New Territories in 1937. The officer with his
back to the camera at left is sitting on a War Department marker stone.

Lieutenant Colonel R.C.B. Anderson, M.C., the first Regular to command the Volunteers, shading his eyes, watches machine gun practice in the New Territories, in about 1937.

Volunteer machine gunners on exercise in the New Territories in 1937.

Seen relaxing at camp in the late 1930s are members of Number Two, Scottish, Machine Gun Company.

Rifle practice is carried out on two days a week throughout the year at King's Park Rifle Range, Kowloon, and at the Peak Range.

Equipment — The four 15-pounder breech-loading guns on loan from Commander Royal Artillery were withdrawn during March, 1908, and are to be replaced by four 15-pounder quick-firing guns, two of which have already been received. [The term quick-firing is applied to a gun, the charge of which is contained in a brass cartridge case which expands on firing to seal the escape of gases. A breech-loading gun is one where the propellant or charge is placed in a silk or cloth bag and the gases are prevented from escaping by the use of a pad fixed to the face of the breech screw].

Table 6.1 Breakdown of Membership in the Corps (1907–8)

Staff	7
Troop	40
Right Half No. 1 Company	45
Left Half No. 1 Company	55
Right Half No. 2 Company	56
Left Half No. 2 Company	48
Engineer Company	44
Total	295

A total of 174 Volunteers were listed as 'Efficient', with more than 30 drills; 62 as 'Efficient', with less than 30 drills. Among the 'Non-Efficient' were 33 people on leave, two with medical certificates, 12 recently joined, and 12 non-efficients who were to pay a fine. Four of those included in the overall list, exclusive of the Staff, had completed over 100 drills, and 74 men had completed between 50 and 100 drills. A Corporal A.E. Wright had achieved the highest number of drills attended — turning up on no less than 123 occasions during the year.

An ambulance class was formed in April, 1907, under Surgeon Captain Forsyth. At the conclusion of the course this class was examined by Lieutenant Fraser, R.A.M.C and nine members passed a satisfactory examination.

On 1st May, 1907, a Semaphore Signalling class was formed under the Staff Officer. This class was examined on 3rd and 5th July and 14 qualified.

A special course of instruction was held during September with four attendances a week for N.C.O.s and others desirous of promotion. This course was well attended with most excellent results.

Recruits drills were held twice a week during the summer months and from beginning of September, 1907, to end of March, 1908, there were drills for all members four times a week.

Regular 15-pounder and Maxim gun practice was carried out. 'Musketry practice is very popular with the majority of the members of the Corps,' said the report. 'During the year 52,089 rounds have been fired by members of the Corps and 25,715 rounds have been supplied to the Reserve Association.'

With the rest of the garrison, the corps took part in the King's Birthday Parade on 9 November 1907. The Corps also paraded with the garrison and lined the streets on 20 April that year, when Sir Matthew Nathan departed from the colony. They turned out again on 28 July for the arrival of the new Governor, Sir Frederick Lugard. On each occasion the troop provided an escort.

The Cadet Company grew to 22 members and a bugle band was being established. A miniature rifle range was soon to open close to Victoria School. The new headquarters had been equipped with a complete gymnastic apparatus, purchased out of private funds. Winter clothing had arrived. Alterations in the establishment of the corps, providing for the formation of an infantry company had been approved and would come into force early in 1908.

The camp report said that the annual camp took place at Stonecutters Island from 19 October to 4 November 1907, with 17 officers and 182 N.C.O.s and men attending. The keen members of the mounted troop held a separate camp over the Christmas period. And so, Volunteering continued during the first decade of the twentieth century. Enthusiasm was high and the new headquarters quickly became an important location in the social life of the colony. In fact, men of suitable age were 'expected' to belong to the Volunteers.

The 1911 census included a table listing the 'European and American Civil Population according to race.' The table showed that there were 889 English male residents, 309 Scots male residents, 93 Irish male residents, 27 Welsh male residents, and 839 'other persons of British race not defined as above', giving a total male British population of 2,157. Given the social structure of the time, in trying to guess the size of the pool of potential Volunteers, the 839 'others' can probably be disregarded since the 'others' would be unlikely to be accepted as volunteers, thus leaving a total of 1,318 English, Irish, Scots or Welsh men. Let us assume that half of these were either children, or too old for service, or disqualified for health or other reasons. That leaves 659 men. Nearly 300 were enrolled Volunteers, with another two to three hundred holding membership of the reserve. 'Everyone' was a Volunteer. Well, not quite everyone — there were about another 450,000 people in the colony at the time.

The Volunteer Reserve Ordinance of 1910 regularized the position of the reserve, laying down rules for its administration and direction. Nothing was said about any nationality requirement, but reservists were required to take an oath and declaration stating that they would 'be faithful and bear true allegiance to His Majesty King George V' his heirs and successors. The reserve was allowed to elect its own president and it was governed by a committee consisting of that person and not less than three others elected by the members.

The government was to issue, on loan, a rifle and equipment for each member, together with 100 free rounds of rifle ammunition per head, with more available on payment. In time of emergency the reservists were to become full Volunteers:

The Governor may, by proclamation, whenever it appears to him advisable to do so by reason of invasion or war or danger of either of them, or by reason of any internal emergency threatening the security, to quell which the available civil force is deemed by him inadequate, cause all or any members of the Volunteer Reserve to be enrolled as members of the Volunteer Force; and all the provisions of the Volunteer Ordinance, 1893, and any Ordinances amending the same, shall in so far as they are applicable extend and apply to every such member on being so enrolled to all intents and purposes as if such members had signed the engagement and taken oath under that Ordinance; and every member so enrolled shall remain and continue subject to the provisions of the said Volunteer Ordinances, and shall be entitled to the befits thereof until the Governor shall by proclamation cancel such enrollment wherepon all members so enrolled as aforesaid shall again become subject to this Ordinance as members of the Volunteer Reserve.

The year 1911 saw the Ch'ing Dynasty come to an end. The provisional president of the Republic of China, which officially came into existence on 1 January 1912, was Dr Sun Yat-sen, former Hong Kong medical student and possibly a former Volunteer.

China was hardly a threat to Hong Kong, however. But the success of Japan in the Sino-Japanese and Russo-Japanese Wars and its steadily increasing power and ambition was causing serious thought to be given to the problem of defence of Hong Kong. An article in the *Naval and Military Record*, in Britain, said that in the absence of a battle squadron, Hong Kong would have to surrender immediately if attacked. The editorial in the *Hong Kong Daily Press* of 7 February 1907, did not think much of that point of view, or the author of it, describing him as 'A miserable croaker infected with the yellow peril fever. The disease in his case is virulent because he seems to think he is the discoveror of it … Japan is the power to whom Hong Kong, like another Port Arthur, is to be surrendered in the visible future.'

The paper said that the *Record's* article had stated that the lessons of history taught that sooner or later one of the great nations would have to fight Japan, or Japan and China, for the right to trade and hold what she had in the East. 'Pestiferous moonshine,' thundered the *Daily Press*. Others were more realistic.

Japan was a power to be reckoned with, having demonstrated great naval success and force of will. Japan was also Britain's ally, as the Anglo-Japanese Alliance of 1902 had been renewed for 10 years in 1905. However, the danger to Imperial interests, scattered across Asia and the Pacific from this newly powerful friend were causing causing concern to strategists. This dangerous friend remained Britain's ally for the time being, however, and when the fires of war erupted in Europe it was Japan who guarded British interests in Asia and allowed naval and military might to be diverted to where it was most needed.

Just before the outbreak of war, the Directory and Chronicle of 1913 put the regular garrison at three companies of Royal Garrison Artillery, one company of Royal Engineers, one company of Infantry, Army Service Corps and Royal Army Medical Corps units, four Indian Infantry battalions — of which two were in North China, presumably at Wei Hai Wei — four companies of native Artillery and one company of local native Engineers.

The approaches to the harbour are strongly fortified, the batteries consisting of well-constructed earthworks. The western entrance is protected by three batteries on Stonecutters Island and two forts on Belcher and Fly Points, from which a tremendous converging fire could be maintained, completely commanding the Sulphur Channel. Pine Wood Battery, on the hill above and west of Richmond Terrace, has a wider range of fire. The Lyemun Pass is defended by two forts on the Hong Kong side and another on Devil's Peak on the mainland, and if vessels survived that fire they would then have to face the batteries at North Point and Hung Hom which completely command the eastern entrance. Another battery on the bluff at Tsim Sha Tsui, Kowloon, commands the whole of the centre of the harbour. The batteries are armed with the latest breech-loading ordnance. The colony of Hong Kong pays a military contribution fixed at 20 per cent of revenue.

In addition to the fortifications the colony possesses a small squadron for harbour defence. This consists of the obsolete turret ironclad Wivern, 2,750 tons, now dismantled, three submarines and six torpedo boats. The crews of these vessels are borne in the receiving ship Tamar which is also the headquarters of the Commodore and his staff. The Naval Yard consists of a large dock, an extensive range of workshops and offices east of the Artillery barracks, and the Naval Authorities have another large establishment on the Kowloon side near to Yau Ma Tei.

7

War in the East

1914–1918

THE outbreak of the First World War saw a surge of patriotic fervour amidst the British residents of Hong Kong, reflecting the situation around the Empire.

Most of the regular troops were quickly withdrawn for service in Europe, leaving a seriously depleted garrison. Initially, Volunteers were assigned to man a series of block houses which had been constructed at strategic points in the hills above Kowloon. Then, no German attack having materialized, they moved to Murray Barracks.

One enthusiastic Volunteer recalled that this continued until:

such time as the banks and larger firms began to hint that, while not lacking in patriotism, they were finding it somewhat difficult to maintain the commercial life of the colony, with 60 per cent of their staffs away, playing at soldiers.

An arrangement was made by which we were to pursue our ordinary avocations during working hours, and be soldiers for the remainder of the time.

Half the Volunteers slept each night in tents in Central while the other half supplied guards for the camp in which German residents of Hong Kong were interned, and various vital points around the colony. The two halves changed over each week.

One veteran wrote:

The whole Corps (less those on guard) paraded every evening; and all Volunteers were ordered to be in uniform at all times, and to have their rifles, equipment and ammunition within easy reach. The 'Alarm', a bomb detonated in the Naval Yard, was to be the signal for all Volunteers to converge on the cricket ground. I may add that the alarm never went off, but periodically, the midday time-signal, or an extra-loud Chinese cracker, brought perspiring gentlemen hurtling from their offices, feverishly donning equipment as they ran.

One became accustomed to the sight of men going to their offices, to the club, to social functions in full battle-order. When invited out to dinner one's host said casually, 'Just leave your rifle and gear in the spare room'. We brought the darned things with us to church. I remember attending a soiree at Government House and leaving my rifle and equipment in the cloak-room before going in to shake hands with Sir Henry and Lady May. I would like to be able to say that I had danced at Government House in shorts and ammunition boots; I was dared to, but lacked the moral courage.

Many men of eligible age left Hong Kong to join the forces. Only 17 British commercial ships remained in Chinese waters and these were taken over by the British government, normal commercial activity being suspended.

There were liberal subscriptions to war charities and the Legislative Council, in addition to the cost of local defence and the military contribution, voted a $10 million gift to Britain. A special additional assessment of seven per cent on the rates raised another $2 million. One of the more surprising gestures of support for the mother country was the presentation to an Imperial Air Flotilla of the Royal Flying Corps of at least two Vickers FB5s — the first true fighter aircraft. The first was funded by the Chinese community and the second by the British residents. Both were inscribed with the names of their donors, the former in Chinese characters as well as English.

The China Mail, of Hong Kong, commented:

The Chinese are often accused of being pro-German and many of them doubtless are. It is quite natural that they should be. But whatever their countrymen over the frontier may think, those who know the benefits of British rule and justice in Hong Kong, Chinese and British subjects alike, have showed many striking evidences of their sympathy with the cause of the Allies. The donors could not have chosen a more useful gift, and, though none of them will probably see it, they will have the satisfaction of feeling they have assisted in equipping the forces which are fighting so strenuously to uphold the principles of justice and truth for which the British flag has always stood.

The German population of Hong Kong was put at 342 men and women by the 1911 Census, easily the largest foreign community. On the outbreak of war the women and children were made to leave the colony. German companies had been tough business competition for British interests in China and in 1916 they were taken over by the government and their assets sold. One of the roles of the Volunteers was to provide a guard for the camp at Hung Hom in which Germans of military age were interned. 'About half the prisoners had been sent down from Tsingtao,' recalled one Volunteer. 'But the rest were local German civilians, our erstwhile friends and acquaintances, and quite ready to be effusively familiar. It is embarrassing for a zealous sentry to be hailed vociferously, as "Good Old Bill" and asked whether he has remembered to load his rifle.'

So relaxed were things that the internees were given tools to construct an earthen stage for the camp's theatre hut. The resulting tunnel ran for 180 feet under the wire and nearby railway line.

The intention was to make a mass escape. The first three men got out unseen, the fourth was carrying a white canvas bag which gave him away. A sentry on a "crow's nest" loosed off and hit the bag — which was good shooting. The owner thereupon dived back into the tunnel thereby blocking further egress. It was somewhat of an anti-climax the more so when the other three were arrested next morning near Fanling by an Indian constable.

One of the few old buildings to have survived in central Hong Kong is the old German Club, closed on the outbreak of war. It is now the home of St Joseph's College which can be seen on the left while driving up Cotton Tree Drive, near the Lower Peak Tram Terminus.

Compulsory enrolment in the defence corps came with the enactment of the Military Service Ordinance of 1917. Every British male between 18 and 55 was made liable for military service. The only exclusions were those who were already in the regular forces, who were employed by the regular forces or recommended for exemption by them and ministers of religion.

The ordinance also established a Hong Kong Defence Corps. Anyone who was already a member of the Hong Kong Volunteer Corps or Hong Kong Volunteer Reserve was automatically transferred to the new Hong Kong Defence Corps with the same rank. The corps consisted of a company of artillery, a company of engineers and a battalion of infantry. The prime role of the artillery continued to be mainly related to the coast defences, where the engineers operated the searchlights.

The year was divided into cold weather and hot weather

training seasons, with the changeover taking place in mid-October and mid-April. There were to be 50 parades per year, in
addition to parades and attendances ordered for musketry instruction or practice. The musketry course was to be the same as
for the regular forces. The artillery and engineer companies were
to be mobilized for one month during the cold weather and there
was to be 'a camp of exercise' of the same duration for the infantry
battalion. Minimum compulsory attendance during this month
was eight days, not necessarily consecutive. Men between 45 and
50 had to attend musketry instruction and practice, but only 24
other parades and four days of camp per year. Men over 50 were
to do 'such modified training as may be prescribed by the General
Officer Commanding the Troops.'

News of peace in November 1918 was celebrated, in Hong Kong,
as elsewhere, with scenes of tremendous jubilation. The cathedral,
and all the other churches were packed for services at which the
dead were remembered while thanks were given for peace. The
buildings and the ships in the harbour were gaily decorated and a
public holiday was declared for Wednesday, 13 November.

A special meeting of the Legislative Council was held and a
resolution expressing heartfelt rejoicing passed by acclamation,
immediately followed by three cheers for the King. The resolution
was then put to the general public at a meeting held at the Theatre
Royal where there were more speeches and a great deal more
cheering. The Hong Kong Club threw open its doors to all friends
of members and 'the greatest enthusiasm prevailed.'

The most significant speech of all the many meetings and
celebrations was made at that same gathering at the Hong Kong
Club. The speaker was the Japanese Consul, Mr E. Suzuki, and his
words are a telling indication of the feelings of Japan which had
stood with the Allies throughout the War:

Let me celebrate, first of all, this auspicious occasion when the honourable
and well-deserved Armistice with Germany has been signed, which
means a complete victory to the Allies — not simply on behalf of the
Japanese community here but also as a member of the nation which has,
for a number of years, been allied to Great Britain, and has fought to the
end the ruthless enemy for the common cause of humanity and freedom.
(Applause).

I need hardly dwell in detail upon the nature and object of the Anglo-
Japanese Alliance. Suffice it to say that it is one of the most important
pivots of Japan's foreign policy, and aims, among other things, at the

maintenance of peace in the Far East. Consequently it would be quite natural that, if the peace, which it has constantly been Japan's cherished desire to maintain, should be threatened and disturbed by any selfish reasons, she would resort to such measures as would ensure her national honour and safety. (Hear, hear).

Four years ago, soon after Great Britain responded to the arrogant challenge of Germany, whose aggressive intention had been revealed by the advance of her troops over the Belgian frontier — in avowed violation of the Treaty ensuring the perpetual neutrality of Belgium, to which Germany herself was a party, though she afterwards said that it only amounted to a 'scrap of paper' — Japan, in full deference to the spirit in which the Alliance was originated, sent an ultimatum to Germany, demanding of her that Tsingtao which Germany had extorted from China under some pretence, and which had proved to be the basis of evils menacing the Far Eastern peace, should at once be surrendered.

War naturally ensued, Tsingtao was speedily taken by us, and since that time no shadow of a soldier or ship of enemy origin has been seen in the East. But if anyone even thought that Japan's task in the war ended with the capture of Tsingtao he certainly made a mistake. Inspired by the sense of righteousness and humanity, and actuated by her duty and responsibility, Japan decided to extend her sphere of activity, sweeping the enemy away from the Pacific and Indian Oceans in co-operation with the British Navy, and assisting in the enduring work in the Mediterranean, in addition to her latest efforts in Siberia. (Applause).

Remote as Japan is geographically situated in the Far East — where, thanks to our combined efforts, no hostile influence has been allowed to exist — it has never made any difference to her unswerving determination to stand by the Alliance and to render all possible assistance to the common cause, because this has been a struggle for liberation against oppression, which has now been defeated.

Distant as she is from the centre of the horrible scenes of the war, it has only served to increase her sympathy with those brave men from every part of the Allied countries, because it was a war to resist Prussian militarism, to prevent world-domination, and to preserve the international freedom and peace for which we have been striving for centuries and which is now being attained. Indeed, it will not be simply my own personal view that the Allies have been fighting in the firm belief that the sword, once unsheathed to defend the majority of nations of the world, both from neutral and material slavery, should never be laid down until the final victory was won — and that is now an accomplished fact. (Cheers).

It is with the greatest pleasure that I say that Japan has played a part in this epoch-making war, discharging her obligations contemplated in the Treaty of Alliance, and I can assure you of my belief that, whatever course events may take after the war, the ties of friendship which have, happily, been subsisting between the two nations under the Alliance will ever be augmented and cemented. (Applause).

Finally, with all my heart, I say that the vindication of Right against Might is so unmistakable as the sun appears when the clouds are dispersed, and that the solution of the problem of the present war has really rested with those who deserved it. (Applause).

Joining in the applause were the the the Officer Administering the Government, Mr Claud Severn, the G.O.C., Major General F. Ventris, army and navy officers and members of the Defence Corps.

The Consul's speech is explained by a look at the historical background. Hong Kong had seen a joyful round of parties and entertainment in the run up to the mid-summer of 1853. An American squadron was in the harbour, under the command of Commodore Matthew Galbraith Perry. The black sailors of the *Susquehanna* were particularly popular, providing music and amateur dramatical entertainment. However, all good things must come to an end and eventually Perry and his four ships set out northwards. Japan's isolation from the world, established in 1637 came to an end in July 1853 when Perry sailed into the harbour of Uraga. Fifteen years of turmoil followed, ending with the overthrow of the Tokugawa Shogunate and the restoration of Imperial rule under the Meiji Emperor.

The new Japanese administration was determined that Japan should not end up as a colony or dependency of a foreign power in an age of western expansion. A constitution which produced national unity, industrialization and a strong army were seen as the keys to future independence and prosperity. An old slogan 'fukoku-kyohei', implying a strong country and a strong military became the guiding maxim.

The Japanese decided that an island state needed a powerful navy and with the Meiji restoration of 1868, the Imperial Japanese Navy came into being. Britain was the world's prime naval power, and so ships were ordered from her and Royal Navy officers became the first instructors at the newly-established naval academy. Throughout the latter part of the nineteenth century, Japan continued to draw upon the shipyards of the west and to develop its own construction capabilities, taking care to note all advances around the world. In August 1877, the first vessel bearing a Japanese flag sailed into the port of London, captained, nonetheless, by an Briton. In 1891, the Admiralty produced as complete a list as it could of all known Japanese war vessels. The fleet stood at 59 vessels, ranging from small torpedo boats up to large cruisers.

War with China followed a short time later. Both countries distrusted each other's intentions towards Korea and at the start of the 1890s it was clear that China was gaining the predominant interest there. The Korean government asked the Chinese to help it put down a rebellion and tension rose.

The Anglo-Japanese Treaty dating from the initial opening of Japan was revised in the summer of 1894. Britain was the first nation to agree to a revision of its treaty and this created much good feeling in Japan. Nine days later the Sino-Japanese War began and the result was a whole series of impressive victories for Japan both at sea and on land, and culminating in the Treaty of Shimonoseki. A small nation had taken a big step on to the world stage. It had almost annihilated Chinese naval power, and it had taken Korea completely, before moving across to the Liaotung peninsula to take Dalien Bay and the great fortified base of Port Arthur. China's final humiliation came at Wei Hai Wei with the suicide of its admiral and surrender of its fleet.

The Shimonosekei treaty laid down that both China and Japan recognized the independence of Korea; Formosa, the Pescadores Islands and the Liaotung Peninsula were ceded to Japan, which received all rights enjoyed by European powers; new treaty ports were opened; economic concessions were made and a large indemnity was set. A supplementary treaty gave Japan tremendous commercial advantages.

But what Japan had won by force of arms it could not keep in the face of diplomacy. Russia, France and Germany 'advised' Japan that 'in the interests of peace' it could not keep the Liaotung Peninsula. This key spit of land jutting into the Bohai Sea housed the vital harbours of Port Arthur and Dalien. The Russians had had their eye on Port Arthur, a warm water port, for decades. Germany was worried that if Russia did not get its way in the east it would look westwards.

That stunning loss of face to Japan was compounded when, in 1898, the Russians calmly forced the Chinese to grant them a lease of the vital Liaotung Peninsula. France took a base at Kwangchow, south of Hong Kong, the British leased Wei Hai Wai at the same time as they took over the New Territories, and

Germany established a naval base at Tsingtao, Kiachow, near Wei Hai Wai. Only the Italians lost out, being refused a concession. The Americans, meanwhile, were busy taking over the Philippines from Spain.

Japan drew the conclusion that national dignity required not only greater naval and military might — but allies. The Japanese played an active part in the allied expedition to Peking in 1900. At the same time, Russia occupied southern Manchuria and the Koreans looked towards Russia as a counterweight to Japan.

However, secret negotiations were going on, the results of which were to stun the world. In February 1902 it was announced in London and Tokyo that a full Anglo-Japanese Alliance had been signed. No longer did Japan stand alone in the world and, significantly, neither did Britain — which had not had a full-scale alliance with anyone for almost a hundred years. Both sides wanted the same thing, containment of Russia. That country's dual alliance with France was now neutralized. The agreement between Britain and Japan stated that each party would assist the other if attacked by or two or more other powers and would remain neutral if the other was at war with one other power. If France had joined with Russia in a war with Japan, then Britain would have been at war with its neighbour across the Channel.

Germany politely declined Russian approaches for assistance, saying it was only interested in trade in Asia.

In 1902, a massive programme of Japanese naval expansion was approaching its culmination, with the completion in the United Kingdom of the world's strongest battleship, the *Mikasa*. All of Japan's big battleships had been built in Britain.

Russia was now to learn, once and for all, the strength of its eastern neighbour. Without bothering to declare war, Japan attacked the Russian fleet at Port Arthur. The Russian Baltic Fleet, rushing around the world was destroyed at the battle in Tsushima Strait and the Japanese army achieved success on land.

America acted as a mediator between the two combatants and peace was signed in September 1905. Japanese primacy in Korea was recognized, and Japan took over Russia's interests in southern Manchuria — including the Liaotung Peninsula containing Port Arthur. It also acquired the southern half of the island of Sakhalin. Korea was quickly brought to heel, being annexed in 1910.

A second significant event in 1905 was the renewal, for 10 years, of the Anglo-Japanese Alliance. Coverage of the alliance was extended as far as India and now each party would come to the aid of the other if attacked by only one other power.

As pointed out by the Japanese consul, in his November 1918 speech to the Hong Kong club gathering, in 1914 Japan had not been slow to declare war on Germany after rejection of a demand for the withdrawal of all German warships from Chinese waters and the handing over of Kiachow to Japan for eventual return to China. The warships did depart, though it is unlikely that this was in response to the Japanese demand being due instead to a desire to concentrate naval force where it was most needed. The German warships made a run for home across the Pacific but met their end at the First Battle of the Falklands.

An unlikely Japanese-British force (significantly, under Japanese command) assaulted Tsingtao, and the garrison there surrendered in November 1914, giving the allies one of their first victories of the war. China pressed for the return of the former German territory but in January 1915 received in response the notorious 'Twenty-One Demands'. These were split into five groups and the first four included: Japanese control of Shantung, Manchuria, Inner Mongolia, the southern coast of China and the Yangtze valley. As if this were not bad enough, the fifth group demanded the employment of Japanese advisers in Chinese political, financial, military and police administration and the purchase by the Chinese of at least 50 per cent of its munitions from Japan.

Although the weak Chinese government eventually agreed to all that was demanded, public opinion was inflamed and a tremendous surge of nationalism resulted, born of a fear that China would virtually cease to exist as an independent nation. Students returned from education abroad to provide impetus and direction to the national outrage.

As the war ended, it was Japan, ally of the powers that defeated Germany, that was supreme in Asia. No western power had any stomach for expansion following the exhaustion of the great war. But, as Consul Suzuki put it to the cheering throng at the Hong Kong Club, most of whom would have been members of or associated with the defence forces, Japan viewed itself as:

the nation which has, for a number of years, been allied to Great Britain, and has fought to the end the ruthless enemy for the common cause of humanity and freedom ... The vindication of Right against Might is as unmistakable as the sun appears when the clouds are dispersed ...

8

The Turbulent Twenties

1919–1934

WITH the cessation of hostilities after the First World War, the need for compulsory military service in Hong Kong had passed and volunteering made its reappearance with the Volunteer Ordinance of 1920.

The colony was facing up to considerable problems and there was turmoil in China. The Versailles Peace Conference at the end of the war considered the question of Shantung.

Japan went into the talks well prepared. In 1915 Japan had made its infamous 'Twenty-one Demands', which would have made China almost a subordinate dependency. Russia had recognized the Twenty-one Demands in 1917. Britain had agreed to support Japan in its claims on Shantung and on German Pacific possessions north of the equator, with Japan agreeing to support Britain in its claims to German Pacific islands south of the equator. Other agreements were made with Italy and France. The United States concluded an agreement in November 1917 recognizing Japan's special position in China in return for a commitment to an 'open door' policy. Finally, Japan made a secret pact with the Chinese warlord government in Peking, granting it a big loan but gaining in return the right to build railways in Shantung and to a military presence at key points.

However, the members of the Chinese delegation to the Versailles conference, which was made up of representatives of Peking and of Sun Yat-sen's government in Canton, arrived with high hopes of the West, which appeared to be devoted to the causes of freedom and national self-determination. They hoped that everything, including 'unequal treaties' in their entirety, was to be discussed. Not so, said the other parties. Only matters relating to the end of the war were on the agenda. That meant, so far as

China was concerned, that only formerly German Shantung was to be discussed. The delegation pleaded, but without success and the Japanese finally revealed their secret agreement with the Peking rulers. Under their secret treaties the allies supported Japan. When news reached China, the student movement was incensed. On 4 May, a huge demonstration took place in Peking to protest at the betrayal of China. Ten students were arrested and this led to a general strike in the capital. The protest was taken up in major cities and the strike was joined by workers and business interests all over the nation. A massive boycott of Japanese products began, together with a refusal to use Japanese steamers or to unload Japanese goods at the docks. The confused Peking regime left the decision whether to sign the Versailles agreement to the delegation itself and boycotted the signing ceremony. The intellectual fires of revolution in China were inflamed and many, disgusted at China's treatment by the West, and by their own country's continuing ineffectiveness, turned towards Marxist principles.

The overthrow of the Ch'ing dynasty in 1911 had been greeted with rejoicing in Hong Kong, but a series of problems, disputes and boycotts followed. In 1916, President Yuan Shih-k'ai declared himself emperor but had to withdraw this claim for lack of support and died soon afterwards. Years of war were to follow as various factions fought for control of China. It was not until October 1928 that the National Government of the Republic of China was established, controlled by the Kuomintang, although even then, the Kuomintang was not in control of the whole country.

Hong Kong had remained quiet during the First World War, but at the end of the decade in which it took place there were considerable internal problems. An outbreak of cerebro-spinal meningitis killed a thousand people; shortages of rice and the resulting price increases caused much hardship and some rioting; an influx of refugees from China drove up rents; inflation was soaring and wages were static, leading to serious labour unrest. A strike began in the dockyards in 1920 and this developed into a major stoppage throughout the colony. The government was forced to use the army and navy to keep essential services running.

It was against this background that the Volunteer Ordinance of 1920, gazetted at the start of February, must be viewed. This was a very detailed piece of legislation, carefully and comprehensively drafted. A new Volunteer Corps was to be set up consisting of a company of artillery, a company of engineers, a machine gun company and a battalion of infantry. The latter could consist of a mounted infantry company, a light infantry company, a Scottish company, a Portuguese company, a reserve company, and "such other companies as may be found desirable."

The most significant paragraph of the ordinance, however, was the following:

In case of great national emergency, or in case of actual or apprehended invasion or of attack on the Colony, or of serious local disturbance, the Governor may, by proclamation, call out any volunteer for actual military service.

For the first time the Volunteers had an internal security role. Becoming a Volunteer entailed a more serious commitment than had been the case in the more relaxed pre-war days.

An oath or declaration of allegiance to the King was required, and everyone joining the corps was to serve for a period of three years, with stiff conditions being laid down before early resignation could be considered. Even if these conditions were met, if a man wished to leave without good reason, or was discharged, penalties applied — $60 if he left before completing a year's service, $40 before completing two years' service and $20 before completing the full three years.

No such penalties had ever been attached to Volunteer service before, and there was no mention in the ordinance of such gentlemanly customs as requirements for proposal and seconding before a man could join. Provision was made, however, for men to be recommended for appointment as officers by members of the companies in which the vacancy existed. The same applied to N.C.O.s. In both cases, this was conditional on the individuals having passed the relevant examinations. On first formation of the new corps this system of recommendation applied to the selection of company commanders. It did not apply to the commandant and staff.

The corps was liable to call out for actual military service and if that happened, then any man who was not incapacitated who did not report was to be considered a deserter. Corps members were not liable to serve or proceed on duty outside Hong Kong without their consent.

During actual military service the Volunteers were to be subject to the same regulations, receive the same pay, allowances and quartering as the regular forces and to be subject to the same regulations 'so far as may by the Governor in Council be deemed applicable to the volunteer corps.' If a man had to leave family members unable to support themselves while he was on actual military service, they were to be eligible for relief. Injury qualified the volunteer for pensions of up to a $1,000 per year, with gratuities payable should a man be killed on service or die of wounds, or as a result of fatigue or exposure, within 12 months.

Strict discipline rules were laid down, with the provisions of the Army Act applying to Volunteers if on actual military service or training with the regular forces, except that the sentence of death was not applicable and no sentence of a court martial could be carried out unless confirmed by the governor.

The Constitution of the Corps detailed its units and added:

The machine gun company will be for heavy machine guns e.g. Vickers guns. Lewis gunners will be distributed throughout the platoons of the infantry battalion ...

The reserve company shall consist of men who have reached the age of 40 years ...

Signallers will be distributed throughout the various companies and units ...

... the Corps shall be under the orders of the General Officer Commanding the Troops, subject to the general control of the Governor.

The company of artillery shall be under the executive command of an officer of the Corps, and shall be under the orders of the Officer Commanding the Royal Artillery of the Garrison for training and inspection.

The company of engineers shall be under the executive command of an officer of the Corps, and shall be under the orders of the Chief Engineer of the Garrison for training and inspection.

The machine gun company shall be under the executive command of an officer of the Corps, and shall be under the orders of the General Officer Commanding the Troops for training and inspection.

The infantry battalion shall be under the executive command of an officer who may be either a volunteer officer or an officer of His Majesty's Regular Forces. If this officer is a volunteer officer the Adjutant of the corps shall be an officer of His Majesty's Regular Forces, appointed with the consent of the General Officer Commanding the Troops, unless no regular officer is available.

The Administrative Commandant of the Corps shall be the officer commanding the infantry battalion, and he shall be assisted by an administration staff.

The constitution also included provision for the establishment of cadet companies.

Under the training schedule, the usual winter and summer periods were detailed. To qualify as efficient, a certain number of parades — in addition to an annual inspection and musketry instruction and practice — had to be completed by the volunteers (see Table 8.1).

Table 8.1 Number of Parades Required by Volunteers for 'Efficient' Rating (1920)

A.	Artillery Company	20
B.	Engineer Company	10
C.	Machine Gun Company	20
D.	Infantry Battalion	10

Members of the Reserve Company who were under 50 had to complete a modified course of musketry training and practice and an annual inspection, with camp attendance optional. No training was required of those over 50.

The artillery and engineer companies were to be mobilized for one week during the cold weather and, during the same season, there would be a camp of exercise for the machine gun company and infantry battalion. The minimum attendance at camp required for efficiency was three days, not necessarily consecutive.

The early 1920s saw events take place in far away Washington D.C. that were to have a dramatic effect on the defences of Hong Kong. A world exhausted by war seized upon the suggestion of the United States that a series of meetings be held in Washington to hammer out agreements which would attempt to prevent a damaging arms race and further conflict.

One of the agreements reached after much discussion was the Naval Armament Limitation Treaty of February 1922, which was signed by Britain, Japan, the United States, France, and Italy. This treaty limited the number of warships of more than 10,000 tons displacement to a ratio of five each for Britain and the United States, three for Japan, and 1.67 each for France and Italy.

Significantly for Hong Kong, this agreement also laid down that no changes were to be made to fortifications in the possessions of the powers between latitude 30 degrees north and the equator. Singapore was, however, excluded from this ban. At this time the great naval base which was captured at Singapore in 1942 had not been developed, and it was estimated that it would take about three months for a fleet to move from the nearest major British base — Malta — to Hong Kong in the event of a threat to its docks, yards, maintenance facilities, defences and supply depots.

There was little money or enthusiasm in Britain for matters of defence. In 1919, the government had laid down that the estimates for the fighting services should be based on the theory that there would be no war for the following 10 years. This greatly restricted defence planners seeking money from hard-pressed governments. In 1925, the Cabinet specifically directed that war with Japan was 'not to be seriously apprehended' within the next 10 years. In 1928, the 10-year rule was made self-perpetuating, with the expiry date extending by 24 hours with every day that passed. The forts of Hong Kong were left untouched. Huge 9.2 inch rounds laboriously hand-carried up to the guns at Mount Davis remained in storage, neatly ordered and maintained. It was to be 1941 before any of them were fired.

For Japan there was a severe shock in store at the Washington talks — its ally, Britain, abandoned the alliance it had signed in 1902. The alliance had been of tremendous emotional importance to Japan; the first it had signed with a Western nation and seen as a sign of the country's standing in the world. The alliance had been renewed in 1905 and 1911 but, after 1918, the spectre of Russian ambition in Asia had diminished with the revolution and Britain was keen to maintain close links to the United States. For their part, the Americans were viewing the growth of Japanese power with considerable unease.

The actual formal ending of the alliance came with the Four Power Pacific Treaty, agreed in December 1921. This treaty laid down that all four would be consulted if any two of them were involved in a dispute over any Pacific question and that they would respect existing rights relating to Pacific possessions.

During the early 1920s, pressure had been building up in Hong Kong. The turmoil in China had led to a great influx of people into the colony. The Census, taken in April 1921, showed the total population to be 625,166, but the Census Officer estimated that, for various reasons, the normal population was greater than that by 30,000. It is interesting to note that the non-Chinese population consisted of 32 nationalities, the main ones being:

British	7,889
	(4,706 males; 3,183 females)
Portuguese	2,057
Japanese	1,585
USA	470
Filipino	232
French	206
Dutch	104
Danish	36
Italian	56
Spanish	59
Russian	36

The Census Officer estimated the number of British nationals of European race at 4,300 and he put the number of British children of European race at about 500 of all ages.

Militancy in the labour force was increasing. A major strike occurred in January 1922, when a claim from the newly established Chinese Seamen's Union for a pay rise of 30 to 40 per cent was rejected. Attempts at settlement came to nothing and at the end of the month labourers and port workers also came out on strike. The workers ensured that few food supplies reached Hong Kong and the government reacted with banning orders against the unions. By the end of February a general strike had been proclaimed and emergency legislation was rushed through giving the government sweeping powers. The settlement that was eventually reached in March was widely seen as a victory for the workers. The government learned a lesson, however, and preparations were made to meet any further such disturbance. Stockpiles were gathered, and Britain was asked for an extra battalion of troops.

In China, the struggle for power was continuing. The death of Sun Yat-sen in March 1925 intensified the factional struggles. Then, on 30 May 1925, municipal police in the International Settlement at Shanghai opened fire on a crowd, killing nine people and wounding others. Demonstrations took place across China and there was talk of another general strike in Hong Kong. This soon developed as seamen and other workers began to leave their jobs.

On 23 June, a huge demonstration took place in Canton as thousands of people marched along the city side of the man-made creek which separated the foreign enclave of Shamien from the rest of the town. Shots were fired and British and French troops opened up on the crowd, killing 52 people. News of this enraged China.

In Hong Kong, the Volunteers had been called up on June 21. 'The members of the HKVDC received a general calling up order last night to parade at HQ immediately, and many were assigned to special duties, which mainly took the form of patrols in different districts,' said the *Hong Kong Daily Press* of 22 June.

The call out was made in a *Government Gazette Extraordinary* which was published by Section 12 of the Volunteer Ordinance of 1920, which stated: 'In case of great national emergency, or in case of actual or apprehended invasion or of attack on the Colony, or in case of serious local disturbance, the Governor may, by proclamation, call out any volunteer corps for actual military service.'

The *Daily Press* said that the Volunteers had been mobilized on the Sunday evening: 'They have been given instructions how to act if called upon, but at present their orders are simply to "stand by". Uniforms have to be worn and rifles and ammunition kept ready to hand. All ranks, also, have to make such arrangements as will enable them to be communicated with rapidly.'

No-one wrote to dispute the editorial comment: 'Never before have the British community been so united and so well-hearted in their determination to establish itself (sic) once and for all as masters in their own household. This strike, engineered from outside, is regarded as a direct threat to our liberty and must be resisted.'

Harry Owen Hughes remembered of this time:

When I came out to Hong Kong in 1922, one of the first functions I attended was the Annual Inspection of the Corps on Murray Parade Ground and I recall being shocked by the standard of drill. But who was I to criticise?

It was on the foundation of those keen Volunteers that we were able to rebuild the old HKVDC, and that did not begin in earnest till 1924 when we young men who had arrived in the Colony after the War had come to our sense. It was as well that we did because the Corps was called up for six weeks in 1925 during the general strike engineered from Canton when we worked in our offices all day and patrolled the streets and guarded hospitals and vulnerable points all night.

Regular and Volunteer troops were posted at key points throughout the city and sailors kept cross-harbour ferries running. Civilians were responsible for keeping essential services functioning and many served as police. The Volunteers appealed for people with motor-cycles to join them: 'They must provide their own cycles and side cars. Oil and petrol will be provided. An electrician and fitter will be in attendance at Volunteer Head-quarters. Work will largely consist of patrolling the roads of the Colony. Recruits must join up permanently, not for the period of the strike only.' But it was not only motorcyclists who flocked to join the Volunteers, for it was reported on 4 July that 'Since the date of mobilisation, some 117 recruits have joined the Hong Kong Volunteer Defence Corps. They have all been posted to the various companies and include among their number Portugese and Chinese volunteers.'

The latter fact is particularly interesting, for this report in the *Daily Press* is one of the first specific references to Chinese serving as Volunteers. Chinese had probably been serving earlier, as this report makes no special significance out of the fact that they were Volunteers in 1925.

On 8 July, the paper carried an article on the 'valuable work being done in many departments' by Chinese during the strike, saying that many had come forward to support the authorities and '... Chinese have joined the Hong Kong Volunteer Defence Corps.'

It does not appear that the Chinese served as a separate unit but, rather, that they were distributed through the different Volunteer units. It is not strange that Chinese should have come forward, for many of the richer Chinese had an obvious interest in maintaining the stability of Hong Kong. It is unlikely, however, that many would have been interested in entering the strange environment of the British military tradition until the impetus of the great events of 1925 took place. Certainly, there was never any question of Chinese being excluded from service with the Volunteers by regulations or other administrative device.

In 1954, an exhibition was mounted at St John's Cathedral Hall and this included a faded picture of the Armoured Car Company in 1926 featuring the Hon. Sir Man-kam Lo as a private. Oxford-educated Lo, related through marriage to the wealthy and influential Ho Tung family, would have had little difficulty in fitting in with the Volunteer environment. However, the question of who was the first Chinese to serve as a Volunteer remains unanswered. A Private Ho Leung, perhaps related to the Ho Tungs, was listed as a member of the Armoured Car Company in July 1925, in a report in the *Daily Press*. In another link with the Chinese community, Cadet corps had been formed in various institutes providing education for Chinese children.

It is interesting to note that it was in the summer of 1906 that the first unit of Volunteers organized on a western model was formed in Shanghai. In 1907 a Chinese unit was added to the Shanghai Volunteer Corps.

In Hong Kong in 1925, displays of strength formed an important part of the tactics of the authorities during the general strike. The *Daily Press* of 8 July reported:

Yesterday evening, the First Battalion The East Surrey Regiment, the Hong Kong Volunteer Defence Corps and a detachment from the British naval boats in harbour made a demonstration march through the city. The Surreys, headed by their regimental band and the naval contingent 1,000 strong, from HMS Titania, HMAS Brisbane and from submarines, headed by a Naval band, went through the Western district. The Volunteers marched via Happy Valley to the Eastern district and returned through Wanchai to Headquarters ...

The flow of new recruits continued, with the total on 16 July standing at 164 and on 20 July at 170.

By September, firm measures by the government meant that the worst of the strike was over, though a serious trade boycott of Hong Kong caused significant problems.

In early 1926 there was talk of another general strike as the dispute between Hong Kong and the government in Canton dragged on. In September 1926 the British sailed up the Pearl River, as they had done so many times before, and marines dealt with pickets at the docks there. A gunboat was left behind to prevent any further trouble. At about this time, Chiang Kai-shek's northern expedition had arrived at the Yangtze but it had been halted at Wuchang. This, and the threat of further British naval action, led the Canton government to look for a settlement and, after negotiations, the boycott formally came to an end on 10 October.

Against the background of the troubles of 1925 and early 1926 the Governor, Sir Cecil Clementi sent a long secret despatch to London, accompanied by maps and appendices, on the subject of the defence of Hong Kong. Contrary to some glib assertions, the general defence of the colony against external threat was always a subject of much thought and discussion. The Clementi despatch, dated 17 February 1926, gave a realistic picture of the situation.

Clementi, who had become Governor in October 1925, wrote that he, the naval commander in chief and the general officer commanding the troops had for some time been engaged in considering how Hong Kong could be defended against attack. They had received assistance from a Hong Kong General Defence Committee and from the officers of the aircraft-carrier HMS *Hermes*.

The Governor felt that 'Under existing conditions we could do no more than defend the island of Hong Kong and temporarily deny the enemy the use of Hong Kong Harbour but that we could not hold the mainland.' This blunt statement was proved true 15 years later.

Elaborating, Clementi said that the New Territories had been acquired 'because it had for many years past been recognised that the extension of Hong Kong territory is necessary for the proper defence and protection of the colony.' The problem was, however:

It now appears that the naval and military forces at present available for the defence of this colony would not be able to hold any part of the New Territories against a powerful enemy, and that it would therefore be open to such an enemy to establish himself along the ridge of the hill range above Kowloon, which completely dominate Hong Kong harbour, and from which position he could direct fire upon the principal docks, forts, and naval and military establishments of the colony as well as upon all shipping in harbour.

A British fleet would take six to eight weeks to reach Hong Kong and even if the colony had been able to hold out for that length of time the damage done would be so great 'as to make Hong Kong of little further strategic value for a considerable period.' The suggested action was the strengthening of local naval forces (to prevent any landings nearby) and of the military garrison (to allow for the defence of the New Territories). Furthermore, it was suggested that an air force be provided.

In a detailed report it was stated that the aim should be to retain the island at all costs with operations on the mainland 'being limited to such delaying action as could be practically carried out without seriously weakening the forces available for attaining this object.'

To protect the harbour, more navy ships were needed, the present garrison would have to be nearly doubled to four battalions of infantry supported by 1,200 other troops, and aircraft would have to be available. 'There appear to be only two alternatives, viz. either to increase the defence forces, or to ac-knowledge the fact that in the event of an oversea attack, the place would not for long be useable as a base for the British fleet.'

In the attached Appreciation, the Object of the Defence was stated to be, firstly, to hold Hong Kong for use as a British Naval base; secondly, if that could not be attained then to prevent the enemy using it as a naval base and thirdly, to ensure that the resources of Hong Kong which would make it valuable as an enemy base were destroyed.

At that time, the strength of the defence forces was one flotilla of submarines, four sloops and five river gun boats, 3,000 regular troops and 600 Volunteers, with additional expansion in an emer-gency, and no air force.

It was put plainly in the report that an enemy would have almost complete local command of the sea, it would have greater military force and it would certainly use air power. The nature of the country would make it difficult to move troops quickly to repel a landing. The central ridge of hills along the island would be an effective obstacle but there would be problems if the landing took place on the mainland. To add to the problem, there were no serious navigational difficulties in landing troops.

The colony's fixed armament in the forts was:

Probably sufficient to deter hostile ships from coming under fire. The range of the guns, however, is much less than that of modern ships' guns, and there is a large extent of water, within their range, which they could not cover with observed fire. Under existing conditions, they could not, therefore, prevent the enemy bombarding the harbour, if he wished to do so.

The movable armament consisted of pack, field and medium artillery.

In assessing the courses of action open to an enemy it was suggested that the attacker might try using long range naval bom-bardment to induce surrender. There could be no reply by the garrison and much damage could result. However, the expendi-ture of ammunition would be high, there would be considerable wear and tear on ships' guns and bombardment would not, alone, bring about surrender. Therefore, this scenario was considered unlikely. What was stated as more realistic was that the enemy would stage landings at several places around the island and the mainland at the same time and make a multi-facetted attack.

There appeared to be no means of preventing this, said the report. The naval defence forces were too small to seriously interfere with landing operations and troops were too few to cover numerous and widely-spread landings. Neither could they offer much resistance once the enemy forces were on the ground and advancing from several different directions.

This whole despatch was remarkably prescient, its only failing being to anticipate that an enemy might first have invaded southern China and would advance from the land.

During 1926 there were two amendments made to the Volunteer Ordinance of 1920. The first laid down that the governor could entrust the general administration of the corps to such officer as he thought fit, rather than requiring that the officer commanding should be the commander of the infantry battalion.

Also, in November of that year, the previous schedule which required different minimum numbers of parades for the various parts of the corps was rescinded and all Volunteers were required to attend 15 drills a year of at least an hour's duration, to carry out range practice and to carry out preliminary range practice of not more than three hours. Attendance at camp for four days was required with at least two of the days being consecutive and including a night. Attendance at the annual inspection parade was also required. There were a number of other minor changes made subsequently.

One person who joined the Volunteers in the mid-1920s was H.A. de Barros Botelho, whose family, like many others, had arrived in Hong Kong from Macau on the founding of the British colony.

My father was a special constable in the 1914–18 war ... There was the big strike in 1925 and I was made a runner. My father was very insistent that I should wear my white and blue arm band and carry a truncheon. I was delivering orders for various people to go on duty and it was no picnic having to walk to Shaukiwan or Wanchai and other places to deliver these orders, so I though it would be better to join the Volunteers.

I went along to the headquarters and joined as a private. We trained one night a week and there was an annual camp held at Volunteer Slopes at Fanling where tents were pitched. We had parades, exercises, shooting, pickets, withdrawals and all the usual things.

On the formation of the Portuguese Company he transferred, recalling: 'When they formed the company we had a Portuguese

Consul here in Hong Kong and he queried the ability of Portugese citizens to swear allegiance to the King. The Governor of Macau at that time was called Barboza. J.P. Braga talked it over with him and the subject was allowed to die a natural death.'

The Scots already had a strong identity within the Volunteers. During the general strike of 1925, a Canadian section had been established. This was a part of the infantry and all Canadian residents were invited to join. A maple leaf badge was planned, though it is not clear whether this was actually worn.

It was in 1926 that the Portuguese took up their separate identity within the H.K.V.D.C. The Portuguese community had always been an important part of the population of Hong Kong. Indeed, as the 1921 census showed, the Portuguese were second in terms of numbers only to the British in the non-Chinese population. The list of the original 'Ninety-Nine' of 1854 contained many Portuguese names.

The *Hong Kong Telegraph* commented on 17 July 1926:

We note with the liveliest satisfaction that there is a movement for the purpose of forming a Portuguese Infantry Company of the Hong Kong Volunteer Defence Corps.

In Shanghai there is a very strong unit of Portuguese in the Volunteers ... and there is certainly no lack of men who would be entitled to enroll in the proposed new company.

The paper said that there were already many Portuguese volunteers — certainly enough to form the nucleus of the new company. With the large Portuguese community resident here, there should be no difficulty in raising at least 200 men, and from this it should be possible to form two platoons.'

From one standpoint, the Portuguese unit of the Defence Corps, once established, should become one of the strongest companies in the whole Corps because most of the Portuguese here are permanent residents of the Colony. They are all duly appreciative, also of the security and protection which they enjoy under the British flag, and, as we have shown, they have not hesitated in the past to render extremely useful service to the community in general.

Once such a unit were formed, we have no doubt that its members would show their pride by striving might and main to make it one of, if not the most, enthusiastic and efficient companies in the Corps.

As predicted, the Portuguese were quick to establish their presence firmly.

During the strike of July 1925, several Portuguese joined Number Four Platoon of the Infantry Company and more signed up over the next few months so that by 1926, the platoon came to be comprised exclusively of Portuguese. In February and March 1927, a further batch of about 30 men enrolled to bring the total up to about 60. Then recommendations were made that a Portuguese Company be established and on 1 April 1927, it was officially announced, through Corps Orders, that sanction had been received to form the Company.

Captain R.R. Davies took over command, with Lieutenant S. Jarvis, M.C., as second in command. At that time, no Portuguese had been commissioned, the highest rank held being that of Company Sergeant Major. However, the first commission came soon afterwards and by 1930 there were four Portuguese officers on active service with another on the reserve. The company then had a strength of about 130.

It was during the 1920s that horses became an integral part of the Volunteers. Cavalry have always thought themselves a cut above the rest — and why should the Volunteers' have been any different? The 1920 Ordinance had provided for a Mounted Infantry Company and, by 1921, there was a small unit of 12 members. The ponies were the private property of the members who received a subsidy of $15 a month if, in the opinion of the commanding officer, attendance at parade was sufficient. The ponies were kept at the Jockey Club stables under the care of two riding boys, called 'Keyhole' and 'The Polo Kid.'

During the seamen's strike of 1922, the Mounted Infantry was sent to Fanling where it established headquarters in the Golf Club clubhouse. Patrols of the hilly passes were carried out to attempt to stop people who were trying to reach Canton.

One effect of the general strike of 1925 was that the Mounted Infantry received their own stables. The attendants at the Jockey Club had threatened to stop work unless the 'British War Horses' were withdrawn. The ponies were moved temporarily to Kowloon before returning to new stables at Causeway Bay.

By mid-1926 it could be reported,'The Mounted Infantry is enjoying a boom not only because it is the most practical and cheapest avenue of approach to hacking, hunting, polo, racing and chasing, but also because it now enjoys opportunities for real efficiency.'

The *Hong Kong Daily Press* of 7 July noted:

New stables, specially for the use of the Mounted Infantry, have been erected at Causeway Bay. This is a tremendous asset to the unit. In the old days the ponies were kept in Jockey Club Stables. When the members of the unit paraded, their ponies were brought out to them on the Polo Ground; they mounted, did a drill, and then handed over their ponies to mafoos who led them back into the sacred and, to many, unknown precincts. Recruits in due course learned to ride through the usual cavalry movements and attended the usual field days. Enterprising members even undertook the adventure of unescorted rides across the Island. But what is the use of learning to sit in a saddle, if you have never put a saddle on?

With their own stables, the Mounted Infantry could now learn the skills of stable-management properly. Indians were used in place of Chinese. They 'took the place of mafoos from the time that those latter objected to doing anything for the white man's war horses in times of emergency.'

It was firmly pointed out:

In no climate is it more true than in Hong Kong that the best thing for the inside of a man is the outside of a horse ... There are, of course, some Jonahs in Hong Kong who, with mystic reference to the Pampas, or the Belvoir, will tell you that it is not worth while, because Hong Kong is not a place for riding. The enterprising and public-spirited gentlemen, or rather ladies and gentlemen, who last year founded the Fanling Hunt may be supposed to have settled that argument by showing that there are miles and miles of Hong Kong territory over which China ponies can gallop three or four days a week for months, without a lame leg.

Scorn was poured on pedestrians, motorists and golfers who thought they knew the countryside of Hong Kong:

But the horseman knows the fascinating tracks from Taipo to Un Long [Yuen Long] and from Fanling to Chuk Ying. He knows the little hills between Sheung Shui and Lo Shu Ling, and the whole length of the frontier from Sha Tau Kok to Lok Ma Chau. He has ridden round Taipo Harbour and Plover Cove. He has been in the enchanted ground round Pineapple Pass before the road went there, and had ridden through Leadmine Pass. Much of that is heart-breaking country for the infantryman. He is blind with fatigue half the time. But the China pony goes merrily along, hopping over the half-hidden ditches, making no mistake on those difficult little bridges of one stone slab, and climbing steps where necessary, while the mounted infantryman scans the country at ease and knows exactly where he is.

As well as the joys of soldiering, the Mounted Infantry was prominent in all mounted sports. Gymkhanas featured such items as 'Wrestling On Horseback', 'Balaclava Melee' and tent pegging, the latter somewhat unusual: 'Tent-Pegging is an exercise seldom seen in Hong Kong. There is a popular superstition that if you get a China pony into a sufficiently rapid gallop to lift a peg you won't stop him inside a mile. Others say that if you brandish a lance near his head he will go mad.'

The Volunteer horsemen were keen supporters of the Fanling Hunt. Two individuals had brought out hounds but were finding the project rather too expensive to continue. The idea of making it a subscription hunt was suggested and the Mounted Infantry went up on a Saturday for a drag hunt and 'a very social evening.' The next morning the hounds were out again. 'Enthusiasm was such that the Masters decided then and there to continue running their hounds, and to send out a subscription list.'

It was from the Mounted Infantry that the Volunteers' involvement with armoured cars sprang. A number of individuals who were injured, or otherwise could not ride approached the unit with the suggestion that they form a Mounted Infantry Transport Section. They had in mind the acquisition of armoured cars. Apparently, several people in Hong Kong had noted with interest the armoured cars which had been sent to Shanghai in the early 1920s by the British and felt that Hong Kong should be in on this new development.

An approach was made to wealthy businessman and community leader Sir Paul Chater and he agreed to donate $1,500 for the purchase of a suitable chassis. 'We were fortunate to be able to obtain locally a Dennis chassis from Alex Ross and Company. On this chassis a body was built by the Hong Kong and Whampoa Dock Company and many hours were spent over at the dock by "Sailor".' This latter was a reference to Lieutenant 'Sailor' Moncrief. "We were also lucky in being able to obtain from Commodore Grace (son of the famous W.G. Grace) a few sheets of high tension steel for the vital parts of the body. This was Number One car.' The vehicle had mountings for two machine guns.

Some years later a six-wheel Thornycroft lorry chassis, which had been brought to China for the purpose of demonstrations, was purchased and again the dock company effected the transformation into an armoured car. One wag commented that 'these two cars, in fact, had so much ship's armour incorporated that it was a toss-up whether they were driven or sailed.'

In 1933, a second Thornycroft chassis was obtained and a third armoured car built.

Out of the Armoured Car Section, came yet another unit — the Motor Cycle Section. The appeal to motorcyclists to come forward during the troubles of 1925 brought an encouraging response and it was therefore decided to form a section from them. The original strength was 14, all of whom, with one exception, were mounted on solo machines. The single cycle and sidecar combination was eventually converted to allow for its use as a machinegun carrier. In 1928 the authorities agreed to provide proper machinegun combinations and two A.J.S. machines were acquired. By 1934–5 there were eight machinegun combinations and several privately-owned machines.

Meanwhile, Hong Kong was slowly recovering from the troubles of the mid-1920s. In China, and, particularly in Canton, the struggles for mastery continued.

In 1927, the Volunteer Amendment Ordinance made some changes to the 1920 ordinance. These included provision for auxiliary units to be raised and a number of other minor changes. Discipline rules were tightened up, with provision being made for the forfeit of $25 in the event of unsatisfactory performance. A new section was inserted giving the commandant the power to order any volunteer to attend court martials or courts of enquiry and providing for a fine of up to $250 if refusal was made.

Provision was included for the establishment of an Army Service Corps Cadre and a Lights Section Cadre.

On the world stage, the power of Japan continued to increase. Hong Kong was given tangible evidence of that power when a large Japanese fleet sailed into the harbour in 1928. Three battlecruisers lay at anchor, together with a cruiser and 16 destroyers. This was Japan's First Battle Squadron. Huge crowds watched the arrival of the fleet and there was much ceremony and pomp. The admiral and his staff officers were met at Queen's Pier before visiting Government House. Later, the Governor, Sir Cecil Clementi, went on board the flagship. Many arrangements were made to entertain the Japanese sailors during their five-day stay. There were visits to the races, a reception and dinner at Government House, trips by tram and bus around the island and New Territories, special cinema performances and a sports meeting.

The *South China Morning Post* reported on 10 April that 'The officers of the visiting squadron will be admitted to temporary honorary membership of the Hong Kong Club, the Royal Hong Kong Yacht Club, the Kowloon Golf Club, the Club De Recreio, the United Services Recreation Club and the Royal Navy Officers' Sports Club.'

Over 5,000 packets of cigarettes were printed with crossed British and Japanese flags on them and these were distributed to the men of the Japanese squadron as souvenirs of their visit to Hong Kong. In all, there were about 6,000 men in the fleet — including a prince who was serving as a navy lieutenant.

The highly successful visit closed with the Japanese Consul-General entertaining representatives of the fleet and the Hong Kong community to a large dinner at the Hong Kong Hotel. The Consul-General, Mr Y. Murakami said:

it gave him great pleasure to have the company of the leading and distinguished personages of Hong Kong and Japan and to express high appreciation of the good will manifested towards Japan and her Navy by all sections of the Hong Kong community. In the firm belief that with close relations between the two Powers of Great Britain and Japan would be strengthened more and more, he had the honour to propose the health of His Majesty the King.

The governor made a suitable reply and proposed the toast to the Emperor of Japan.

One man who must have been present and drinking the toasts was the Japanese admiral Kato Kanji. This individual was a leader of the many Japanese navy men who felt outraged at the ratios imposed by the Washington agreements — in fact he later said he felt the roots of Japan's involvement in the Second World War could be traced to these. Kato believed in the supreme destiny of Japan to rule under the leadership of its God-Emperor. In the 1930s Kato played a vital part in shaping the attitudes of many of Japan's naval officers. In Hong Kong, in 1928 he bowed and smiled and raised his glass in toasts.

While the large Japanese fleet was in Hong Kong news of the King's approval for the grant of Colours for the H.K.V.D.C. was received.

In May 1928, the Volunteers paraded for the presentation of these colours which had been donated by the women of Hong Kong. The leading lady in this project was the wife of the Governor, Lady Clementi. This was the first time that the Volunteers had received colours, the proposal and design having been approved by the monarch. Theirs was a King's Colour and a Regimental Colour.

On 6 May, the Volunteers drew up on the Murray Parade Ground, surrounded by spectators and well-wishers. Many VIPs were in prominent positions. 'The colours were unfurled and placed on the drums in the middle of the ground, the corps having been drawn up in a hollow square formation. The official party advanced towards the centre of the ground and His Lordship The Bishop dedicated the Colours which were then presented to the Corps by His Excellency.'

Speaking afterward the ceremony, Clementi referred, wrongly, to the foundation of the corps in 1866. He was obviously unaware of the 1854 date. Still, it seems unlikely that anyone present knew any better. Clementi said that volunteering in Hong Kong had grown to become the present Hongkong Volunteer Defence Corps, which consisted of Artillery, Engineers, Mounted Infantry, the Armoured Car Company and eight platoons of infantry (including one platoon of reserves for men over 40 years of age) — 39 officers and 533 other ranks in all.

The Governor praised the enthusiasm of the Volunteers during the First World War when they had taken over many duties from the regular forces. In addition a considerable number of Volunteers had returned to the United Kingdom to enlist, with others going to India and other parts of the empire. The corps and the reserve had both been mobilized on the outbreak of war when their strengths had been 392 and 318 respectively. The Roll of Honour of the Volunteers showed that 24 of those who were members of the corps at the outbreak of the war were listed. Members of the corps and of the reserve who served during the war elsewhere accounted for another 49 names. The number of men now in the corps who had war service stood at 29 officers and 181 other ranks, he said. 'Since the war the Corps has twice been mobilised, in 1922 and 1925 by proclamation in the Gazette of a "State of Emergency" in the colony consequent to strikes and unrest in Kwangtung province,' he added.

Sir Cecil said that during its long history the corps had never possessed colours. A recommendation was made in December 1926 that this situation be remedied by the grant of a King's Colour and a Regimental Colour. The G.O.C. supported the recommendation and Sir Cecil then forwarded it to London with his own enthusiastic endorsement. Subsequently, the King had given his approval. The ladies of the colony then set up a subscription scheme to pay for the new colours.

Gentlemen of the Hongkong Volunteer Defence Corps, I charge you to remember that the colours which have been presented to you this day are a gift from your Sovereign and from the ladies of Hong Kong. In days of yore knights did their devoir manfully in service of their leige lord the King and for their lady's favour. Military duty nowadays is less colourful than it used to be; but it demands from the soldier even greater gallantry and devotion than in bygone times. Let these colours always be treasured among you as emblems of loyalty to the Crown, to the Colony and to your own homes.

An impressive march-past then followed and the ladies were the guests of the officers at Regimental headquarters. That same morning a memorial to the Chinese who died in the service of Great Britain during the First World War was unveiled in the Botanical Gardens. It remains there today, an archway near the lower entrance, with an inscription added to commemorate the dead of the Second World War.

At the close of the 1920s, the Volunteers continued their busy round of training and drills.

Toiling up Garden Road in the heat of the sun on Friday afternoon two khaki-clad Defence Force Lieutenants paused, removed their topees and mopped their perspiring brows with their handkerchiefs. Just at that moment a large Buick saloon car containing two privates drew in to the kerb. One of the privates beckoned the officers. 'Would you care for a lift to Headquarters, Sir?' queried one of the men. 'What Ho!' replied an officer cheerily as he and his companion clambered into the car. The private who owned the car was the junior partner of a firm of shipping agents. The officer was his secretary. They were on their way to take part in the annual inspection of the Defence Force on the Murray Parade Ground.

Thus said the *Hong Kong Weekly Press*, of 1 March 1929.

Such is the spirit of camaraderie in Hong Kong's splendid Volunteer Defence Corps. That discipline is also one of the strongest points of the Corps was evidenced ten minutes later when the officer reproved the private for having a dirty rifle.

The annual inspection was a considerable occasion, with relatives and friends of Volunteers present in large numbers.

Heads of local firms who had given leave to their staffs who were members of the Corps strolled up to mingle with spectators, seemingly oblivious to the presence of Corporal Smith or Private Jones who had forsaken their pens and office stools to shoulder a rifle for the afternoon. Yet these chiefs were seen to beam with pride in several instances and were heard to remark to each other on occasion, 'You see that smart-looking chappie in the rear, there? He's my number one salesman.' Or else, 'That hefty-looking sergeant with the pukkah swing is my secretary.

The corps was inspected by Major General C.C. Luard, the retiring G.O.C.

The companies marched exceptionally well, and the swinging kilts of the Scotties made a brave sight which was accentuated by the flashing glint of swords and bayonets. At the halt in front of the General, the wings of the Corps formed left and right companies respectively, the parade taking the shape of three sides of a square. The General then bestowed long-service medals on C.S.M. Green and Sergt. Jack. He then made a farewell speech.

The General spoke warmly of the progress made by the band. This was their first appearance at an annual inspection and they had done extremely well, he said. The four years he had spent in Hong Kong had proved to him the value of the Corps as a defence force, and, as a trained body of men, they were a decided asset to the Colony. They were a credit to their energetic and painstaking Commandant, Lieut-Col Bird.

Many changes had taken place, and new companies had been formed in order to cope with modern demands. The Corps was now working on right lines and he assured them that if they were needed in an emergency, they would take their places as a recognised unit side by side with regular forces.

Other favourable remarks followed from the general, though he expressed a wish to see the British display a keenness to join that would match that of the Portuguese.

And now,' he concluded, 'I wish you goodbye and good luck.' With the tang of the trombones and cornets and the steady beat of the drum keeping them in step, the Corps swung in fours from the Parade Ground and marched back to their headquarters. Today they have donned their civilian clothes and are back again at their office desks wondering if 'the boss' was there and if he noticed them and their drill.

The annual Hong Kong Volunteer Rifle Meeting was held at the Stonecutters Island range, the *Weekly Press* reported on 5 April 1929. There were a record number of entries and a good attendance in spite of threatening weather. Conditions were, however, good with only a slight wind. In view of the large number of entries, shooting began at 9.30 a.m. and did not stop until 6.30 p.m. In the open events for revolver shooting, entries were received from the army and navy and from the police reserve 'Sharpshooters' Company'. The two-day event was a tremendous success with many firers obtaining perfect scores.

Looking back over the 1920s, the emergence of the Volunteers as a well-organized, well-trained, force with a particular role to play in the defence of Hong Kong can be discerned. Several other units came into being, as well as the Mounted Infantry and Armoured Car Sections which have already been dealt with.

The Army Service Corps cadre had its roots in 1925, when the unit was set up:

With the object of providing, under military control, a means of fulfilling the A.S.C. requirements as to transport which the peacetime establishment in the Colony does not provide. The cadre originally consisted of one officer, two warrant officers and ten other ranks, mostly men whose civilian employment qualified them technically for the control and upkeep of motor vehicles.

Provision for the cadre was made in the 1927 ordinance, but it seems to have existed in name only until 1931 when the unit was rejuvenated.

In 1927 the Corps Signals was established as a separate Volunteer unit. But soon afterwards, enthusiasm began to flag.

Apart from the usual hard nucleus of veterans, personnel was drawn from those sources which could provide trained men — Post Office Telegraph Offices and, as it was known in those days, Eastern Extension Telegraph Company. A large number of these men were of Indian origin.

Unfortunately, this was a period of 'between war' doldrums for the Volunteers and the various companies and units within the Corps, not particularly strong, were too busy with unit training to bother much about signals. Apart from the gunners, who had their own telephonists, there was no training on a large or battalion scale which would have emphasized the need for telecommunication. As a result, Corps Signals like most of the units of those days, pretty well 'paddled their own canoe'.

A Signal Section was set up in 1924, with most of its personnel coming from the Engineer Company. Instruction was given in the use of telephones, in daylight signalling lamps and in the use of flags. The following year, two Marconi XPI Duplex Wireless Telephony Sets were purchased, 'which aroused considerable interest.' Erecting the sets required considerable hard work, as two steel masts, each 48 feet high, had to be set up on suitable ground 300 feet apart. The aerials were strung between them and the transmitter and receiver were placed under, and connected to, the aerials. Power came from a small battery-driven motor.

In 1926, a Morris chassis was acquired and an armoured body was built upon it. The vehicle was used for transporting the wireless equipment. The enthusiastic signallers embarked upon a series of experiments and the sets were adapted to short wave working with the heavy steel masts being scrapped in favour of light copper versions. But the geography of Hong Kong, in particular of the New Territories with its many high hills, caused considerable problems. Eventually, in 1931, short wave was abandoned in favour of the standard army pattern 'C' Trench Wireless Telegraphy Set Mark II.

The Scots have played a crucial role in the history of Hong Kong and it is not surprising, therefore, that the Volunteers should have had a strongly Scottish tradition. Scots had always been members of the Volunteers and, after the end of the First World War, much agitation took place for the formation of a Scottish Company. In 1919, a meeting was held which was attended by the Chieftain of the colony's St Andrew's Society, A.S. McKichan, and other leading Scots. But 'before the meeting was concluded the proposed Scottish Company became an established fact.'

The command was first offered to Captain T.W. Hill, of Bradley and Company, a large trading firm, but he declined, saying he was a gunner not an infantryman. J.H. Gordon, who had served with the Argyll and Sutherland Highlanders became, therefore, the first commanding officer. Hill later took over command, however, when Gordon was posted to Shanghai. The Gordon tartan was chosen for wear by the Scots, in tribute to their first commanding officer and in 1920 a pipe band was formed. In 1924 the official headdress became the Glengarry.

During the visit of the Prince of Wales to Hong Kong in 1922, the Scots company provided a Royal Guard of Honour: 'With the large membership at that time, this created an impression among residents that is still remembered.'

In 1924, the company comprised three platoons — one based in Hong Kong's central district, one at Taikoo where there was a large dockyard, and one at Kowloon.

The Scots had an active social as well as military life, with a constant round of dinners including those after the annual sports day and at Halloween. Highland games were well supported. A report of the Halloween dinner of 1932 gives a snapshot. The *Overland China Mail* of 9 November reported:

Scott and Sassenach alike gathered at the Hong Kong Volunteer Defence Corps Headquarters to celebrate the Scottish Company's eighth Halloween Reunion

Ushered in to the swirling music of the pipes the haggis, brown and steaming, was the motif of the evening. The passing round the official table of the bowl with a 'wee sma drappie' was also carried out with due ceremony. The loyal toast was proposed by the officer commanding the company, Captain H.R. Forsyth which was followed by a spirited rendition of 'Scots Wha Hae.'

Pipe selections were given by pipers under Pipe Major Mackie, while songs were sung by the Company and the Sawdust Club Trio. Second Lieutenant T.P. Saunderson delighted with a sword dance.

Captain Forsyth reviewed the company's activities during the year:

Since coming back from leave last September he had found a very virile Company and he commended Lieut. Brown on his work. In the rifle meets the speaker continued the Company had acquitted themselves well, and special mention should be made of the performance of the No.7 Platoon 'B' team at the Easter meeting, when they retained the tile rifle shooting trophy. The 'A' team had also done exceedingly well.

The company held a dance during the year, but he was sorry to say that it was not a financial success. In September, the Scottish Company had fired in an Interport shoot. A team from Singapore which should have competed was very unfortunately unable to compete, but Shanghai took part. Hong Kong shot on September 25 and Shanghai the next. The Hong Kong Scottish Company did not shoot up to their usual standard, and Shanghai won by a very narrow margin.

The strength of the company stood at 61, Forsyth said, and training in machine gun work was progressing particularly well.

The President of the St Andrew's Society, Mr K.E. Grieg, replied on behalf of the visitors, praising the company. 'The Scots, particularly the older ones, looked to the Volunteers to bring Scots to the fore, and it gave them very great pleasure to see them doing so well,' he said. Grieg meant what he said, and he and his wife were hosts to their fellow countrymen after the annual Church Parade of the Scottish Company, held at the Union Church, in November

1932. The company marched to the church with pipes and drums playing and the service was attended by many dignitaries, including the Governor and the GOC British Troops in China.

Volunteers played a key role at the forts of Hong Kong in manning the lights, without which the guns would have been useless at night. In the years prior to the First World War the Volunteer engineers were to be found practicing at Belcher's Battery or at Lyemun.

The activities of the Company were many and various and besides the training of Coast Defence Electric Light, which formed the major portion of the training programme each year, it was found possible to attain a certain proficiency in Field Company Field Telephone training while attending the annual fortnight camp, which in those days before the war were looked forward to so eagerly by every member of the Volunteers. Although a certain amount of theoretical knowledge of trench construction (for instance) was acquired, it was not found possible to acquire the practical art of using pick and shovel at the same time ...

It was, however, in Coast Defence Lighting that the chief interest of the company lay, and proficiency either as an electrician or an engine driver was a necessary qualification of each member of the company. August 4th, 1914, found the company about twenty strong together with the other companies of the Volunteers at Headquarters awaiting orders as to their future movements. That night found the Engineer Company billetted in an obsolete Fort, which was to be their home for some weeks after. From then on the strength of the company increased by leaps and bounds and it was not long before they were able to man all the searchlights in the Colony.

In the enthusiasm of the first weeks of war, employers were happy to let their staff take a half day's leave after they had worked from midnight to 6.30am on the lights. But this consideration did not last and the Volunteers spent their days at their offices and their nights at the forts. However, most had only to do one duty a week by the end of the war.

The 1920s ordinance provided for the setting up of an Engineer company and this became, during that decade, one of the strongest units in the corps. The company was eventually split into 'field', 'signal' and 'light' sections. The engineers were very busy during the general strike, functioning as infantry and patrolling streets and mounting guards.

During the 1920s the Volunteers' long association with artillery continued in the form of the artillery company. In 1926 the armament of the unit was the 4.5 QF howitzer. Two six-inch breech-loading howitzers were acquired during that year but these appear not to have been a success and the gunners reverted to the 4.5s. Practice took place at Tai Lam and good links were established with the Fifth Battery of the Hong Kong and Singapore Royal Artillery. Drills continued at the forts.

The Machine Gun Company appears to have languished somewhat in the early part of the 1920s but, like the rest of the Volunteers, the troubles of 1925 led to an upsurge in recruiting. 'In 1926 the Lords of War who had watched a sewing machine working faster than a sew amah, applied this important lesson to the Company and said: "We believe they could shoot faster if we gave them proper machines." So they sold the company Vickers guns and made them learn how to use them.'

Provision was made for the establishment of naval Volunteers in 1923. In December that year, the Naval Volunteer Defence Force ordinance was to be gazetted, but it is unclear whether or to what extent a naval unit was established, for it was not until 1933 that naval volunteers were properly organized.

9

Problems All Around

THE 1930s opened in Hong Kong with a range of problems to be faced. Like the rest of the world the effects of the great financial crash of 1929 were starting to be felt. Also, events in China were reflected, as ever, in Hong Kong.

From 1928 (when the Nationalist government had established itself at Nanking) onwards, there was a constant stream of incidents involving warlords, communists, and, above all, the belligerence of Japan. All these factors led to the continued influx of immigrants into Hong Kong and the 1931 Census put the population at 849,751.

The Volunteers were looking for recruits. At the annual smoking concert and presentation of prizes held in May 1930, the Officer Commanding, Major Dowbiggin, felt 'That more of the younger men of the Colony, particularly the recent arrivals, ought to make it a point to join up, quite apart from patriotic sentiments, as the Volunteer Corps was really the best and cheapest club in the Colony.'

The *Hong Kong Weekly News* and *China Overland Trade Report* of 6 June said that Dowbiggin 'Firmly believed the efficiency of the Corps had suffered through the discipline being made too easy. He had served in several other similar bodies in the East, and from his experience he found that the higher standard of efficiency was aimed at, the keenner the men are to enroll.' The General Officer Commanding British troops, Major General J.W. Sandilands, said, 'I quite agree with Major Dowbiggin that possibly this unit might be more efficient, but I can only say that in my official report of this year, I stated that in my considered opinion the training and especially the life you live in camp compares favourably with that of any territorial units in the United Kingdom (applause).'

The Volunteers were well to the fore when, on 3 June, Hong Kong celebrated the King's birthday. Over 2,300 troops took part, drawn from the various military and naval units. There was a ceremonial march-past at the Cenotaph and a march through the streets of the city. Large crowds were present. The Governor, Sir William Peel, was escorted to the parade by the Motor Cycle Section of the Volunteers, five machines in front and five behind.

The Volunteers took part in the march-past, marching to the sound of their own band.

The Volunteers made a brave showing this year, quite an encouraging number taking part in the parade. They were headed by their own band, followed by the various detachments of their infantry, with the mounted section bringing up the rear. The China ponies used by the Volunteers, however, compared unfavourably with the chargers used by British and Indian officers on parade ...

Development of the fortifications of Hong Kong continued to remain at a standstill, but the potential threats to the colony were worrying many residents. On 19 February 1931, a leading article in the *China Mail* said that Hong Kong was now more important than ever to Britain in view of the British withdrawal from Wei Hai Wei. Concern was expressed over Kowloon: 'Because of the intimacy it enjoys with Hong Kong it is more likely to betray it; its very flat plain-like expanse, backed by hills which over shadow the whole colony, is a potential threat to our security. The very place to be guarded, it is as open to invasion and bombardment as are the plains of Waterloo.'

The paper felt that landings on Hong Kong island would be unlikely to succeed, but the Kowloon hills made an ideal artillery position for any enemy.

Whatever attitude China adopted in a future conflict in the Far East, the present strength of her armies could do little or nothing to resist the wholesale invasion of Kwangtung by a superior power which had as its object not the conquest of China, but the destruction of Hong Kong as a dangerous base of British military operations.

Attention paid to defence was the simplest form of wisdom, but the Labour government was 'fighting for its life' and the 'Singapore Naval Dock Scheme' had been postponed, 'so it is unlikely that the Ministry of War will be concerned with Hong Kong.' If the London authorities were not overly concerned about protecting Hong Kong, the authorities in the colony were. The General Officer Commanding made what were by now the usual remarks about recruiting when he carried out the 1931 annual inspection. These comments annoyed at least one man, who wrote to the press. His letter appeared in the *Overland China Mail* on 16 April, saying that the G.O.C.'s 'perennial grouse about the "slackers of the colony"' was noted but that he personally had no intention of Volunteering. Volunteering was fine, he wrote, for fit young men in their early twenties 'for whom it is an excellent form of sport.' He continued:

What I object to is the current military point of view towards volunteers in its relation to the citizens of this colony.

The late lamented holocaust that swept over Europe brought to light one very strong fact, and it is that 'cannon fodder' can be manufactured at remarkably short notice. It may not be very good material, in the light of strict efficiency, but it was willing, and it was good enough for its purpose. This being so, I fail to see why presumably intelligent human beings should spend hours of their life — and spare time — in learning to form fours, hit bulls' eyes and so forth.

He went on to say that the type of man who was a Volunteer would be commissioned in a future war and, therefore, he would receive all the training that he needed then before being put in command of troops. 'I maintain, therefore, that our Volunteer Corps, as it is constituted today, serves no useful purpose.' The claim that regular training was needed if a man was to be of any use was 'bosh'. 'In five days any normal Sergeant Major can knock as much into the average man's head as the Volunteer Corps could in five years!'

Until the corps was organized as an Officer Cadet Corps it was not fulfilling its real duty, the writer went on.

To my way of thinking every man in the corps should be able to get out in front and drill his own company, and at the least 60 per cent of the Corps should be able to put the entire Corps through battalion drill. Every man should be instructed in the rudiments of military history, and the elements of tactics and strategy, with particular reference to the newer forms of warfare — mechanical, aerial, bacteriological etc.

He said he was puzzled by the constant references made to the use to which the corps would be put in times of military emergency. 'Trade is the life blood of the Empire,' he stated, and asked what use would be the Volunteers in 'civil emergency similar to the military ones always so much feared.'

This letter sparked a lively debate. The writer did not identify himself, using a pseudonym 'Lai Tee' but he claimed that he had spent more of his life in regular and volunteer armed units than a normal, non-professional, military person. However, another correspondent disagreed with his views, pointing out that 'The five days which 'Lai Tee' thinks sufficient to turn the average citizen into a soldier, or at least a Volunteer, would be just enough for an enemy faction to wipe out a city.'

An editorial in the *Daily China Mail* of 13 April said that the letter had certainly given a lot of publicity to the Volunteers and years of experience had shown that they were essential. Many methods had been tried to increase recruiting, the editorial continued, but while some business houses had virtually every man in the Volunteers, others did not have one. The writer pointed out that there was no co-operation between the Volunteers and the Police Reserve: 'It is known that some prefer the quieter life of a Police Reserve to the triflingly more arduous duties appertaining to a Volunteer.' No person, the paper suggested, should be allowed to become a police reservist unless he had served first with the Volunteers. It went on to say that the G.O.C.'s remarks, anyway, were not directed at men such as 'Lai Tee' who had considerable military service, but at the young men of the colony. 'Let each citizen examine his conscience and ask himself whether he has really performed a citizen's duty by remaining outside the Corps.'

One individual who claimed to have responded to the call to arms was actor Errol Flynn, though his tale is tremendously confused in his book, *My Wicked, Wicked Ways*. In the early 1930s, Flynn found himself in Hong Kong.

We strolled into the commercial area of Hong Kong, wondering which way to turn next. A huge poster of a young Englishman in uniform pointed straight at me, saying 'England and China Need You. Join the Royal Hong Kong Volunteers.

Like two idealists off on a crusade, we headed for the recruiting station. We'd check the Yellow Peril from Japan and preserve it for the exclusive use of the Chinese. Actually, I still don't know the rights and wrongs of that embroglio. In 1932 we knew that Hong Kong was in danger of being swallowed up. Everywhere there was talk about the possibility of evacuation. How far would the Japanese go?

It is not clear what Flynn joined, though it can hardly have been the Volunteers, for he says that he sailed for Shanghai to serve there.

On a more serious note, meanwhile, the militarists had been growing in influence in Japan, pouring scorn on civilian leaders who had accepted the 'humiliating' 5:5:3 ratio at Washington and its reaffirmation by the London Naval Agreement of 1930. Their eyes were on the Chinese territory of Manchuria.

As a part of the peace settlement of the Russo-Japanese War, Japan had taken over the Russian leasehold in the Liaotung Peninsula and Russian economic and railway rights in Manchuria. The 'Kwantung Leased Territory' came into being and the army there began to plan for a complete takeover. Eventually, the military authorities set themself the target of the spring of 1932 for the occupation. However, this was brought forward and, following a bomb incident which was stage-managed in September 1931, the army authorities struck. Although Tokyo knew of the invasion plot, the government took no action to stop it. Field officers had taken the initiative. Japan was led 'Onto the road of militarism, conquest, and ultimately, destruction. In the view of many, the Mukden Incident of September 18, 1931, sowed the seeds of World War II,' said the historian, Immanuel C.Y. Hsu.

Within five months, the whole of Manchuria was overrun. On 9 March 1932, the puppet state of Manchukuo was created and the last Emperor, Pu Yi, was made Chief Executive. Flushed with their success, the militarists began to dream of further expansion in North China.

After the Japanese invasion of Manchuria, rioting occurred in Hong Kong together with arson and looting and the murder of six members of a Japanese family. Eventually, the army was called in to support the police and the Armoured Car Company and Motor Cycle Section of the Volunteers were mobilized.

The economy was faltering, the world recession was in full swing, the Canton authorities were in frequent dispute with the government in Nanking, and China raised its tariffs. Furthermore, the Hong Kong dollar had halved in value against the pound, due to a fall in the price of silver.

However, 1932 saw the formation of three new units in the Volunteers — the Anti-Aircraft Light Automatic Company, the Army Service Cadre, and the Anzac Company. The Army Service Cadre unit had, of course, been around since the mid-1920s, but in 1932 it was reorganized and there was an influx of new men.

A dinner was held to mark the setting up of the three new units at which the G.O.C., Major General Sandilands, put forward a very forceful warning:

The tendency often is to ask what we are going to defend ourselves against. You all know what has happened recently, what has happened on the China Coast. Cast your mind back to Empire Day last year. No one in the Colony then realised that Chapei would be in ruins, and that the whole neighbourhood would become a devastated area.

This was a reference to the Japanese attack on Chinese Shanghai, staged as a diversion of international attention from what was happening in Manchuria. Chinese troops fought bravely but were defeated and a truce was arranged in May.

Sandilands went on:

We are living in one of the most important colonies in the British empire and it behoves us to be prepared for any eventuality. As regards the units here tonight, all will be of the greatest use should such an unfortunate thing happen as war. We have thousands and thousands of armed men in England, but we all know that there are no means of getting them here in time and we must rely on the British population to come to our assistance.

The *China Mail* commented:

The GOC, without any alarmist speech has quietly, but forcibly, demonstrated a fact which is not sufficiently recognised. The Volunteers, after all, sacrifice much time and labour in a purely honorary fashion, and are actuated by motives which include a sincere endeavour to assist in safe-guarding the Colony. Public support is disappointing and the apathy of so many citizens is inexplicable in view of recent happenings in the Far East. Much of it is no doubt due to ignorance of conditions and a blind faith 'that things would turn out all right somehow.

The value of an efficient Volunteer Force was clearly demonstrated in Shanghai during the recent outbreak when the Volunteers proved invaluable in assisting the Regulars in picketing, guarding property and lives, and generally doing a soldier's job. The Force is extremely well-organized in Shanghai, the comprehensive scheme in operation including an establishment of a Russian Company which is paid in full-time. It is not suggested that Hong Kong should move to such an extreme, but it would be very welcome if some of the public enthusiasm and support given to the Shanghai Volunteers were shown here.

In 1932, the idea for the establishment of an Anzac company

came from a group of young Australians and New Zealanders who met originally to organize a ceremony to commemorate the famous landing at Gallipoli, on 25 April 1915. A committee was formed and a programme drawn up. The service started at 10.50 a.m. at the Cenotaph with a wreath being laid by Mr C. de Saille-Robertson, M.M. He was an old resident of Hong Kong who had been a member of the original First Australian Division and who had been present at the landing at Gaba Tepe as well as the evacuation. A wreath was also laid by a party from the First Battalion of the South Wales Borderers, whose Second Battalion had formed part of the landing parties at Cape Helles on the same day. The ceremony was followed by a dinner that evening at the Hong Kong Hotel with a table arranged in an 'A' shape.

The press reported that at the dinner, de Saille-Robertson called on those present to form a company of their own in the Volunteers. The response was astounding, for 'of the assembly of forty, thirty names were handed in at once.' Before 30 April, a new machine gun company had been formed, known as the Anzac Company. De Saille-Robertson was gazetted Lieutenant to command it. By the end of the year the strength had risen to 50.

At the Anzac Day dinner, de Saille-Robertson had said that Australians and New Zealanders in Hong Kong had much to be thankful for in living under the protection of the British flag and the best way to demonstrate their appreciation was by the formation of an Australasian unit in the Volunteers. The idea had the support of the corps commandant, Colonel Bird.

He is quite as enthusiastic about it as I am, and if you are willing to prove your Anzac spirit, which I know you possess, and are willing to join up in sufficient numbers he will be only too pleased to start a special Australasian unit which will wear the badges of Anzac and its distinctive uniform.

The slouch hats that we Aussies love and which were to the fore in all the battles during the last war shall be seen among the Hong Kong Volunteers for the first time in its history.

The choice of the machine-gun as the weapon for the new unit was appropriate, he said: 'The machine gun was pre-eminently the weapon of Gallipoli, and it is in recognition of this, that the new Unit will be so armed.'

The first parade of the Anzacs took place on 10 May 1932, with 31 members being present:

Nothing in the way of drill was attempted, the unit assembling in the Headquarters Lecture Room, where they were congratulated, and the new members welcomed to the Corps by Lieut-Col. L.G. Bird, D.S.O., O.B.E., who urged the men to regularly attend parades and to turn up at camp, assuring them that they would be very happy in the Corps.

The Adjutant, Capt. W.H.G. Goater, then explained the Volunteer Ordinance and told the men what would be expected of them. He then mentioned that the hats for the unit had been ordered from Australia, and he hoped that the time would come when it would not be necessary to order from there, and that the Anzac unit would be strong enough as to necessitate the carrying of local stores.

The position of the Anzac Company in the defence scheme, it was intimated, would be allotted later.

The Anzacs surprised most people by winning the Machine Gun Trophy in their first year of existence.

The annual parade in 1933 took place on 11 April, when the corps fell in at Volunteer Headquarters and, led by the pipers of the Scottish Company and the band of the South Wales Borderers they marched to the Murray Parade Ground. The strength of the Corps on parade was 27 officers and 360 other ranks. After the march-past they formed up in a hollow square to be addressed by the new Garrison Officer Commanding, Major General O.C. Borrett.

This is the first occasion on which I have had the honour of inspecting you and I must congratulate you on your appearance and movements.

It is always a pleasure as well as an honour to be connected even in a small way with a patriotic body of men like yourselves, who are willing to give up a great deal of time to fit yourselves for what is the most important duty of any man, defence of his country.

As you know, ever since the War the fighting forces of the Empire have been reduced again and again and as the professionals are reduced so much more is reliance placed on the territorials and Volunteers increased. The part the Defence Corps has to play in the protection of this Colony is one of the greatest importance and is one which cannot be played by a man who only turns up at the moment of crisis.

It takes a considerable time to get a working knowledge of machine guns or to become proficient in working search lights and performing many other duties you are undertaking. Although on the face of it there appear too many units and sub-units already in the Corps, yet there are other duties I would ask you to undertake if only you could enlist the available man-power which exists in the Colony, such as taking over part of the anti-aircraft defence, guns and lights.

Because the Empire is supposed to have its face set steadily towards Peace, that does not make armed forces a luxury. The idea was exploded long ago in the motoring world. However good a driver a man may be he always insures himself against the other man. Even if we have good drivers at the head of the Empire they cannot prevent the other man running into us, and I therefore appeal to you all to do your best to get the potential man-power in the Colony to join up.

I have it on good authority that at the moment there are over 1,000 available men in the Colony who are not undertaking any part in its protection. Untrained, they will be unfit to go into your ranks in a crisis, and can only be utilised in labour Corps. Trained, they can make Hong Kong still more impregnable than it is at present.

Borrett's remarks on the organization of the Volunteers were followed up the next month, when the Volunteer Ordinance of 1933 was gazetted, repealing the Volunteer Amendment Ordinances of 1926 and 1927 and the 1920 Volunteer Ordinance. Under the 1933 regulations, the revised organization was laid down (see Table 9.1).

Table 9.1 Organization of the Corps under the Volunteer Ordinance 1933

UNITS OF THE CORPS

A Corps Headquarters.	I. Machine Gun Company.
B. The Corps Band.	J. Scottish Company.
C. The Battery.	K. Portugese Company.
D. Engineer Company.	L. Anzac Company.
E. Corps Signals.	M. Flying Section.
F. Machine Gun Troop.	N. Medical Section.
G. Armoured Car Section.	O. Reserve Company.
H. Motor Machine Gun Section.	P. Reserve of Officers.

AUXILIARY UNITS

A. Army Service Corps Cadre.
B. Anti-Aircraft Light Automatic Company.
C. Lights Section Cadre.

The ordinance laid down in relation to membership that 'It shall be lawful for the Governor, in his discretion, to accept the services of any person desiring to be enrolled as a member thereof.' However, officers had to be British subjects, commissioned by the Governor. The commanding officer could be either a Volunteer or a Regular. But if he was a Volunteer the adjutant would have to be a regular — and vice versa. Foreign nationals were particularly welcome to join the Army Service Corps Cadre and the Lights Section Cadre and they should be 'individuals whose previous training has rendered them fit to perform such duties as they may be required to perform if called out for actual military service.' A special declaration was laid down for members of the two cadres and of the Anti-Aircraft Light Automatic Company. This excluded the undertaking 'to be faithful and bear true allegiance to His Majesty King George.' However, if a man was to be called out for actual military service, then an oath or declaration including the phrase had to be taken.

Members of the two cadres were not required to attend any training, parade or inspection and no uniform was provided for either them or the Anti-Aircraft Light Automatic Company unless called out for actual military service. The Reserve Company was for men aged over 40 and details were given of the Reserve of Officers, which was to consist of former officers. Tremendous detail was given of disciplinary regulations, with fines laid down for men who quit without good reason.

What constituted actual military service was carefully specified.

In cases of great national or local emergency, or in case of actual or apprehended invasion of or attack on the Colony, or in case it may be desirable to take precautions against the possibility of serious local disturbance, the Governor may, by proclamation, call out the Corps or any portion thereof for actual military service.

An offence of obstructing or resisting a member of the corps in the discharge of his duty was laid down, with a fine upon summary conviction not exceeding $250 and imprisonment for up to six months.

The ordinance continued with a great deal of detail, covering matters such as stores, books to be kept, equipment, retirement ages, appointments and promotions. The training year remained divided into hot weather and cold weather periods, the former ending on 14 October and the latter on 15 April.

The minimum training required remained the same as in the 1926 and 1927 ordinances, consisting of attendance at 15 one-hour drills, range practices, preliminary range training, attendance at camp for four days, and attendance at the annual inspection parade. Once a Volunteer had proved himself 'efficient' for three years, which did not need to be successive, the training load was reduced. Members of the Reserve company had only to receive Musketry instruction and carry out practice, attend the annual inspection and make an optional appearance at camp.

The term 'recruit' included every Volunteer who had not served for at least one year in the Royal Navy, Regular Army, Royal Marines, Militia, Special Reserve, Imperial Yeomanry, and Volunteer force in His Majesty's dominions, or in the Territorial Force, Royal Irish Constabulary, permanent forces of any part of His Majesty's dominions outside Great Britain, or any university Officers Training Corps.

A major Army, Navy, and Air Force exercise held in April 1933, demonstrated the perception of the threat to Hong Kong and resulted in the crucial engagement taking place at Wong Nei Chong Gap, scene of much fighting eight years later. Although the Volunteers do not appear to have been involved in the exercise it is interesting nonetheless. The 'Blueland' force was made up of two companies from the Lincoln Regiment and about 200 marines. The marines were landed at Gin Drinkers Bay with the object of attacking the Standard Oil Company's storage tanks at Lai Chi Kok. But this was merely a feint to cover the main landing at Repulse Bay where the two companies of the Lincolns disembarked from the *Medway* in boats towed by pinnaces. The landing was carried out well, with a first wave securing the beach for the main landing.

The 'Redland' forces were made up of the South Wales Borderers stationed at Wong Nei Chong Gap, and the remaining two companies of the Lincolns, the Fifth (Howitzer) Battery of the Hong Kong and Singapore Royal Artillery stationed at Happy Valley who 'fired' over the hills to Repulse Bay, and the Jat Regiment at Lai Chi Kok. The other units of the garrison were standing by ready to repel any attack. 'Aeroplanes sighted the hostile fleet, composed of the *Berwick* and *Medway*, at about 5 p.m. yesterday,' it was reported. 'This was reported to the Officer Commanding the defence force and destroyers and submarines, with their lights out, stalked the invading fleet all night.'

Colonel Nosworthy, who was commanding the Redland forces, waited until he was sure of the landing place of the enemy and then called on his reserves which were stationed at Kowloon. He had to wait to make sure which of the two landings was the main one. The marines at Lai Chi Kok were met by a small force of Jats, but fought their way to the oil tanks which they technically set on fire. The Jats then brought up their reinforcements and the marines, having destroyed the tanks, re-embarked on the *Berwick*.

The main battle took place at Wong Nei Chong Gap. The invading Lincolns after their landing on the beach at Repulse Bay, marched up the Repulse Bay Road to the Gap where they were held up by the South Wales Borderers. Fierce fighting ensued and the Borderers called up the Redland Lincolns in support. The Redland Lincolns carried out an encircling movement and after reaching Deep Water Bay were in the rear of the invaders. The Blueland Lincolns were then held between two bodies of their opponents, and the war was declared finished. All troops then returned to barracks.

Although the Volunteers did not play a part in this engagement they were busy with their own training — much to the annoyance of some people, as the *Overland China Mail* reported on 8 February 1933:

Heavy howitzer firing by a section of the Hong Kong Volunteer Defence Corps at Castle Peak on February 5 and especially during the tiffin interval has raised the indignation of Mr A. Smith, Manager of Messrs. Whiteaway, Laidlaw and Co., Ltd., who was spending the day in a new house he had recently built at Castle Peak.

Mr Smith told the *China Mail* that live shells were being fired over the road, even with traffic in progress, and in the vicinity of newly constructed houses which were occupied. 'Of course,' said Mr Smith, ' the firing has been done in the past and will always be done, I suppose. You know it's no use complaining. You get no satisfaction from the Military. What's the use of making a lot of fuss about it?' he added.

Mr Smith said that during last summer, heavy firing was the cause of the breakage of much crockery in the bathing matsheds. But at the time there were no houses in the immediate vicinity. 'I do think, though,' Mr Smith went on to say, 'the firing should cease when there is traffic along the road.'

Not everyone in Hong Kong felt that the Volunteers were the correct response to worrying events in China, and, in January, 1933, the Hong Kong Peace Group was formed. The Revd Dr E.L. Allen told the first annual meeting, held at the Helena May Institute on 31 January 1933, 'For you in China, the real enemy is not Japan. For you in Japan, the real enemy is not China. It is something within yourselves. Defeat is to surrender your souls to fear and suspicion and hate; victory is to suffer anything rather than incur so terrible a loss.' The group had been formed as a direct result of the Sino-Japanese conflict and membership had grown to 30.

In February, the arrival of the field battery of the Shanghai Volunteers who had come to Hong Kong for live round practice was reported.

The annual inspection and parade of troops took place on 3 June and one interested observer present was Captain Takashi of the Imperial Japanese Army.

During 1933, the Japanese army was proceeding with its aggressive acts in North China. The League of Nations had refused to recognise the legality of Manchukuo, but the Japanese were unconcerned, attacking passes in the Great Wall in January 1933 and withdrawing from the League in March. At the same time, elsewhere in China, the Nationalists and the Communists were fighting for supremacy and in October 1934 the Long March began.

The trade depression in Hong reached its depth in 1935.

In the middle of the 1930s as a result of the Washington agreements, Hong Kong's coast defences had been left largely in the state they had been prior to the First World War. But although the coast defence of Hong Kong does not seem to have excited a great deal of interest in the United Kingdom, it was a topic of continuing worry in the colony and residents constantly pointed out the needs they saw for upgrading and modernization. Imperial fixations were elsewhere, however; Singapore to be exact.

The construction of the massive base there was to overshadow almost everything else in terms of the defence of British interests in Asia. Britain had chosen Singapore for its major base in the region and, for this reason, Singapore had been specifically excluded from the non-fortification agreement made in Washington. Though the decision to develop the base was made in 1921, it had become the victim of much political infighting and delay. The Labour government of 1924 cancelled the whole scheme; Baldwin's government of later that year re-started it. Shortage of money was a perennial problem and, in 1926, the original plans were scaled back but work continued. Contributions for the cost of the base came from Hong Kong, which had an obvious interest in seeing a main battle fleet stationed in its vicinity, from New Zealand and from Malaya. Labour came back to power in 1929 and, again, development was halted. On the return of the Conservatives in 1932 construction started again.

Though it was a political football, the base on Singapore did slowly progress and there were spin-off benefits for coast defence as a whole. The construction of the big base meant that interest in the usually 'Cinderella' subject was maintained. New systems were worked out and tested, new guns designed and personnel training maintained. It was to be the mid-1930s, however, before serious action was taken to assess and improve the defences of Hong Kong. The citizens of the colony had, as stated, been watching Japanese aggression in China in the 1920s and early 1930s with increasing worry. They called on the Home government to improve Hong Kong's defences but, due to lack of money, the Washington limitations, and political inertia, nothing was done.

At the London Conference, which was held in January 1930, Japan had demanded that its standing in the 5:5:3 ratio be improved. This was rejected, to the fury of the hawks, but a complicated compromise was arrived at. It became apparent in the first half of the 1930s, however, that the rules were being stretched to, and beyond, the limit by both Japan and Germany. In 1933, the British government decided, reluctantly, to abandon its 'ten-year rule', which assumed that there would be no major conflict for 10 years, on a rolling basis. In December 1934, the Japanese gave notice of two years, as required, that at the end of 1936 it would no longer consider itself bound by agreements on naval limitation.

At last, serious thought started to be given to improving the fixed defences of Hong Kong. Even though the fact had been pointed out decades before, the southern side of the island was still, for all practical purposes, defenceless.

About the only military presence was at the naval dockyard at Aberdeen. The old barracks at Stanley, erected in the 1840s, had long since fallen into ruin. The great dams at Tai Tam, vital to the city water supply, were open to attack. As was demonstrated by exercises, an invading force could land at virtually any of the bays which corrugate the coastline and it was doubtful whether a quick and effective response could have been made.

Plans were drawn up, or dusted off, to move defences away from the inner harbour area, where they had been sufficient to deal with the threats of the previous century, and out to the south side of the island where the real danger now lay. The battle was now to be fought out at sea, at least in its initial phases and not at the eastern and western edges of the crowded harbour. Defences were to go up at Stanley, at Chung Hom Kok, at Cape D'Aguilar, lower Mount Davis, Cape Collinson, Brick Hill, Aberdeen, and Shek O, and the coastline and hills were to be peppered with pillboxes.

The workhorses of the coast defences were to remain the big 9.2 inch guns, of which there were the original five at Mount Davis and three at Devil's Peak. It was decided to set up two big new forts to house 9.2 inch long-range guns at Stanley and Cape D'Aguilar. Six-inch guns, to meet the closer range threat, were to go in at Chung Hom Kok, lower Mount Davis (Jubilee Battery), Cape D'Aguilar, and Cape Collinson, in addition to those already in place at Lyemun and, possibly, Stonecutters Island. The question of exactly how all these developments took place is somewhat vexed by the absence in Hong Kong of detailed records.

It was decided to remove two of the 9.2 inch guns from Mount Davis to Stanley and this operation was carried out in the middle of 1936. During the same period, the large barracks and other facilities at Stanley were constructed. The defences at Devil's Peak were no longer considered appropriate, following the decision to move the forces southwards and outwards. The top gun at Devil's Peak, Gough Gun, was removed in the mid-1930s to become the third gun at Stanley. The two guns at Pottinger Battery, also at Devil's Peak, were taken out in 1940 and set up at Cape D'Aguilar. As well as the guns, a sophisticated system of observation posts and fire commands was set up.

By 1941, the coast defences of Hong Kong were as shown in Table 9.2.

The year 1935 saw the publication of the first Hong Kong Defence Corps Yearbook — covering the previous year as well. The yearbook was then published annually up until 1940 and fascinating reading the editions make. In its introduction, the first yearbook stated: 'The Hong Kong Volunteer Defence Corps, although it has existed since 1868, lacks a historian.' That, presumably, is why the writer was unaware of the 1854 genesis of the organization. 'A visit to Headquarters will reveal Rolls, Photographs and newspaper cuttings to the interested, but there has never yet been undertaken a systematic attempt to record the year-to-year life of the Corps, in which, at one time or another, almost every foreign resident of the Colony has served.'

Table 9.2 Hong Kong's Coast Defences (1941)

Battery	Location	No. of Guns	Size
1. EASTERN FIRE COMMAND			
a. 8TH COAST REGIMENT ROYAL ARTILLERY			
12th Coast Battery	Stanley	3	9.2″
30th Coast Battery	Bokhara (D'Aguilar)	2	9.2″
36th Coast Battery	Cape Collinson	2	6″
36th Coast Battery	Chung Hom Kok	2	6″
b. HONG KONG VOLUNTEER DEFENCE CORPS			
Fourth Battery	Pakshawan (Lyemun)	2	6″
First Battery	D'Aguilar	2	4″
Second Battery	Bluff Head (Stanley)	2	6″
2. WESTERN FIRE COMMAND			
a. 12TH COAST REGIMENT ROYAL ARTILLERY			
24th Coast Battery	Mount Davis	3	9.2″
20th Coast Battery	Stonecutters	3	6″
b. HONG KONG VOLUNTEER DEFENCE CORPS			
Third Battery	Aberdeen	2	4″
Third Battery	Belcher's Fort	2	4″

This table clearly demonstrates the integral role of the men of the Hong Kong Volunteer Defence Corps in the fixed coast artillery defences of the colony.

Lieutenant Colonel H.B.L. Dowbiggin, O.B.E., Commanding Officer, sent a message to all members of the Corps. He had been a member since 1906 and he wrote:

Undoubtedly the best recruiting agents for the Corps are the members of the Corps itself. The more efficient and keen they are the more likely good fellows will want to join the Corps. No fellow wants to join up with a Unit which just does the minimum amount of parades. No keen fellow minds how many parades he does provided that the work done appeals to his intelligence and is of a progressive character, and that is where the efficient officer is called upon the pull his weight in the boat.

The artillery had been given an important role in Hong Kong's defence plans and Colonel Dowbiggin particularly wanted to see more recruits to it.

The First Battery entry in the yearbook gave a quick sketch of its recent history:

A few years ago, in 1926, to be exact, the armament of the unit was the 4.5 QF Howitzer, but in October of that year the powers that be thought that this fine body of men might be able to stand a louder bang when they went to camp. It might make them jump to it a bit more. So two six-inch B.L. Howitzers were produced at HQ much to the disgust of our worthy Quartermaster. However, after we had carried away the doors regularly every two months and cut up the grass and fired them at Tai Lam, we thought, let's have a smaller piece to train on, so we changed back to the 4.5 Howitzer. By this time, owing to the energy of Capt T. Addis Martin, we had the honour of being affiliated to the Royal Regiment and were permitted to wear R.A. on our shoulders, a privilege which has not been granted to many Volunteer Batteries.

Early in 1935, it was said, the battery had been changed into 'concrete gunners' and it was now training regularly at Belchers once a month from 6 p.m. to 10 p.m. with the rest of the drills being completed at headquarters. The title had changed to First Battery, but it was unlikely that a Second Battery would be formed in the near future. Unfortunately, no illustrations could be provided: 'It is rather difficult to produce photographs of the unit nowadays as it is "verboten" in three different languages to take photographs in the fort.' The Nominal Roll showed that the battery was organized into a headquarters, a depression range-finder detachment, signallers, Number One Gun detachment and Number Two Gun detachment. Two officers and 30 other ranks were listed.

The Corps Engineers' entry said that it had a long tradition in the Volunteers and the present training concentrated on defence electric light instruction interspersed with infantry work. Lighting had also formed the main focus of activity during the First World War.

It was, however, in Coast Defence Lighting that the chief interest of the company lay, and proficiency either as an electrician or an engine driver was a necessary qualification for each member of the company.

August 4th, 1914, found the company about twenty strong together with the other companies of the Volunteers at Headquarters awaiting orders as to their future movements. That night found the Engineer Company billetted in an obsolete Fort, which was to be their home for some weeks after. From then on, the strength of the company increased by leaps and bounds and it was not long before they were able to man all the searchlights in the Colony ...

To begin with, it was quite pleasant, being part time soldier and civilian, as the firms were rather sympathetic towards those of their staff who were Volunteers.

However, as has been mentioned, shorter working hours did not last.

There are pleasant recollections of the time spent in the 'Fort' when one had to subsist on Army rations every day and the Volunteer cook could only make Irish Stew; but it did taste good. Of attempts to wash the spare shirt and to dry it so that it appeared as if it had been ironed. Of rags in the huts after lights out when boots, putties and anything handy were used as missiles to repel attacks from the other hut and the consequent confusion next morning when one had to get on parade...

Although the Engineers had been well supported during the troubles of the 1920s, when they had a field, signal and light section, the enthusiasm had fallen away until the field section was disbanded, with the signal section transforming into Corps Signals. The Corps Signals entry repeated something of its history, noting that short wave had been abandoned when, in 1931, it acquired a standard Army pattern 'C' Trench Wireless Telegraphy Set Mark II which was still in use. 'It has been proved to be extremely efficient, mobility is all that can be desired, and communication can be established very quickly — five minutes only being required to get going.'

In addition to wireless equipment, the Signals also had a ten line cordless telephone exchange with the required telephones and cables. In the event of mobilization of the Volunteers, the Signal Section would come under the command of the Chief Signal Officer, China Command. During the year personal equipment had been changed from webbing to leather to conform with that worn by the Royal Corps of Signals. 'This change is appreciated by all.'

The Yearbook recorded the combination of the several machine gun units into a Corps Machine Gun battalion. A battalion headquarters was established with its own signal section. Number One Machine Gun Company consisted of a headquarters and four platoons.

The Scottish Company consisted of a headquarters, two platoons and three Honorary Pipers. 'While the present numerical strength of the company is not what it has been, or could be if every eligible Scot were to come forward, there is no doubt that it has been depleted by the departure to the Homeland through the present economic depression of many of its stalwarts in the past three years.'

Number Three (Anzac) Company consisted of a headquarters and two platoons.

The training carried out during last season was of a very interesting nature. For the first time beach defence was thoroughly gone into and as there is no training laid down for this type of defence each member of the Company had much more individual thinking to do, thereby exploding the time-worn regular army sergeant-major's phrase 'you're not paid to think in the Army.'

The Corps Infantry was very well supported, with a head-quarters and four platoons of four sections each. Each of the four sections was divided into two rifle sections and two Lewis Gun sections. The total strength of the company stood at about 130 men.

The Portuguese Company (now known as the Corps Infantry) was formed by half-a-dozen men, who, in July 1925, (during the strike) joined the No. 4 Platoon of the Infantry Company. In September, 1925, a few more men enrolled and it was suggested by Captain S.J. Jordain, M.C., (now Major) E.J.R. Mitchell and Mr R.R. Davies (now Captain, Reserve of Officers) that a special section composed of Portuguese be formed. This was done. During 1926 about twenty more joined up and the No.4 Platoon of the Infantry Company became composed exclusively of Portuguese lads. Mr Davies was appointed Officer In Command.

In February/March 1927, a batch of about thirty men enrolled, bringing the total to about sixty. Then recommendations were forwarded to Headquarters that a Portuguese Company be formed. On April 1, 1927, it was officially announced, through Corps Orders, that sanction has been received to form the Company.

Captain R.R. Davies took over command with Lt. S. Jarvis, M.C., (now Captain) as second-in-command. There were no Portuguese officers, the highest rank attained by a Portuguese in those days being that of Company-Sergeant-Major. From 1927 onwards, the number of men enrolled increased substantially. On August 3, 1928, the Commandant, Lieut-Col. L.G. Bird, D.S.O., announced at the Company's concert, that one of the members of the Company would be given commissioned rank and at the end of the same month, a Portuguese was gazetted as 2nd Lieutenant.

The yearbook stated that 'The Troop' had now been converted from Mounted Infantry to a Machine Gun Troop and it had a skeleton formation for four guns. The ponies were stabled for the hunting season at Fanling and in Hong Kong during the summer so that members could indulge in both hunting and polo at appropriate times of the year.

The training programme is roughly as follows: — When the ponies come back to Causeway Bay from their winter quarters, recruits are put through the Riding School under Sgt Maj. Charles, whilst the rest do Pack Saddle drill with machine guns. After the recruits have passed out of the school, they are instructed in loading Pack ponies, and then the whole Troop does mounted drill with Pack ponies and machine guns. This leads up to the Alarm Race, which is contested by the subsections at the gymkhana. The ponies go to Fanling about the middle of November, and parades during the winter months are at Volunteer Headquarters, and comprise elementary instruction on the gun for Recruits and more advanced subjects for those members of the Troop who are already proficient.

The Armoured Car Section noted that its Number One car had recently been condemned as its steel was too heavy for the roads of the colony. However, the chassis was now being used by the A.S.C. Cadre. The call out of the anti-Japanese riots of 1931 was duly noted:

You should have seen us serving our King and Colony in September 1931. What action! What superb fearlessness! At the call of duty, we leapt 'to it,' hardly pausing to fill the Tundice or even arrange for a fresh supply, and proceeded to our posts. Through the first anxious hours we remained steady, while the heaps of 'dead men' grew around us, and with grim determination guarded the Polo Club, and other strategic centres; truly a remarkable effort.

The Motor Cycle (M.G.) section noted that it was stronger than ever and was actually the only unit which was above establishment. Training concentrated on machine gun work, but other instruction included map reading, musketry and revolver firing, driving, maintenance of machines and anti-gas training.

An interesting exercise to demonstrate our flexibility was carried out during Camp last year. One section in action on Dodwell's Ridge were ordered to evacuate and take up another position near Lok Ma Chau. The distance between the two points is approximately four miles and slightly less than twenty minutes elapsed from the command 'cease fire' in the first position until fire was again opened in the second. It will be thus realised that we can justly claim to be the most mobile unit in the present corps.

The motorcyclists also noted their involvement in the troubles of 1931. 'In October 1931, during the anti-Japanese riots, the Section was mobilised and assisted the Police in maintaining law and order on the Peninsula. During this period many drivers appreciated the issue of steel helmets as protection against numerous missiles, including flower pots, which were directed against patrols.'

The Reserve Company had two officers in its headquarters and two sections.

The Reserves, or Reserve Company as it is now called was formed in 1914 out of the Reserve Association by Sir Henry May, K.C.M.G., the then Governor of Hong Kong. It was an entirely separate unit from the Volunteers, with a distinctive uniform patterned on that of an Officer.

During the early years of the War the Reserves became one of the most important arms in the fighting forces of the Colony, and at one time had on its rolls no less than over 700 men. The first Commandant was Major G.H. Wakeman and the Headquarters of the Reserve Company were situated at the Courts of Justice.

Later on in 1916 or 1917, the Reserves were united with the Volunteers and then became known as the Reserve Company. On the reorganization of the Volunteer Corps in 1920 the Reserve Company still had an attraction for many older men and a number joined again.

Though the training commitment was light, there could be no doubt that the Reserves had a role to play in the defence of the Colony.

The report of the Medical Section traced its history back to the early part of the century and it had been mobilized with other Volunteers during the First World War and the 1920s — and this gives another tantalizing glimpse of early Chinese Volunteer involvement.

In 1925 the unit was mobilised with the Corps owing to local conditions of emergency, and the raison d'etre of the Section was amply justified by the manner in which numbers of fully qualified medical men joined up as privates, making the unit, in a day almost, fully equipped to perform its whole task. It is interesting to note that among those who answered the call were nearly all the foreign Medicos, and they were supported by several of the Chinese Doctors of the Colony.

Could these latter have been continuing a tradition of Chinese medical service in the Volunteers started by Sun Yat-sen?

In 1935, the Medical Section provided the nucleus of a Field Ambulance since it was again expected that in time of trouble doctors and other personnel would quickly join up. The officers were civilian doctors, of whom there were four, the one Warrant Officer and ten other ranks being trained nurses, dispensers, X-ray experts and other medical specialists. 'The requirements of stretcher bearers and for menial tasks would be enlisted from the best of the Chinese Coolies or Chair-men.'

On 1 October 1934, a unique unit had been acquired: 'Almost certainly the only unit of its kind in existence out of the United Kingdom which is administered by any Volunteer Force, and that is, from conception to birth, a product of the women of the Colony.' This was the Nursing Detachment and, on that day, 76 women signed on. Some of the women were already qualified and others started a programme of study. A four-day camp was held in November and a full training schedule was subsequently organized. The detachment was commanded by Mrs J. Durran and there were 75 other members.

During 1935 there will be progressive classes in first-aid work, and a series of lectures on chemical warfare, that form of frightfulness which everyone, the world over, has at last realised will never be omitted from future wars; truly a pleasant outlook for those to whose energy and foresight this Detachment owes its existence.

The enrolment of women in the Volunteers led to much humourous comment. One article maintained that it was womanizing the defences, and continued with the following:

Parades

A. Corps Signals — Parade at Headquarters at 5.30pm. Pte Freda Freckleface is specially commended for the way in which she signalled the O.C. across the Rose Room of the Peninsula the other night.

B. Corps Machine Gun Battalion — Unit will parade at Headquarters at 5.30pm on Wednesday for instruction in Bridge and Whist. Afternoon tea will be served.

C. Mobile Unit — The next parade will be held at 8.30pm on the Peak Road, when instruction will be given in holding hands, whispering, canoodling and snuggle-pupping. Snuggle-pups should be brought by individual ranks.

D. No 3 (Anzac) Company — Parade at H.Q. for Gas Drill, 5.30pm Friday. Gossip will be issued during this parade. Members will bring their own scandal.

E. Corps Infantry — Members are requested to leave their infantry with the amahs during to-morrow's parade. Following the parade, a sale of work will take place on the parade ground.

In the spring of 1930, the Volunteers took to the air with the establishment of a Flying Section. This did not constitute a separate unit in the ordinary sense, but consisted of two officers and some half a dozen other ranks who were to receive instruction concurrently with the instruction they were receiving in their respective units. Volunteers were keen to join the new section but only those who showed good performance in their other duties were allowed to join. As much as possible, each branch of the Corps was allowed to provide one man.

Training was carried out in co-operation with the recently-formed Hong Kong Flying Club which started out with three planes but two were quickly lost in accidents. More problems followed:

Weather conditions proved a constant and depressing handicap. Elsewhere in the world the early morning had almost invariably been found to be the best time for elementary flying training. Accordingly, and also in order to avoid inconveniencing private members of the Flying Club, the Volunteers repaired to Field Cottage, on the Kai Tak Aerodrome, twice every week, where they remained overnight, in order to be ready to fly at crack o'dawn. Early morning weather, however, proved to be unsuitable for flying instruction and after a time, the excellent breakfasts were held hardly to justify the discomforts of the nights preceding — rarely did any flying follow — and thereafter Volunteers came out to Kai Tak when and how they could for their training. Even so, adverse weather conditions often put a stop to flying for weeks at a time.

Eventually, the great day came when it was found possible on one clear Saturday afternoon to send three Volunteer aviators off on their first solo flight. They all returned safely and were feeling pleased with themselves. A civilian then took the plane up and crashed it. That was the end of the first phase of Volunteer involvement with flying and, not surprisingly, the Hong Kong Flying Club closed its hangar doors for good. A short time later, however, the Far East Flying Training School was in business. In return for a government subsidy, it was committed to train ten Volunteer Air Arm pilots. The 1934–5 Yearbook said that it was hoped that there would soon be ten pilots with 'A' Licences, flying time would then increase to 50 hours each, with service training to follow on that.

In June 1936, a major King's Birthday Review was held in Hong Kong — the first for several years. This large display involved Royal Navy, Royal Marines, 9th Heavy Battery R.A., Anti-Aircraft

Brigade, RA, Hong Kong and Singapore Brigade, R.A., Fortress Royal Engineers, 2nd Battalion East Lancashire Regiment, 2nd Battalion Royal Welch Fusiliers, 1st Battalion Royal Ulster Rifles, 1/8th Punjab Regiment, Royal Army Service Corps, Royal Army Ordnance Corps, Hong Kong Mule Corps, Royal Air Force, Hong Kong Naval Volunteer Defence Force, Hong Kong Volunteer Defence Corps, Hong Kong Police, and St John's Ambulance Brigade. Over 4,000 troops took part in the review and the Motor Machine Gun Section of the H.K.V.D.C. provided the escort for the Governor 'as on all occasions.'

In the yearbook for 1935, dated 1935–6, the G.S.O. 1, Colonel H.C. Harrison, D.S.O., gave an impression of the role of the Volunteers, saying he had been pleasantly surprised by the keenness displayed in Hong Kong.

'A team in training' ah — that, the thing we want in Hong Kong more than anything else! I obviously can't go into details here but all of you know — whether you are machine-gunners, artillerists, engineers, armoured carmen, signallers, service corps or infantrymen — that in the execution of your role you are split up into 'petits paquets,' dotted here and there in the gaps of the necessary 'thin red line.' So the whole of the Hong Kong land-cordon demands, from Volunteers and Regulars alike, the existence of a 'team in training' to an extent which is unparalleled elsewhere. That team has got to have brains and brawn, accustomed to each other's strength and weakness — but each equally fit.

During the year, four week-end camps were held, in the latter part of November and the start of December, while on the social front both the Machine Gun Battalion and the Corps Infantry held successful balls. In fact, all units reported an interesting year. A Machine Gun Battalion Signal Section had been formed in order that the battalion should be complete in itself and conform to the organization which existed in a regular battalion.

The Anzac Company appears to have been disbanded by 1935 — for there is no reference to it. Instead, there is a Number Three (M.G.) Company. This, it was explained, was formed from a nucleus from Number One Company and its main object was to defend the beaches on the mainland. 'We have not commenced Machine Gun training yet but Command Headquarters have been so impressed with the personnel of the Company that they have already allotted Beaches to us and our popularity is such that each Member of the Company has been given a Beach all to himself.'

Flying training was progressing well with a constant stream of would-be pilots. The women of the Nursing Detachment were also very busy, studying nursing and other practical subjects. They attended camp and received instruction in such subjects as map-reading and anti-gas precautions. Stretcher drill caused problems. 'To the uninitiated, it might appear a simple matter to pick up a wounded man. This is far from being the case. It is indeed a most difficult procedure, well-nigh impossible, necessitating a marvellously complex system of movements, based on the drill book, which none of us had seen.'

In 1936, the Volunteers received their first Regular Army Colonel. Lieutenant-Colonel H.B.L. Dowbiggin retired and his place was taken by Lieutenant-Colonel R.C.B. Anderson, M.C. He was an Argyle and Sutherland Highlander, having served as Adjutant of his Battalion while it was stationed in Hong Kong and Shanghai from October 1931 to November 1934. He became adjutant of the H.K.V.D.C. in October 1935.

The yearbook for 1936 contained a message from Major-General A.W. Bartholemew, the G.O.C.

I haven't seen many Volunteers, but I like all I have seen. I like them in Shanghai, I like them in Tientsin and naturally I like them best of all in Hong Kong.

Of course one finds different standards in different places. I have heard it remarked that 'The Shanghai Volunteers are the best in the East.' Maybe, but the Shanghai Municipal Council is the best Fairy Godmother. Given unlimited money, any unit can be first class. I am sure your Commandant would love to present each Volunteer with a Rolls Royce and establish a 'Jimmy's Kitchen' on each beach.

All units reported that they had been busy with training during 1936. The nominal roll of the new Number Three (M.G.) Company was given in the yearbook and this included a good number of Chinese names. Chinese were now serving on a routine basis as Volunteers. The Air Arm reported that it now comprised three flights, a training flight, an active or service flight, and a reserve flight.

A new Railway Operating Detachment Cadre had joined the Volunteers. No explanation was given for its setting up, but, during the year, the unit had been concerned with two movements of a military nature. The detachment co-operated in the annual camp, providing special trains on the Kowloon–Canton

Railway, 'thus enabling the personnel to gain experience in the entraining of troops and to familiarise the members of the Corps with the methods associated with the movement of troops by rail.' Regular army operations involved the unit in February 1936, moving certain units from Kowloon City to Tai Po Market.

The train which left Kowloon at 00.10 consisted of 420 officers and men, 57 mules, equipment and baggage, and amounting to 52 axles in all. The detraining was completed at Tai Po Market Station at 1.50 hours. The troops were again entrained at 11.50 hours the same morning at Fanling Station. The train left Fanling at 12.00 hours on a fast train timing and arrived at Kowloon at 12.35 hours. It was agreed that the exercise provided valuable experience.

The cadre was to have a Construction Section which would concentrate its attentions more on demolition than construction.

10

Japan Comes Closer

IN Japan during the 1930s, the militarists had been building their power through a continuing programme of murder and coups d'etat. Having easily overrun Manchuria, covetous eyes were being cast on the rest of North China and a series of incidents inspired by the Japanese occurred. The Chinese people responded with protests and a nationwide boycott of Japanese products. In 1936 Japan signed the Anti-Comintern Pact with Germany and the clouds of war gathered, ever darker.

In Hong Kong, the danger was well appreciated. A fascinating insight into the perception of the threat to Hong Kong is provided by the secret Hong Kong Defence Scheme of 1936. This shows that the dangers that were facing the colony were very clearly appreciated and disproves any claims that there was a failure to realize that a storm was coming. Interestingly, the scheme was only downgraded from its 'Secret' status in 1986 — though this seems to have been delayed so long only because no-one thought about it, rather than because of any sinister motive.

The report began by considering the general defence problem. The first part of the scheme outlined details of the area to be defended, saying that the city of Victoria was the 'keep' of the colony.

The April 1931 Census estimated the total population of Hong Kong at about 853,000, including 20,000 non-Chinese. The total number of males of military age between 16 and 50 stood at 266,580 but 'The local Chinese can be taken as useless for combatant purposes.' Victoria was very congested, and flanked by the suburbs of Wanchai and Kennedy Town. Though protected by the hills to the south, it 'must always be peculiarly vulnerable to air bombardment or incendiarism.'

Details of the harbour, supplies, fuel stocks and water were given and the vulnerable areas of the colony were identified.

Localities most likely to be selected as objectives for air attack and long-range bombardment are concentrated on the shores of the Harbour. The more important are:

a. The closely populated area of the City.
b. The naval and commercial dockyards.
c. The naval and military magazines.
d. The W/T installations; particularly on Stonecutters' Island.
e. The anchorage.
f. The food storage.
g. Wharves and other harbour facilities.
h. Oil fuel depots (North Point, Lai Chi Kok, Gin Drinkers' Bay and Texaco (1462)
i. Kai Tak Aerodrome.

Fire risks posed a problem. 'In the native quarters of the city of Victoria, the closely built Chinese dwellings, warehouses etc, render the City liable to large outbreaks of fire resulting from bombardment or air attack. The scrub covering the hillside is, after a period of dry weather, readily ignited by shellfire, bombs, or even Very lights.' Roads and ferries were assessed, as were submarine and cable links with the outside world.

The approach to the land frontier, then 10 miles long, of which four miles was formed by the Sham Chun River, consisted of the railway. However, there were no metalled road crossings, although four roads leading up to the border were identified in Chinese territory.

Kai Tak was the only permanent air landing facility. There was a small landing site at Kwanti Race Course, near Fanling, which was used by both large and small aircraft, but this was considered to be unsafe. Emergency landings could be made at the Fanling golf course but these would be difficult. Night flying facilities existed only at Kai Tak. An additional aerodrome was nearing completion at Pat Heung. The waters around the island were admirably suited for seaplane or flying-boat work, said the report, and there were numerous inlets and bays in the new territories. But all sites lacked back-up facilities. The report continued:

Hong Kong could be reinforced from Singapore in two days, provided Saigon was available for our use, but, failing this, the route would have to be Kudat (near Borneo), Manila (if available), and then on to Hong Kong. It is noteworthy that Hong Kong could also be reinforced from India in two days, via Calcutta–Mandalay–Bhamo–Yunnanfu and Nanning, provided Chinese co-operation was assured and refuelling facilities could be made available at those places.

The report then dealt with local conditions affecting the defence.

The island of Hong Kong consists of a central East and West Ridge with spurs running out in a northerly and southerly direction. This ridge is pierced by some eight passes as follows:

Tytam*, Quarry, Stanley, Wong Nei Chong*, Wanchai, Magazine*, Victoria, Mount Davis*.

* = carries motor road.

Immediately north of Kowloon runs the Kowloon Ridge, pierced by some six passes as follows:

Customs, Grasscutters, Sha Tin, Lai Chi Kok (carries main frontier road), Smugglers, Railway Pass.

The main side of the ridge is precipitous; the northern side, though steep, provides sufficient depth for the organization of a defensive position. This is now in the course of preparation.

The Hong Kong and Kowloon Ridges thus form a natural amphitheatre in which lie the harbour and the vulnerable areas mentioned in paragraph 15 above, and as long as they are denied to the enemy direct hostile observation over the harbour is to a very large extent prevented. There are a few isolated points from which observation can be gained, but only at a distance and from considerable heights.

The report noted the great difficulty in movement:

Movement of troops by other than the Railway, the metalled first- and second-class roads, and the Chinese footpaths is practically prohibited by the rugged nature and overgrown condition of the terrain. The Chinese footpaths are very narrow and often steep, and are suitable only for infantry and pack in single file. In the New Territory there are considerable areas of paddi, which are passable for infantry and pack during the winter (November to March, but not when flooded during the remainder of the year. There is no paddi on the Island, except near Little Hong Kong [Near Aberdeen].

The nature of the eastern and southern coast lines with their frequent indentations resulted in the existence of many possible landing beaches, many of which had excellent access to metalled first-class roads, particularly on the south coast of the Island. 'In

180 SECOND TO NONE

order to gain a footing in Hong Kong, a landing force would be obliged to seize a number of separate beaches, since there is no single beach which offers adequate forming up and deployment facilities.' The report identified the most likely landing areas on the Island as being the Dragon's Back–Stanley area, the Repulse Bay–Aberdeen area and the Aberdeen–Mount Davis area. In the New Territories, landings might come at Starling Inlet or Tolo Harbour, at Hebe Haven–Port Shelter or at Tsun Wan–Castle Peak Reach.

The report commented:

In view of the small strength of the garrison now available, or likely to be available, for the defence of the Fortress, the length of the perimeter to be guarded must always form a serious source of weakness. Delay must be obtained by such devices as Beach Machineguns, advanced detachments and obstacles, but, in the main, chief reliance must be placed on mobile reserves maintained as strong as possible.

Mobility and early information are absolutely of first importance. The former involves not only careful administrative arrangements for the use of motor transport and certain extensions of the existing road system, but also great physical fitness on the part of the troops and an intimate knowledge of the country. The latter entails not only an efficient system of Coast Watching, but also adequate air and sea reconnaissance.

After identifying climatic and hydrographical details, the report went on to consider potential enemy advance bases at Bias and Mirs Bays.

The report then gave: 'Reasons for Undertaking Defence' which were, firstly, as a Naval Base, secondly, as a base for further operations, and thirdly, as a commercial port.

Hong Kong is therefore a strategic point vital to the conduct of the operations of our Fleet, Army and Air Force. The loss of Hong Kong would be not only a serious blow to our prestige, but to the potential value of our Fleet in the China Sea. It would prevent British naval, military or air operations being undertaken against Japan until considerable preparation and operations had been undertaken either to effect its recapture or to open a temporary base elsewhere.

Hong Kong has not only the positive values outlined above, but a negative value in the sense that its retention would deprive an enemy of the use of the territory of the Colony as an additional base for his operations in the Pacific.

The object of a First-Class Power in attacking Hong Kong would therefore be to deny to the British the use of the Naval Base and other facilities referred to above, and if possible to capture it in such a condition as would render it useful as an advance base for operations against the British.

The report went on to consider the likely scale and form of attack.

Strategic and other Considerations concerning probable Nature of Attack by Sea, Land and Air.

The only States possessing the means of attacking Hong Kong are the United States of America, China and Japan.

a. Hostilities between the United States and the British Empire appear at present out of the question. In any case the main theatre of naval war would be in the Atlantic and no extensive operations against Hong Kong need be anticipated for many months after the outbreak of hostilities.

b. China. The Chinese Republic is in a position to attack the Colony of Hong Kong across the land frontier. The quality of the Chinese Army is such that it should be well within our power to hold in check any force that might be brought against Hong Kong, until adequate reinforcements can be brought from overseas. Improvements under foreign tuition are, however, noted and require watching. Their recent progress in aviation in particular has been remarkable. In this connection the possibility of their taking air action against the Colony can no longer be ignored.

c. Japan possesses the means to attack Hong Kong by sea, land and air, and moreover in the event of war with the British Empire it has been pointed out that for strategic reasons she is virtually compelled to attempt the seizure of Hong Kong as early as possible after the outbreak of hostilties. It is accordingly with regard to a war with the Japanese Empire that the defence scheme is prepared.

The British China fleet normally consists of cruisers, destroyers, submarines and an aircraft carrier. it is markedly inferior to the Japanese Fleet and could not hope to engage the latter successfully. It is, however, a menace to the safe passage of a Japanese Overseas Expedition.

The British Main Fleet, which is superior to the Japanese Fleet, is in peace time stationed in European waters. The Japanese will therefore at the outset enjoy a Naval preponderance in the Pacific which will terminate with the arrival of the British Fleet.

It is therefore of great importance to Japan to seize Hong Kong in sufficient time to consolidate their hold before the British Main Fleet has annulled the initial Japanese naval preponderance. On the other hand, whilst the retention of the Island of Hong Kong is of primary importance, the essence of the problem of defence is that the actual water of the Harbour should be available for use of the Main Fleet on its arrival. The scheme of defence has therefore been drawn up with this object in view.

Role of the British China Fleet

The composition of the British China Fleet is such that it constitutes a serious menace to an enemy Expeditionary Force on passage to Hong Kong. The larger the Expeditionary Force is, the more readily would it be detected and located; also more difficult would it be for the escort to afford it protection.

It follows that it will be of great importance to Japan to employ the smallest and most compact Expeditionary Force consistent with the attainment of her object. This consideration is likely to have a considerable influence on the scale and form of attack.

Restrictions in View of a Future Fleet Action

The Japanese must recognise that ultimate victory may depend on their ability to meet the British Main Fleet in battle, and for this purpose they will need the concerted efforts of modern war vessels. The risk to such ships, if employed against Hong Kong, will tend to limit the employment of the full Japanese naval strength.

Isolation of Hong Kong

From the outbreak of war our forces in Hong Kong will be isolated. They will therefore have to maintain the defence until the arrival of the British Main Fleet, with only those resources in man-power and material which exist in the Colony in time of peace, supplemented by such additions which it may be found possible to introduce into the Colony in anticipation of war. The enemy will therefore appreciate that economy of force, morale and material is of singular importance to the defence. He may therefore be expected to carry out all possible forms of destructive and harassing action with a view both to morale and material destruction and to embarassing the defence with problems of protection and control of the civil population.

Surprise

Our temporary loss of Naval superiority facilitates the development of a surprise attack on Hong Kong. The size of an Expeditionary Force designed to capture Hong Kong may therefore be limited by the requirements of secrecy in preparation. This consideration applies principally to the initial attack, and particularly if this is planned to precede or follow shortly after the formal Declaration of Hostilities.

The report said that unless the Japanese plan of operations was restricted to a direct attack on the island they would have to land in Chinese territory. Similarly, their shore-based aircraft would have to operate from Chinese soil. The Chinese ability to resist this was seen as slight but it was pointed out that Japanese infringement of her neutrality might enable Britain to demand equal privileges which could be of considerable value to a relieving force. It would also be of great assistance in air actions. Friendly relations therefore had to be maintained with Canton.

In a fascinating part of the report, the scale of attack by land, sea and air was assessed. Assuming that Japan had no assistance from an ally or allies, the report stated that:

The initial scale of a landing attack has been assessed as a covering force of about two Brigades, either on the Island or New Territory within 48 hours of the Declaration of War, followed 12 hours later by the balance of a Division.

A force of the above size, with a small proportion of light artillery and a reasonable allowance of Engineers and Services, could be conveyed to Hong Kong within the time stated without presenting a more than ordinary difficult naval problem.

If a regular investment from the Mainland was contemplated, the force would be reinforced as early as possible with a considerable quantity of medium and siege artillery.

It is estimated that a second division could not arrive for another ten days unless secrecy was sacrificed at an earlier period.

As regards naval support, it must be assumed that the Fortress will be liable to bombardment by capital ships with guns up to 16-inch calibre.

As regards air attack, it is estimated that Japan could in favourable circumstances establish a force of at least eleven squadrons within striking distance of Hong Kong in from 15 to 30 days. A force of two or three squadrons could probably operate from Swatow within a week.

The possibility of the enemy's main attack being preceded by an intensive air offensive, with the object of neutralising the fixed defences, should never be lost sight of.

The report was of the opinion that if the enemy did not land troops directly on the island, then he would do so either in China or in the New Territories. An attack on the island could take place in view of the existence of areas of water close to the harbour entrances which could not be illuminated, the shortage of mines and the existence of many deep water quays. Such an attack would be risky, but, 'Japan has, however, on her Navy List several old armoured ships, the loss of which would not affect the issue of the war. A raid on the island could also be a diversionary measure from the main attack.' If an attack was to come from China, the most likely places for the initial landing were at Au Tau, in Bias Bay, or immediately north of Sha Tau Kok.

The report said that the preparation of troops for an attack would probably take a week or so and therefore there would be a 'Precautionary Period' of some eight or nine days. But it added tellingly, 'On the other hand, it is well known that the Japanese are adepts in the art of secrecy, and it must therefore be clearly understood that there can be no guarantee of this warning.' Equally telling:

Although the initial attack may be expected to be carried out by not more than some two brigades, it is considered that the attack, once opened, will thereafter be sustained, and supported with a continual stream of reinforcing personnel and material, either as reinforcements to an existing force or organized for fresh landings. If an investment from the land side is undertaken, heavy and siege artillery will be brought forward as early as possible.

The table given to illustrate the System of Command in Hong Kong 'In time of extreme peril when His Excellency the Governor has decided that unified command is necessary', showed the clear integration of the Volunteers into defence planning. The Governor was the top man, being also Vice Admiral and Commander in Chief. Beneath him came the Commodore Royal Navy, the Officer Commanding, Troops, and the Officer Commanding, Royal Air Force. Under the O.C. Troops were the various subsidiary commanders of elements such as artillery, engineers, anti-aircraft and reserves — and the Commandant of the Hong Kong Volunteer Defence Corps.

Total strength figures for the H.K.V.D.C. were 51 officers and 826 other ranks, as shown in Table 10.1.

Another table in the report noted that, in addition to the machineguns of regular battalions, the H.K.V.D.C. owned 25 guns with another gun on its way out from the United Kingdom. The R.A.O.C. had another 136 guns which could be called into use.

During any 'Precuationary Period', the total 162 additional guns were to be distributed between the regular battalions and the Volunteers. The latter was to be given 71 guns for its M.G. Battalion, 12 for its M.M.G. Platoon, four for its Armoured Car Section and four for its mechanized M.G. Troop.

The Volunteer Machine Gun Battalion was to man posts around the island coastline at Sai Wan Point, Big Wave Bay, Rocky Bay,

Table 10.1 Volunteer Numbers as Shown in the Secret Defence Scheme
(1936)

	Officers	Other Ranks
Headquarters	6	20
'A' Section	2	34
'L' Section	—	50
'M' Section	1	40
Corps Engineers	2	36
Corps Signals	1	50
M.G. Bn HQ	2	2
M.G. Troop	1	28
Armoured Car Section	1	28
M.M.G. Section	2	36
No. 1 (M.G.) Company	4	45
No. 2 (Scottish) Company	3	48
No. 3 (M.G.) Company	3	77
M.G. Bn Signals	1	24
Corps Infantry HQ	1	4
'A' Rifle Company	5	120
'B' AALA Coy	2	70
Medical Section	5	12
Air Arm	1	9
Army Service Corps Cadre	4	50
Railway O.D. Cadre HQ	2	2
Operating Section	2	36
Construction Section	1	15

Island Bay, East Tytam Bay, Tytam Harbour, Tytam Harbour
Pumping Station, West Tytam Bay, Tweed Bay, Stanley Bay, West
Bay, Five and a Quarter Fathom Bay, Repulse Bay, Deepwater Bay,
Brickworks, Aberdeen Channel East and West, Aberdeen Bay,
Kellett Bay, Rope Pier, Tai Ho Wan, Sandy Bay, Tytam Gap. The
M.M.G. Platoon was to man inland posts at Tytam Gap and in the
centre and right sectors of the inland defences.

On the mainland, the M.G. Troop was to man posts at Starling
Inlet while the Machine Gun Battalion was to man posts at Tai Po,

Tolo Harbour, Tai Po Station, Tide Cove, Wong Uk Island, Hebe Haven, Port Shelter (North, Central and South), the Hung Ha Isthmus, Gin Drinkers Bay and the Texaco Installation.

The M.M.G. Platoon was to patrol the coastline from the brewery at Sham Tseng to Castle Peak Police Station, with an element in Fortress Reserve at Whitfield Barracks. The Armoured Car Section was also to have an element in reserve and to provide a force extra to normal establishment attached to the regular battalions. The Machine Gun Battalion was also to man posts at Stonecutters Island North, East, South, and West.

Though there can be endless argument over what should or should not have been done in relation to the defence of Hong Kong in the 1930s, one fact is perfectly clear from this whole report: the threat was Japan and the authorities fully understood this and planned accordingly.

By 1937, however, the British Chiefs of Staff felt that the four battalions in Hong Kong could hardly be effective without reinforcements. The Japanese had air superiority and would probably knock out the defences within a short period. Hong Kong was very vulnerable. However, the option of writing it off and reducing the garrison was not felt to be practical in view of the loss of British prestige and the likely adverse effect on the morale of China. This thinking was not, of course, public knowledge.

The essential role of the Volunteers in the defence of Hong Kong was stressed by the G.O.C., Bartholomew, at his annual inspection of the Corps in March, 1937: 'If you crack,' he said, 'or if your numbers go down it means that this fortress may not be impregnable. And impregnable it has got to be.' He went on to say that he was pleased at an increase in recruitment, but warned, 'Remember we want every man we can get, as your Corps is a most important unit in the defences of the colony. During the last year we have worked very hard to modernise this fortress and in all our plans you play a vital part.'

The Volunteers were to take part in a major garrison exercise that evening and Bartholomew said:

I hope to see many of you in action in the next 24 hours and I hope that you will have been inquisitive and found out everything that effects the smooth running and efficient working of your respective jobs, so that if I ask anyone about anything concerning your work, I may get the correct answer. When you get in, on the conclusion of the operations, mind you ask the answer to any question which arose and could not be answered on the spot.

Lastly, I hope that we shall 'actuate' most of you tonight; but remember in war there are days or weeks when nothing happens and then suddenly comes the crisis. The answer you make to that crisis is really the vital test of whether you are ready and fit for war. If you get slack in war it is then that the attack will come. If tonight you feel bored — I am sorry — but that too is part of your training and I hope you will have an interesting and instructive night.

The Volunteer inspection took place on Saturday, 20 March but the exercise started on the Thursday night when two brigades of attacking 'Blue' forces landed on the mainland between the Hong Kong Brewery at Sham Tseng and Castle Peak. The defending 'Red Forces', the Kumoan Rifles, Royal Welch Fusiliers and Royal Ulster Rifles, fell back to prepared positions notionally inflicting heavy losses on the Blue troops and holding firm against waves of assault. HMS *Cumberland* engaged the forts and caused heavy damage to the power station but was held to have been badly hit by the shore batteries. A communique issued just before the Volunteers went into action on the Saturday said that the Blue pressure had increased with the landings being developed. The two infantry brigades, supported by light artillery, were pressing forward chiefly from the Kam Tin Plain towards the left flanks of Red's prepared 'inner line' of defence which ran between the Shing Mun Dam and Gin Drinkers' Bay. Blue was opposed by the Kumoan Rifles and the Royal Welch Fusiliers, supported by four artillery batteries. The Royal Ulster Rifles and the Kumoan Rifles held the flank to the east.

On the Saturday night, Blue vessels tried, but failed, to enter the harbour but did manage to put landing parties ashore on Green Island at the west and at Sandy Bay, Pokfulam. Both parties were eventually driven back to their boats — although the latter did manage to enter Mount Davis Fort.

Blue destroyers appeared in Tolo Harbour, but two were judged to have been lost to defending artillery. Landing parties were put ashore between Tai Po and Tide Cove (modern Sha Tin). The Volunteers were waiting for them, however, and several landing parties were judged to have been annihilated. Others managed to demolish the Tai Po Road and part of the railway before re-embarking. In fact, it was said, this caused Red a certain amount of trouble as it had intended to cut the railway anyway.

Elements of the Royal Welch Fusiliers and Royal Ulster Rifles supported the Volunteer machine-gunners in these actions, sustaining serious casualties. Bombardment of the forts continued and it was said that the defences of the Island must remain in the hands of the Volunteer detachments there who deployed into their Island war positions during the Saturday afternoon, ready to repulse any landings. Also involved were the Seaforth Highlanders and a company of the Fusiliers.

Despite all the preparation, however, the Blue troops scored a dramatic blow at the heart of the city. At about 8.30 p.m., under cover of poor weather, two destroyers crept into the harbour undetected, except by a small patrol boat which was sunk, and succeeded in landing troops at Murray Pier. A few minutes later, bitter fighting was taking place in the Naval Yard, after preliminary bombardment by the destroyers, and after a series of sharp encounters with heavy losses on both sides the enemy occupied the Naval Yard. The centre of the city was then taken over and an attack went in on military headquarters where guerrilla fighting ensued.

Yet another dramatic coup was scored at about 9.30 p.m. when a strong force was landed in Kellett Bay (modern Wah Fu estate) near Aberdeen, and patrols cut Pokfulam Road and what is now called Victoria Road, severing communications. At 10.50 p.m. a party of Marines landed elsewhere near Aberdeen taking the defence completely by surprise and capturing a Volunteer machine-gun post on the beach. Another Volunteer post was also captured near Victoria Road.

An attempt to land at Deepwater Bay was driven off, with Volunteer machine gunners exacting a heavy toll. At Stanley, the enemy landed and, after a brisk engagement, captured a machine-gun post manned by the Seaforths. The biggest landing was at Shek O where HMS *Capetown* put ashore 600 men of the Inniskillin Fusiliers who swept all defenders before them. Fighting continued into the Sunday morning when the exercise ended.

This exercise showed a very real appreciation of the threat to Hong Kong, and Japanese agents in the colony must have read the extensive press reports with interest.

In July 1937, the Japanese staged the 'Marco Polo Bridge' incident and started undeclared war on China. Massive troop reinforcements poured into North China from Japan. Peking was evacuated on 28 July and on 30 July Tientsin fell. On 13 August a second front was opened at Shanghai in a bid to destroy China's economic powerhouse. One effect of this was to cause an influx of foreign national refugees into Hong Kong. On 12 December Nanking fell and the Japanese troops engaged in a bloody and indiscriminate massacre of civilians.

The tone of the editorial of the 1937 Yearbook was, not surprisingly, grim: 'Our ships are still being stopped by Japanese destroyers, and even the "Rawlpindi" was "mistaken" for a Chinese vessel. There has been shelling just across the border and towns in South China have been bombed and shelled.' The war was quickly closing up on Hong Kong — a full four years before Pearl Harbour.

The editorial writer found it hard to credit that there were still those who would not join the Volunteers:

The excuses given for not being a Volunteer are many and varied. One man told us he was not going to fight for two shillings per day and we told him that if the occasion arose he would perhaps have to fight for nothing if he wanted to live. Another said 'Oh, I'll be there if any trouble starts, but I'm not joining now.' To which we replied 'Yes, you'll come in handy to dig latrines as that is about all the use you will be without any previous training.' Now is the time for a man to join. It is useless him imagining that if trouble started he could take his place in the scheme of things. He couldn't, and would be more of a nuisance than an asset. You can well imagine how our compatriots in Shanghai felt as they mobilized and those who had not already joined came rushing full of importance 'to do their bit.' They were in the way and served no useful purpose for days, while the trained volunteer was on his job of work at once.

The Commandant's annual report for the year ending 15 April unfortunately, did not give the total strength for the corps. Germans and Dutch had left the corps: 'Of the 108 members who resigned during the last 12 months, 31 are of Dutch and German nationality and their resignations were brought by the fact that they were in danger of losing their national status should they continue to serve.'

Two additional units had been formed in the previous 12 months, an Improvised Battery, affiliated to the Royal Marines in HMS *Tamar* and an Army Service Corps Company, formed out of the old Army Service Corps Cadre, and affiliated to the R.A.S.C. Hong Kong.

During the year, two camps had been held with about 400

members being excercised, and a full and active part had been
taken in combined operations. All ranks had been fitted with Box
Respirators and been instructed in anti-gas measures. An appeal
was made for Volunteers to be exempted from Jury Service, while
the G.O.C., Maj.-Gen. Bartholomew said that the matter of a new
headquarters, with full supporting facilities was now in hand. An
officer, Major E.J.R. Mitchell, and Sergeant-Major Everest, had
represented the Corps at the Coronation in London where they
paraded in uniform with representatives from all over the Empire.

Meanwhile, in Hong Kong, the Volunteers had played a part in
the Coronation Review which was held at Happy Valley Race
Course on 12 May, supplying a company of 35 for the parade with
the Volunteer motor cyclists providing their usual escort for the
Governor. All units of the Volunteers reported a very active year
with a full round of training amply backed up by a busy social
programme.

It was in 1937 that Chinese members really became a significant
part of the Corps. In the *South China Morning Post*, of Saturday, 19
October that year, there was a routine column of Volunteer information where reference was made to 'No.4 (M.G.) Company' with
details of its drills. Although this was not identified specifically as
a Chinese formation, elsewhere in the column various information
on personnel was given and 22 Chinese names were listed — all
assigned to Number Four Company. In the weeks following, there
appeared many more Chinese names, again all in the same company.

Albert Chang Kung-po recalled, in 1954:

In the earlier part of the year 1937, there were no Chinese participants in
the H.K.V.D.C. Colonel Anderson was then the Commandant, and at the
outbreak of Sino-Japanese hostilities in that year, he adopted the sugges-
tion of a minority of Chinese Government servants for the organisation of
Chinese companies. The task of this organisation was shouldered by
Major Branson, then Captain, and in the same year, the first Chinese
Company, the 4th Battery, was formed, and was soon followed by the 4th
Machine Gun Company. As Chinese recruits gradually increased, another
Company, No. 7 (M.G.) Coy., was formed. When Colonel Rose succeeded
Colonel Anderson as Commandant after the latter's retirement, the exten-
sive training given to the Chinese, who responded with a cheerful spirit,
achieved very satisfactory results.

Late March 1938 saw the big combined operations manoeuvres

begin. The story-line was that Hong Kong was a small mainland power with large colonial possessions some 2000 miles to the south. The normal garrison consisted of a brigade of field artillery, a brigade of heavy artillery, a brigade of anti-aircraft artillery, a corps of fortress engineers and an infantry brigade consisting of five battalions together with various ancillary troops. But, a revolt had broken out in the southern colony and the garrison there had had to be reinforced by all available ships, an infantry battalion and the anti-aircraft brigade which had been temporarily converted into field artillery.

At the same time, Hong Kong's northern neighbour 'Pacifica' was acting in a threatening manner. Pacifica had a modern fleet and an army of seven infantry divisions, one of which could be fully mobilized three or four days after a declaration of war. The remaining divisions would be ready to take the field at fortnightly intervals. The Pacifican airforce consisted of about 500 first line machines. Of these, 50 carrier-borne and 50 land-based would be ready to operate against Hong Kong within a few hours of the outbreak of hostilities. A further 150 land-based aircraft would become available as soon as landing grounds could be established on Chinese soil.

The Hong Kong Volunteer Defence Corps took part in the exercise:

On the Island, No. 2 (Scottish) M.G. Coy, covered the left sector, No. 1 M.G. Coy, the centre sector, and No. 3 M.G. Coy, the right sector.

No. 5 M.G. Coy, was manning 'The Gaps' and the Corps Battery was at Belcher's Fort, with the Engineers on searchlights at Belcher's. M.G. Signals, the D.R.s, the A.S.C., divided between the Island and the Mainland.

On the Mainland the volunteers were also deployed, with No. 3 M.G. Coy at Port Shelter and Tai Po. Armoured Cars and Motor Machine Guns provided Tai Po and Castle Peak patrols, and the Mobile M.G. reserves were at Sham Shui Po.

Given the topography of the New Territories and of Hong Kong the scenarios to be practised in any war game are very limited. This exercise, like many others, was an uncannily accurate indication of how an actual battle would go. However, the days of exercises were drawing to a close. The real threat was moving ever closer to the borders of Hong Kong.

During 1938, fighting between the Chinese and the Japanese

had been intense. On 12 October the Japanese landed, as had been feared, on the eastern side of Bias Bay, along the coast to the north of Hong Kong. A further landing was made at Au Tou. The Chinese, lacking aircraft, appeared not to have accurately located the invaders and it was probably not until the Japanese arrived at Waichow that the Chinese headquarters discovered that a heavily-mechanized body of troops equipped with amphibian tanks had passed the defence lines in the East River Area. There were also strong rumours that the Japanese had help from fifth-columnists in taking Waichow.

Having crossed the East River, the Japanese then split into two columns and advanced on Canton, one column swinging to the north and the other following the line of the Kowloon-Canton Railway. The total Japanese troops strength was put at about 30,000. In the *Hong Kong Weekly Press* of 21 October 1938, one Chinese patriot was quoted as saying:

The Japanese, in launching their invasion of Kwantung Province, are challenging us at the very source of our spirit of resistance and nationalism. Our Province was the last to submit to the domination of the Mongols and to the Manchus. It was the first to give expression to the spirit of nationalism which ended the domination of the Manchus over our people. And by their invasion the Japanese have cast caution to the winds and in a frenzy of desperation have invaded the homeland of our Great Leader, Sun Yat-sen.

But the Japanese pushed onwards and soon the decision was taken by the Chinese military to withdraw from Canton and pull back to the hills. The war was now, as the *Daily Press* of 28 November so accurately stated, 'At the doors of the Colony,' — almost three years exactly from the actual attack. It is worth repeating the point, for many accounts of the battle for Hong Kong have paid insufficient attention to the run-up to the invasion, often giving the impression that the 1941 attack was something of a surprise. The military and civil authorities knew full well what the threat was. 'The Japanese Army in its mad adventure in China, has now seen fit to extend the scope of their activities to the very doors of the Colony. Hostilities between the opposing forces are going on in the vicinity of Hong Kong's borders and gunfire can be heard by residents of the New Territories,' said the *Daily Press*.

It seems that the Japanese actually crossed the border on some occasions as they fought for control of Shum Chun (Shenzhen), and a number of British were briefly over-run. The newspaper commented hopefully:

It would hardly appear in the light of the ready Japanese withdrawal from the British posts they have occupied that the Japanese navy have any desire to involve Hong Kong in the fighting and it would seem they are trying to steer clear of anything likely to antagonise the British ... For the present there is little need for apprehension so far as Hong Kong is concerned. The government have the situation well in hand and it would be advisable for the public not to become panic-stricken but to do the best they can by giving the authorities every assistance possible.

It was reported that several people had been killed and wounded in the fighting, some of whom were residents of British territory. Two women were said to have been killed by shell fire, others were machinegunned.

During the Japanese shelling two police officials, Assistant Superinten-dent F.F. Booker and Inspector G.C. Taylor had a narrow escape when a shell exploded a few feet from their car. The Japanese had taken over a British military post on the British side of the river and had hoisted the Rising Sun. An officer produced a map and, in a discussion which took place on the bridge, remonstrated that they had crossed into British territory. The Japanese maintained the border was some eight miles fur-ther south, but, eventually, they withdrew back into Chinese territory.

The Japanese attack resulted in a major influx of refugees into Hong Kong which caused considerable problems. Mrs R. Langley, Secretary of the St. John Ambulance Brigade spoke to the Emer-gency Refugee Council on 24 November, saying that she had just returned from a visit to Shum Chun where conditions were 'beyond all description. There was no electricity and no regular water supply and food was very scarce. Refugees were not flock-ing in by the hundreds but by the thousands.' Adding to the problems was the fact that 'lepers and lunatics' were included in the refugee flow.

The government stepped up preparations for war with black-out and air raid precaution exercises being held. The road to the frontier from Sheung Shui was closed, 'To save possible sightseers from disappointment' according to the notice issued by the Com-missioner of Police.

The worrying events in China, and in Europe, produced a sombre tone for much of the Volunteers' 1938 yearbook. The departing Major General, A.W. Bartholomew noted:

During the past year the East has had a trying time. In August, 1937, when things were particularly bad I had to denude Hong Kong of troops for a few days in order to re-inforce Shanghai. I could only take this risk in the knowledge of your existence in the Colony. It might have been a case of 'No Volunteer Defence Corps — no reinforcements for Shanghai until relief Battalions arrive from the South'. The delay thus caused might have been fatal. So, although you may not have realised it, your very existence has recently been of material service to the British Empire.

And if it ever comes to real war here, I am quite sure that you will come up to the mark. But remember, it is the real thing that you are training for and NOT 'But the scheme ends at 10 a.m. tomorrow, Sir!!', nor 'Let's eat drink and be merry, for tomorrow we go home.' Your training is naturally sketchy and at times may be irksome, but there is rough and smooth to everything that we do in this life, so you've just got to take things as they come and 'play' for all you are fit.

In August 1938, Lieutenant Colonel H.B. Rose, M.C., had taken over as commanding officer from Lieutenant Colonel R.C.B. Anderson, M.C.

During the year, the Corps Infantry (Portuguese) was abolished and in its place two new companies were formed: Number Five Machine Gun Company (Portuguese) and the Anti-Aircraft Company (Portuguese). Number Four Machine Gun Company (Chinese) appeared in the records for the first time. A Pay Section was also set up. Approval was given for a Chinese section of the Engineer Company to be formed for work on the defensive lights.

Many good things had been said about the enthusiasm of the Chinese Volunteers at the Corps Annual Dinner and presentation of prizes, held in May, at Volunteer Headquarters. Lieutenant Colonel Anderson said that the formation of the Chinese company had been most successful:

The creation of a Chinese Company is an innovation in this Corps but I am glad to be able to say that it has already proved a successful one. The anxiety to join and the keenness and enthusiasm exhibited by all those who have been enrolled ensured the success of this company from the very beginning. I congratulate Captain Branson and his staff on the rapid progress that has been made and on behalf of all other units in the Corps, I extend a very hearty welcome to the Chinese Company.

The Governor, Sir Geoffry Northcote, also spoke:

I do not wish to be an alarmist; I do not think that this Colony is about to be plunged into war, but no one can look around the world today without realising its turmoil and how its peace is jeopardized, and at such a time it is the duty of every British subject in this Colony, who in the event of war could be spared from his peacetime duties, so to train himself now, that he may be able to play a useful part.

Northcote had, apparently, been a Volunteer himself:

As I listened to your Colonel's speech my memory carried me back some 40 years when I myself first became a Volunteer; those were the days when they used to call us bug shooters ... If we did not have the complicated training that you gentlemen have today, at any rate I can assure you that volunteering in the last century had plenty arduous in it, as anyone who has doubled along Laffan's Plain or up the Long Valley, in a tight-waisted red coat under a heavy helmet and in Corps boots, will agree. It is with just a trace of pride that I recall that I ran so hard in those days that I was promoted to the rank of Lance Corporal.

He, too, was pleased to see Chinese join the corps:

I am very glad indeed to welcome the Chinese Machine Gun Company. In entrusting to them a part of the armed defences of this Colony, Government has, I feel sure, done a wise as well as a welcome thing. It was with great pleasure that I learned of the willingness of the Military Authorities to rely so largely on this Chinese Company for guarding the fixed defences of the Island and Mainland. Colonel Anderson has been able to pay to that Company's keenness a warm compliment which all heard with much happiness...

Captain V.C. Branson, M.C., officer commanding the new Chinese company was able to offer, in the yearbook, evidence of the enthusiasm with which the Chinese Volunteers were carrying out their duties, despite initial scepticism.

Previous experiments designed to attract new personnel to the Corps have not been uniformly successful and it is not surprising to find a few who regarded the expediency of this new venture with some dubiety. However, encouraged by the records of the Chinese Units in the Shanghai and Malaya Volunteers, Headquarters considered that the inclusion of a Chinese unit in the Hong Kong Defence Corps was fully justified.

The actual inception of the Company dates from June 1937 when ten Chinese recruits were posted to Corps Headquarters. The Company proper, however, was only formed in October of that year, when it was decided to create two platoons of 30 men each as Machine Gunners. It may, therefore, seem premature to attempt a retrospect; however, with practically a year's training behind us, we are in a position to take stock, and can say without suspicion of trumpet-blowing, that in keenness and efficiency a satisfactory standard has been set and attained.

The keenness and hard work of the recruits, who paraded twice-weekly had resulted in much progress even though 'the task of creating a Company out of nothing but a supply of keen but absolutely raw recruits was by no means easy.' Three platoons had now been formed and a fourth was planned to remove more names from the waiting list. In the 1938 yearbook, Capt. Branson went on to pay tribute to the support of the instructors from the Royal Scots and Middlesex Regiments.

In London, in July 1938, the defence chiefs had taken a close look at Hong Kong and had reaffirmed their view that the colony was virtually indefensible. However, prestige and the need to attempt to deny the harbour to the Japanese made a continued British military presence essential. Changes were made to the defence plan. The Washington treaties had lapsed and work was pushed ahead on the construction of defences in the New Territories and the strengthening of the forts and defences on the Island. The decision was made to attempt to hold the enemy on a line which streched for 13 miles or so from Gin Drinker's Bay (the site of the present-day container port) in the west, to Port Shelter in the east. The Gin Drinker's Line thus came into being — the key point being the large redoubt at Shing Mun, at the base of a valley up which ran the road leading over Lead Mine Pass to Tai Po. All along the line, trenches, fire-steps, barbed wire entanglements and obstructions were constructed. Fields of fire and defensive responsibilities were worked out. The threat from the sea was to be held off by the big 9.2 inch guns at Mount Davis, Stanley and Cape D'Aguilar, and by the six inch and smaller guns scattered around the coastline.

But events in Europe were to change the plans.

11

'War Has Broken Out'

THOUGH war in Germany was of tremendous interest to the foreign residents of Hong Kong, the immediate threat to the colony was, of course, Japan. By the time war was declared in Europe in September 1939, the Japanese had been in Canton for almost a year. In early 1939, they had closed up to the border and a series of incidents had occurred. One of the most serious being a major violation which took place in February.

The old military maxim runs: 'Time wasted is seldom spent in reconnaissance. Time spent in reconnaissance is seldom wasted.' In 1939, the Japanese were wasting no time. During the early hours of 13, 15 and 16 February, Japanese planes probed deep into Hong Kong territory. Appearing at about 5.30 a.m., they spent a leisurely hour flying around the border area, Shum Chun and Lo Wu.

The next time the planes returned, they attacked. On 21 February nine planes 'brought death and destruction out of the skies,' the *Hong Kong Weekly Press* reported.

Many people were killed in a major attack on the border area. On the British side, at least eight people, including an Indian police constable and several women and children were killed. On the Chinese side, more than 40 others died in an attack on Shum Chun and there were many other casualties elsewhere.

That the incident did not assume more serious proportions was due to the poor marksmanship of the Japanese fliers. One of their targets was the Royal Scots Regiment some two miles in British territory from the border. Bombs actually fell within the confines of the camp area but fortunately there were no casualties due to the fact that the men were out on manoeuvres at the time of the raid.

Nevertheless, the Japanese machine-gunned and bombed a train between Fanling and Lowu station, claiming several lives and wounding a number of other civilians.

British Post No. 11 likewise received a direct hit and a reinforced concrete building was completely demolished. Here it was that Surdah Singh, the Indian policeman, lost his life, when he refused to leave his post.

The post was just to the east of the bridge over the Shum Chun River. It was quite clearly marked with a British flag.

A *Daily Press* reporter rushed to the frontier:

I arrived at Sheungshui about 11.30am. The first sight that greeted me was the horribly mangled remains of the Indian constable who had been killed at the Lowu Railway bridge across the Shumchun River after having declined to leave his post when told to do so by a British sergeant.

Refugees were pouring along the military road, and the railway track … The bombed ruins at Shumchun were still smoking and the people were at work putting out the flames. Corpses were still to be seen where they had fallen … Poignant scenes were to be witnessed. Wounded had died on the road to the New Territories and the wailing of the relatives further incensed one against the utter brutality of the perpetrators of the raid.

It was clear that the main targets of the attack were the hapless refugees who had fled from inland to refugee camps on the Chinese side of the border.

A refugee worker said, 'We could hear the bursts of machine-gun fire as the planes approached the buildings in which the refugees were lodged. Ten refugees of the camp who were still in the open were machine-gunned. We saw bombs falling from the racks and heard them burst along the railway near the Lowu station.'

The *Daily Press* correspondent wrote:

The first crater I saw in British territory was about 25 yards from Lowu Railway bridge. It had destroyed part of the permanent way. Workmen were digging in the crater for parts of the bomb to determine its size.

Fifteen yards further on, another bomb had scored a hit on a reinforced concrete building alongside which a couple of railway carriages were standing. The building had been demolished and one body was later extracted. The railway carriages had served as the barracks for the Indian policemen on guard at the Lowu Railway bridge. It was riddled with flying metal from the bomb.

Between the building and the railway carriages were six bodies. They had been peasants. It was pitiful to see the small baby and a tiny child which had been killed by the concussion of the exploding bomb.

Hundreds of weeping and wailing refugees, carrying their worldly belongings, were wending their way to safety under the Union Jack. Women and children were bemoaning the loss of their loved ones. Wounded were struggling manfully along the road, forcing back groans of pain.

In the railway compound on the British side of the border:

Gruesome bloodstains, almost everywhere, bore mute evidence of the terrible work of destruction that had been done by the perpetrators if this international crime. The corpses of the barbarism, torn and mangled beyond recognition — men, women and children alike, whose ages ranged from a few months to grown-ups — were being removed in wooden wreckage and placed in wooden coffins provided by the Red Swastika Society.

Heartbroken women and children were forcibly torn away from the coffins which they were clasping and which contained the remains of their loved ones, who had either been done to death in the bombings or who had been mowed down by the machine-gun of the enemies of their country.

There could be no doubt that the attack on the British Post at the bridge was deliberate:

I saw hanging up on the side a huge Union Jack, which likewise had been riddled by Japanese machine-gunners. There could have been mo mistaking that this was our territory. If the Japs could have seen human beings fleeing for safety and used them as targets for their machine-guns, there can be no excuse that their airmen could not have seen the British flag.

About 30 bombs had been dropped on British territory, including the two dropped on the Royal Scots camp after the attack on the train.

As the situation in Europe and in China became ever more serious, the government of Hong Kong took steps to prepare for war. In June, conscription was introduced for all male British subjects of European parentage, aged between 18 and 55. Hong Kong was the first British territory to follow the example of the home country in the introduction of conscription.

Men aged between 18 and 41, who were fit for active service, were assigned to the Hong Kong Volunteer Defence Corps or the Hong Kong Naval Defence Force.

A number of essential service corps, such as the Auxiliary Fire Service, the Air Raid Precautions Department, the Auxiliary Police, and the Auxiliary Nursing Service were set up and men who were not fit, or who were otherwise not able to serve, were posted to these. Women volunteered for the nursing service.

Citizens of the British dominions were allowed three months to volunteer, after that the ordinance would apply to them as well. Many European nationalities and 450 Chinese also volunteered.

Legislative Councillor, Mr Lo Man-kam, stated at a meeting of the council on 27 July that, 'Chinese British subjects have never failed to respond to the Colony's call in time of her need.' He noted that the conscription bill was intended only to apply to British subjects of European descent — purely on grounds of practicality. There could be no question, however, of different treatment should Chinese volunteer:

The Colony is justly proud of its Hongkong Volunteer Defence Corps. But in order that its splendid esprit de corps, its efficiency, may not be impaired, it is essential that all its members should be able to feel that, as fellow members working in union for a common cause, they do in fact receive equal treatment in every respect, and in all matters, without any discrimination between race or creed.

I understand that there has been some rumour as to the possibility of racial discrimination being made in regard to pay on mobilisation, and that this rumour has occasioned some concern.

I need hardly point out that this concern has no reference to the sordid question of mere dollars and cents. It arises from a deep conviction that volunteers working for a common cause should receive equal treatment, and from a just resentment that any racial discrimination should exist in any matter whatsoever.

An official was immediately on his feet to assure Mr Lo that 'his fears on this subject are groundless. This Government fully agrees that all members of the Corps should receive equal treatment in every respect and at all times.'

The G.O.C., Major General A.E. Grassett added:

It want to take this opportunity of informing honourable members of my very high opinion of the efficiency of the Portuguese, the Colony-born and the Chinese units of the Volunteer Defence Corps. These units are expanding and developing and are going on very well indeed. I feel confident and I know honourable members will share my feelings that we can count on the fullest possible assistance from the Chinese and other communities and that they would fight and give their lives and services readily as required in the defence of the Colony, their hearth and home.

Grassett refuted rumours that Hong Kong was not to be defended in the event of an attack, saying, 'These rumours are entirely false. It is our intention to defend the Colony to the end.'

The outbreak of war in Europe had, however, had an immediate effect on defence planning and, as the manpower was simply not available, the decision was taken to abandon the plan of trying to hold an attacker along the Gin Drinker's Line. The plan now was to leave a small force of one regiment to hold the mainland for two days while demolitions were completed and then to stand fast on the island.

Of course, the coming of war in Europe, also had a major effect on the Volunteers in 1939. A year later, Lieutenant Colonel H.B. Rose wrote:

During the year much has happened and there have been many changes in both the size and constitution of the Corps. It has been a strenuous time for all of us and it has only been possible to achieve what we have with the good will and ready service of all ranks.

The main event affecting the Corps has been the recent introduction of compulsory service in the Colony. It was a striking testimony to the spirit of the Colony that by the time the Compulsory Service Ordinance came into operation, practically the whole of the British community of military age had already joined one or other of the defence groups in the Colony.

The keenness and enthusiasm of all ranks during the past year has been beyond all praise, and I am confident that whatever difficulties may lie ahead there is one constant factor that can be relied on, and that is the loyalty and high sense of duty of all ranks of the corps.

Men had also flocked to Volunteer units elsewhere. It was reported that there were now some 4,000 men in the Shanghai Volunteers. Enrolment in the Singapore Volunteer Defence Corps had also grown strongly.

Feelings of patriotism in Hong Kong ran high and many men wished to leave to join the British forces. But the 1939 Yearbook cautioned:

Recently we have met many members of the Corps who are chafing at the delay in getting away to have a 'crack' at the Hun, others have complained in the local papers that they have not been mobilised and so train intensely for the day they will be needed. This is the right spirit but there are many factors to be considered, the least of all being the problem of transportation. Then there is the disruption of business here which must be carried on. Imports — especially from England and her Dominions must be maintained so as to allow those at Home to meet the extra taxation and so enable us to carry this war to a successful conclusion.

In the last war, men of all ages, professions and trades were permitted to enlist at the outset with the result that the services of numbers of technicians and professional men whose services would have been invaluable were lost. Today, there is a place for every man in the organization of war and those who feel that they are not doing enough should be patient and await the time when they are called.

The G.S.O. I, of China Command, Colonel A.G. Neville, reinforced the point: 'One of the things which impressed me most when studying the defence of this Colony was the vital importance of the H.K.V.D.C. There is no single aspect of our defence here in which you do not play a part, whether it be infantry, machine gunners, gunners, engineers or any of the services.'

In 1940 it was reported, however, that the H.K.V.D.C., had supplied 10 officers to the Regular Army, mostly to the Royal Artillery. Considerable reorganization and strengthening had been carried out. In March 1939, there were two artillery units, the First Battery and Second (Improvised) Battery. However, in April, these had been formed into four coast defence batteries, the First, Second, Third and Fourth Batteries, the whole being known as the Corps Artillery. Extra recruitment had been required, but all four batteries were practically up to strength by the end of July. The gunners had worked very hard at the coast defence forts to prac- tice their skills. One problem had arisen with the manning of the defensive lights. Previously, these had been looked after by the Engineer Company but now they were the responsibility of the artillery. However, many of the men who had been on the lights in the Engineer Company transferred to the artillery and were split amongst the four batteries to spread their experience.

In April, the engineers were formed into the Field Company Engineers, absorbing the old construction section of the Railway Operating Detachment. The activities of the company were similar to those of a field company of the Royal Engineers, except that there was a strong tendency to specialization in demolition work. Many practices were carried out in relation to the demoli- tion of the Kowloon–Canton Railway. The company consisted of a headquarters and three sections, further subdivided into three parties.

A new Chinese unit had been formed — the Beach Light Com- pany. This unit was born as the Lyon Light Section of the Corps Engineers. The Lyon lights were new to Hong Kong and they were used to provide illumination for the machine gunners covering the beaches. The first recruits were enrolled on 5 May 1938, and numbers grew quickly, with the unit changing its name in 1939 to the Beach Light Company. During that year, much training was carried out and the unit served on numerous beach exercises where it worked in conjunction with the First Battalion, Middlesex Regiment, which also provided instructors.

The Volunteer signallers had witnessed a rather confusing reor- ganization. It seems that the Machine Gun Signals (formerly the Machine Gun Battalion Signals) absorbed and took over the men of the Corps Signals. The resulting unit was also known as the Corps Signals, though it was smaller than previously.

The Mobile Column consisted of the Armoured Car Platoon and the M.M.G. Platoon.

Number One Machine Gun Company included 'Number Four Troop Platoon', but the ponies had gone from active service now and riding activities were confined to leisure time. But there was still much interest in the annual Dowbiggin Trophy Race, run during the Fanling Hunt's point-to-point meeting. The dinner which followed:

Was its good old usual self; the menu was the same, the thirsts as unquenchable as ever, the speeches — yes, so far as we can recollect — exactly the same, even the jokes had an old familiar tang about them.

But goodbye to all that, in khaki shorts and webbing equipment we now do our best to wear out as many pairs of Volunteer issue boots as possible in a year ... We have for the whole of this summer delved into the intricacies of the finer points of machine gunning. What we don't know about quadrant angles and the combined sight rule is really scarcely worth knowing.

Number Two Machine Gun (Scottish) Company had moved away from its concentration on manning beach defence positions to a more general role. Number Three Machine Gun Company had also had a busy year of training in all aspects of military life. Number Four Machine Gun Company, with its Chinese volunteers, had rapidly been gaining experience and it distinguished itself in carrying off the corps' Efficiency Cup. Many members had slept under canvas for the first time while at camp and the training season was celebrated in appropriate fashion with a company dinner at the Kwangchow Restaurant at West Point.

Portugese volunteers made up Number Five Machine Gun Company, and the Anti-Aircraft Company. Tactical exercises were carried out at Shek O and exercises with troops at Pokfulam and a four day camp was held. Members of the A.A. company were given the opportunity to practice observation from the air by the Corps Air Arm. A handsome inscribed silver rose bowl had been donated by those who had arrived in Hong Kong as refugees from Shanghai in appreciation of the work done by the Portugese Volunteers.

The Air Arm had introduced night flying into its programme during 1938, and took part in an excercise with the Mobile Column in which it was judged that several machinegun combinations were destroyed.

The Army Service Corps Company reported a busy year. It had taken part in the running of two transport pools, one on the island and one on the mainland, during combined operations. The medical men reported that the name of their unit had been changed, from the Medical Section, to Field Ambulance: 'The past year has been one of great moment to the Medical Unit of the Corps; first of all we started off by having parades; that practically shattered the Corps morale, for when the medical unit begins to sharpen knives and to look longingly and knowingly at bones there must be a likelihood of something doing somewhere.' Combined operations had shown that vigorous recruiting was necessary if the unit was to meet the calls upon it and by April it was almost at full strength, with 60 members.

The Pay Section wrestled with the problems of administration and of calculating the various payments and bonuses due to each Volunteer.

Throughout 1940, the mood remained grim. The news from Europe was not encouraging and the Japanese continued their aggressive stance. London continued to hold the view that Hong Kong was an outpost to be held as long as possible but that it could not be relieved or expected to withstand a prolonged siege. Requests for reinforcements were turned down. The defence plan remained that the enemy should be delayed on the mainland long enough for demolitions to be completed, then all forces were to be withdrawn to the Island.

The Volunteers' numbers continued to grow and training became ever more intense, with the introduction of weekly full day's training. A temporary headquarters was in use while preparations were made to start on the construction of a new main building.

The Acting Governor and Commander in Chief, Lieutenant General Edward Felix Norton, told the Volunteers:

I find the Hong Kong Volunteer Defence Corps in an eminently satisfactory state of efficiency. I am struck with the steady and consistent way in which your training is carried out in spite of the fact that most of you are busy men in other departments.

I have wide experience of the Volunteer movement in India and have met there some very fine bodies of men, but those bodies owe their incentive more to the hope of individual emergency commissions than to the prospect of active employment as corporate units. This is where the Hong Kong Volunteer Defence Corps has a great pull. You train for a real emergency and whether this emergency is remote or not matters little compared with the fact that, should it materialize, the role which you will play will be a vital one; your importance in the framework of Empire defence is as great as that of almost any unit in the British army.

You have a fine role for which to train; you have splendid material; best of all, your spirit from all I hear is the real fighting spirit, and that is the thing which really matters. I won't be rash as to wish you active service experience, though I know full well that this is the one thing that the majority of you would hope for. Let me instead quote the old Latin tag — *Si vis pacem para bellum.*

The four batteries had been carrying out regular training. The young second, third and fourth batteries reported that they had grown considerably since their establishment. A new artillery unit had also been established — the Fifth, Anti-Aircraft Battery. This was composed of British and Chinese with a staff of regular gunners.

The engineers were continuing to practice their work of destruction and also trained in throwing up bridges and constructing wire obstacles.

The Fortress Signal Company had come into being in the summer of 1939, at the request of the military authorities, for the purpose of providing regular communications in certain sectors of Hong Kong where the civilian communications were inadequate. The Volunteer signallers had laid down the required lines and equipment and were responsible for maintenance. They could call for advice on the staff of the Hong Kong Telephone Company and used its training facilities.

The armoured cars of Number One and Number Two Platoons of the mobile column had been much in use, practicing patrolling the roads of the New Territories. Similarly, numbers Three, Four and Five, Motor Machinegun Platoons had been very active, although one member commented, 'Withdrawal has been developed to a high state of perfection to the exclusion of all other strategy, and if the fortunes of war ever make it necessary to advance towards the border or beyond it, the scheme would undoubtedly have to be called a withdrawal from Kowloon or we simply couldn't function.'

The efficiency of the Corps Signals had greatly improved, with the standard of signalling being brought up to that required in the regular army. Furthermore, there were now seven machine gun companies and they were were as busy as all the other Volunteer units with a constant round of training, drills and practice shoots.

Many men were in 'key posts' in civilian life and, thus, were not able to make a full commitment to the Volunteers. There was also a need to give elementary training to new recruits and so a training Cadre was established. Recruits passed on into other units after receiving their initial instruction, while men in key posts received basic training which would enable them to be of use should their definition as 'key men' change. The age of members of this unit ranged up to 54 years, and they were in the charge of Major H. Owen Hughes. The 'Hughesilliers' were to play a distinguished part in the coming battle.

Another new unit was the Stanley Platoon, formed mainly by men who were prison officers at the main prison for Hong Kong. Seventy-five per cent of its members were ex-servicemen and it was noted, 'Capturing prisoners is part of our daily routine.'

The Army Service Corps Company had been greatly expanded from its skeleton organization on the outbreak of war in Europe. The Transport Section unit was tasked, in conjunction with the regular R.A.S.C., with doing the transport and supply work for all the troops in the colony not actually done by the transport of a specific unit. The protection of convoys on the move from land and air attack was carefully practiced. A Supplies Section had been established largely involved with food supply. In its ranks were clerical staff, bakers, butchers, supplies issuers and other specialists.

The role of the Pay Section had also become increasingly important, and the training had been stepped up considerably with the Volunteers finding out all sorts of obscure but vital information:

We had learned the stoppages against a man admitted to hospital, and how he was allowed one penny per day for hair cutting whilst in hospital, not forgetting that he does not receive a penny for the day of admission, (presumably his hair does not grow on that day) though actually he does receive the penny, inasmuch as he draws full clothing allowance on the day of admission. We had learned that a man (unfortunate enough to be found out) sent to detention barracks, was charged sixpence per week for washing, noting in passing that if in the jug for only seven days there was no charge, but if in for more than seven days, up to thirteen days he was charged sixpence, whilst 14 days would cost him one shilling.

The medical section had been expanded into a full Field Ambulance and there was an intense programme of training.

The government had been involved in a storm of protest by its insistence, in 1940, that women and children be evacuated from Hong Kong to Australia. Many meetings had been held and the highly-emotive subject had been the cause of much bad feeling. In June, more than 3,474 women and children had been shipped out.

Many of the women who did remain served with the Nursing Detachment of the H.K.V.D.C.

At the beginning, many of us desired and even attempted to return home to be nearer to the sphere of War, so that we might feel that we were doing more for our wounded country. But our job lies here, and since the outbreak of hostilities we have steadfastly gone on with our training, so that we might be prepared to carry out our allotted task, when and where required.

Four members of the Nursing Detachment had travelled with the military medical staff accompanying the evacuees to Australia. 'Their task was no sinecure and added to this was the anxiety of knowing that there was an enemy raider in the vicinity, an uneasy thought with a shipfull of women and children.'

The fact that some women had been allowed to remain after the evacuation had led to criticism, but the Volunteer nurses responded, 'Sticks and stones may break my bones but names will never hurt me.' By November, London had agreed that those women who had not already left the colony would not be compelled to depart — but that those who had already gone could not return.

The Secretary of State asks that any woman with children should be strongly urged to leave the Colony, even though the compulsory powers are not at present being exercised. It must be emphasised that, should the situation further deteriorate no facilities to leave the Colony can be guaranteed and those not willing to avail themselves of the facilities now offered will in any case have to give preference to those temporarily exempted under the original scheme. The Secretary of State also expresses the hope that all those remaining in the Colony should feel it their duty to do all they can to assist in the Colony's defence scheme.

The Volunteer nurses were doing just that. Training was very intense, with some weeks requiring attendance on four or five days. The women steadily passed examinations which confirmed their skills.

As 1940 dragged on, so the preparations for war went on. In November, a large number of American citizens left Hong Kong, complying with their government's advice that American nationals should leave the Far East. Japanese also started to leave, although of their own accord: 'Mr K. Okazaki, Japanese Consul-General in Hong Kong, said that they were not doing so on the advice or instructions of the Japanese Government. "I have received no such instructions from my government".'

Air Raid tunnels were being constructed, though there was much corruption in the Air Raid Precautions Department. A decision not to build public shelters was reversed in June 1940, and a flurry of excavation started. Some tunnels were very large, such as that at Leighton Hill: 'It has been found that the tunnel there, which will be built to run right through the hill, may be able to take in anything from 8,000 to 10,000 people.' By December, it was reported that 55 pen-type air raid shelters had been constructed which could protect 165,000 people. The shelters would protect 300 people against splinters and blast from a 500 pound high-explosive bomb exploding at a distance of 50 feet. Reinforced roofs would protect against low flying planes attempting to machine gun the shelters. Ten thousand gas masks were available for sale at $2.50 each, though only a handful had been purchased.

In the waters around Hong Kong, Japanese navy vessels harassed local shipping and junks, seizing crews and cargoes. But appearances were maintained and on 3 December, a cocktail party was held at the Hong Kong Hotel for the new Japanese Consul, Mr. Seiko Yano, who was taking over from Mr. Katsuo Okazaki. Yano had come from a post at the Chinese Affairs Board in Tokyo and he had served as First Secretary at the Japanese embassy in Nanking. He had also served in Canton and New York. Present at the party were Major General Grassett, the newly-arrived Commodore A.C. Collinson, R.N., and many other leading names in civilian, military and naval life — including Volunteers such as Lieutenant K.M.A. Barnett and the Commanding Officer of the Hong Kong Naval Volunteer Reserve, Commander J. Petrie.

Japan strengthened its hold on South China throughout early 1941. Press reports of the time give many details of troop movements and occasional reports of Chinese successes, such as the assassination of collaborators, attacks on rail lines and guerrilla assaults. However, it seems that the effectiveness of the Chinese attacks was eagerly over-stated in a Hong Kong desperate for good news. By September, British residents of Japan were being advised to leave. Japanese warships were masters of the seas around Hong Kong. Nonetheless, the issue of the compulsory evacuation of women and children continued to raise tempers with many protests at the policy.

In January 1941, it was reported that manoeuvres were being

carried out by the Japanese and Cantonese puppet forces near Nam Tau, where landing operations and shore defence exercises were being practiced.

In early February, the Japanese actually landed in Bias Bay and struck inland towards Tam Shui from three directions. The landing was supported by aircraft flying from a carrier, a cruiser and three destroyers. The Chinese had withdrawn some time ago and so the landing was unopposed. About 3,000 troops were thought to have landed at the two ports of Hachung and Au Tau, the same ports where the Japanese landed in 1938, at the start of their attack on Canton.

The thrust of the attack was the important city on the East River of Waichow, or Huizhou. Another force, put at about 6,000 men, advanced from the west. The city was heavily bombed, but the Chinese put up a spirited resistance, with guerrillas attacking the advancing forces. Few civilians were left in the town, though foreign missionaries refused to be evacuated.

Meanwhile, the Japanese were busily constructing roads and airstrips in the area to the north of the border with Hong Kong. 'Two Japanese aircraft are alleged to have flown over British territory near the New Territories border yesterday morning. One of the machines appeared to be out of order. Both planes came from the North East of Shum Chun presently to land at the newly completed landing field between Nam Tau and Shum Chun', it was reported.

It was also noted that the Japanese had finished a series of strong motor roads and that motor traffic could now travel from Taiping, near the narrow entrance to the Pearl River known as the Bocca Tigris or the Bogue, to the border area.

Wide roads between land points on the shores of Bias Bay and interior towns are being constructed day and night, while other paths are being widened for mechanised transport. The Japanese have assembled some 1,000 military trucks at Namtau and are laying telephone wires from Bias Bay to the Pearl River delta. At Au Tau where the Japanese have just completed a landing field for aircraft they have assembled some 60 military motor vehicles and a large quantity of stores.

Daily raids by planes based in Swatow and from an aircraft carrier took place on towns and villages still in Chinese hands.

In March, 500 officers and men of the Volunteer Corps Artillery paraded together for the first time and were inspected by the

G.O.C., Grassett. In April, the Commander in Chief, Far East, Air Chief Marshall Sir Robert Brooke-Popham, visited Hong Kong and he detailed successes in the Mediterranean and Africa as encouraging. But, he cautioned, Hong Kong must be on its guard:

Hong Kong threatens no one, nor did Yugoslavia. Strength is the only guarantee against aggression and with the world as it is today, only the strong have friends.

The only way that we can ensure against attack in Hong Kong is to convince any would be attacker that such an operation would be too costly.

Our first duty, therefore, is to ensure that all defence preparations are so maintained as to be ready at any moment to work at the highest degree of efficiency. The defences are already strong, much has been done and all credit is due to those responsible. But we must never rest satisfied with the stage that the preparations have reached.

What everyone must remember is that defence is not the concern merely of a Navy, an Army and an Air Force. No place can be considered as being adequately protected unless every man and woman takes his or her full share in an active or passive defence.

During my two visits to Hong Kong I have been very pleased to find that the civil and military authorities are in full cooperation and that all sections of the community are working together admirably.

He went on to say that every possible contribution must be made to assist other parts of the empire and its allies and to reduce demands on shipping.

Remember that people in England are on strict rations of such things as sugar, tea, butter and jam; that women and children are being subjected to more than mere discomfort by air attacks. Every pound of imported goods you can spare means more space available to provide urgent necessities elsewhere.

Here is a question that everyone should be continually asking himself or herself 'Is there any more that I can do to help on the war effort?' No nobler cause than that for which the British Empire is now fighting has ever inspired mankind.

Meanwhile, the government gazetted a series of 'Protected Areas' on the island which were placed under the Defence Regulations. These included the Tai Tam area, the D'Aguilar Peninsula, part of Chung Hom Kok, Brick Hill at Aberdeen and Shouson Hill.

A semi-official census taken by the Air Raid Precautions

Department put the population at 1,420,629 Chinese, including 154 000 people living on boats (see Table 11.1).

Table 11.1 Breakdown of non-Chinese Population
(figures from Air Raid Precautions Dept. — 1941)

British*	7,982
Indian	7,379
Portuguese	2,922
'European'	2,905
American	396
Miscellaneous	2,094

* including the naval and military establishments

The Volunteers were heavily involved in the many exercises which took place throughout 1941. A camp held in early March was washed out, however, by torrential rain. Orders were given to strike camp and the soaked Volunteers returned to town to carry out the rest of their training during daily stints at headquarters for the period of the camp.

In early September there was a major exercise which involved a night's total blackout. Restrictions were strictly enforced with all lighting, including advertising, forbidden. Street lights were extinguished. The scenario saw troops practicing moving across the harbour by night under blackout. Other troops took up defensive positions on the island. It was reported that:

Troops in full kit and some sections of the Volunteers took part in the exercises ... It is understood that so far the manoeuvres have proved very successful and have provided good training for the men.

The exercises gave the colony a somewhat realistic atmosphere — particularly motorists, some of whom encountered barriers on the roads in various parts of the colony, where they were stopped by men in full war paint, and then told to proceed. This was a little startling on lonely roads, and more so to those who suddenly came across a lone soldier camouflaged among the trees, or detected suddenly at the road side at the business end of a machine gun.

Bathers on several beaches were interested in sea planes and land planes flying overhead, sometimes thrillingly low. Several planes were seen to drop 'parachutists' and the rattle of machinegun fire told its own story. These exercises, it is understood, were designed to give the local garrison practice in repelling troops of the type encountered in Greece and Crete, where large numbers of airborne troops were landed from enemy planes and gliders. At night the searchlights probed the sky and fastened their beams on solitary 'raiders' looking like 'Tootsie' toys.

Press reports generally tried to offer encouragement, with one despatch, dated 3 September, from Swatow claiming that the Japanese commanders had held a conference in Amoy to discuss the possibility of withdrawing garrisons from occupied areas of South China. 'There is fear among the Japanese about the defence efficiency of their garrisons in view of the intensified activities of Chinese guerrillas and regular troops.'

Sunday 7 September was declared a day of intercession throughout the Empire at the request of the King and services were held at many of the colony's churches.

A bill was published in the *Government Gazette* stating that if war broke out, the Police Force, the Hong Kong Police Reserve, the Police Force regulated under the Naval Establishments Police Ordinance, and special constables appointed under the Peace Preservation Ordinance, or any of them, would be liable to perform combatant duties as militia.

Meanwhile, in Singapore, Brooke-Popham, and the Commander in Chief, China Station, Vice Admiral Sir Geoffrey Layton, were making encouraging noises, saying they were not afraid of any threat. On 7 January 1941, however, Churchill had written in response to a request for reinforcements for Hong Kong:

This is all wrong. If Japan goes to war with us there is not the slightest chance of holding Hong Kong or relieving it. It is most unwise to increase the loss we shall suffer there. Instead of increasing the garrison it ought to be reduced to a symbolical scale. Any trouble arising there must be dealt with at the Peace Conference after the war. We must avoid frittering away our resources on untenable positions. Japan will think long before declaring war on the British Empire, and whether there are two or six battalions at Hong Kong will make no difference to her choice. I wish we had fewer troops there, but to move any would be noticeable and dangerous.

However, Brooke-Popham had argued strongly as to the importance of Hong Kong in relation to British interests in Asia, saying that it should be properly defended and that two additional battalions of infantry were needed. This opinion was shared by Grassett, the G.O.C., and when he returned to London he argued for the reinforcement. In the face of such views, the Chief of Staff recommended the request and the decision was made, in September, to send two battalions of Canadian infantry to Hong Kong to reinforce the four battalions already there.

War was coming.

12

A Worthwhile Gamble

I submit that although I and my forces may have been a hostage to
fortune, we were a detachment that deflected from more important objectives, such as the Philippines, Singapore, or perhaps even Australia, an
enemy force that consisted of two first line divisions, one reserve division,
corps artillery, about 80 aircraft and a considerable naval blockade force.
Strategically we gambled and lost, but it was a worthwhile gamble.

Major General C.M. Maltby, M.C., G.O.C., British Troops in China.

Military writers will argue for many a day why the defence of Hong Kong
collapsed so abjectly. Those of the Anglo-American school will, of course,
explain that 'the garrison was hopelessly outnumbered,' and will prepare
for the school books of their children glowing accounts of the excessive
gallantry of the defenders. Of the fighting men in the front lines, or some
of them, left entirely without air support and with rapidly diminishing
artillery aid, this may be true. In general, however, the truth is that the
Imperial Forces of Japan were superior in every department. Their
strategy was superb, and their tactics of equal quality.

Hong Kong News, 1942.

DURING the early afternoon of on Christmas Day 1941, the
G.O.C., Maltby, asked Colonel Stewart, Officer Commanding the
First Battalion, Middlesex Regiment, how long he thought he
could hold his positions. 'One hour' came the answer. The British
headquarters had lost contact with the remaining forces holding
out at Stanley and the overall situation was extremely grim.
Maltby talked to naval and military officers. 'At 15.15, I advised
His Excellency the Governor, that no further useful military resis-
tance was possible and I therefore ordered all Commanding
Officers to break off the fighting and to capitulate to the nearest
Japanese Commander, as and when the enemy advanced and the
opportunity offered.'

That evening the Governor, Sir Mark Young, accompanied by Maltby travelled to the Peninsula Hotel where the Japanese commanders had established themselves. Was the surrender unconditional, they asked. 'I replied that I had made no conditions,' said Young.

* * *

The Japanese attack was expected by the military commanders in Hong Kong. Given the history of incidents, over-flying, naval harassment and general belligerence in the border area, this could have hardly been different. 'That war was inevitable seemed clear to me,' said Maltby. However, civilian opinion was more optimistic. People doubted generally that Japan would declare war against the allied powers, the intelligence system was weak and there was an impression that Japan was only bluffing. But the attack on Hong Kong on 8 December 1941, went in at the same time as the attack on Pearl Harbour, with the date differing only due to the international date line.

Shortly before the assault, the defence plan had changed again with the decision to send two battalions of Canadians to reinforce the garrison. The Royal Rifles of Canada and the Winnipeg Grenadiers arrived on 16 November, just 23 days before the Japanese attack. The existing British strength in Hong Kong had been four battalions of infantry: the First Battalion, Middlesex Regiment, the Second Battalion, Royal Scots, the 5/7th Battalion, Rajput Regiment, and the 2/14th Battalion, Punjab Regiment.

In addition there were headquarters elements of the Royal Artillery, together with the 8th Coast Regiment, the 12th Coast Regiment and the 5th Anti-Aircraft Regiment, the Hong Kong and Singapore Royal Artillery, the 965th Defence Battery. In support were the elements of the Royal Ordnance Corps, the Royal Army Service Corps, the Royal Army Veterinary Corps, the Royal Army Dental Corps, the Royal Army Pay Corps, the Hong Kong Mule Corps, Indian Medical Services and, of course, the Hong Kong Volunteer Defence Corps.

The Royal Air Force consisted of two elderly Walrus Amphibian planes and three Vildebeeste Torpedo Bombers. The

Royal Navy consisted of the equally elderly destroyer, HMS *Thracian*, four gunboats, eight motor torpedo boats and a some patrol boats. Two other destroyers, the *Scout* and *Thanet* were ordered to sail for Singapore as the Japanese attacked.

With the arrival of the Canadians, the defence plan reverted to the concept which had originally been established in 1937. This called for the main resistance rather than just a delaying action to be made on the mainland.

Formerly, the Punjabis were to have fought the delaying action, falling back to the Devil's Peak Peninsula in the west where another defensive line, the Ma Lau Tong Line, had been erected. The Field Company Engineers, of the H.K.V.D.C., were to operate on the mainland, being responsible for road and railway demolitions. The defenders of the 'island fortress' would have been the Rajputs, the Middlesex Regiment, the main Volunteer force and the artillery and supporting units.

Now, the stand was to be taken along the line of the only partially completed Gin Drinker's Line. The Royal Scots were to hold the left, or west, sector, including the Shing Mun Redoubt, the Punjabis the centre sector, and the Rajputs the right. This might have sounded fine in theory, but the line covered some of the most difficult country in the territory, and each unit had an extensive front which it found difficult to cover adequately, especially at night. Provision of reserves was also problematic. However, intensive work started to strengthen the defences and to reconnoitre their approaches.

The two Canadian battalions were stationed on the Island, together with the Middlesex Regiment who were specialists in beach defence. The new plan did not require the H.K.V.D.C. Mobile Machine Gun Company to cover the Volunteer engineers, who would, instead, be protected by regular troops, so its members were split between Number One and Two Companies.

Also in the forward area were the Volunteer armoured cars. At Kai Tak airfield, providing local defence and standing by as a reserve for the Gin Drinkers Line, was Number One Company. One platoon of that company had recently been equipped with bren carriers and these had the job of patrolling the coastal Castle Peak Road.

The remainder of the H.K.V.D.C. were stationed on the island. At the start of the battle, therefore, the Volunteers were stationed as shown in Table 12.1.

Table 12.1 Volunteer Emplacements (1941)

First Battery	Cape D'Aguilar
Second Battery	Bluff Battery, Stanley
Third Battery	Aberdeen (Ap Lei Chau)
Fourth Battery	Pak Sha Wan Battery, Lyemun
Fifth AA Battery	Sai Wan Hill, Lyemun
Field Company Engineers	New Territories, responsible for demolitions of bridges, tunnels, road and rail links, installations likely to be useful to the enemy. Later headquartered at Tai Hang, Hong Kong Island
Corps Signals	Peak Mansions
Armoured Car Platoon	Mainland patrols. After mainland withdrawal headquartered at West Brigade HQ
Number One (Rifle) Company	Kai Tak Airfield. In reserve for Gin Drinkers Line. One platoon with bren carriers patrolling Castle Peak Road. After withdrawal, Tai Tam Valley
Number Two (Machine Gun) Company	Pottinger Gap and Big Wave Bay
Number Three (Machine Gun) Company	Two platoons on Stonecutters Island, initially. Then Jardine's Lookout
Number Four (Rifle) Company	High West, Victoria Gap and Mount Kellett
Number Five (Machine Gun) Company	Mount Davis
Number Six (AA) Company	North shore of Island
Number Seven (Rifle) Company	Magazine Gap, Wanchai Gap, Middle Gap
Army Service Corps Company	Headquarters at Deepwater Bay
Hughes Group	North Point Power Station
Supply and Transport Section	Initially at HKVDC headquarters, Garden Road, later moved to Peak Mansions
Field Ambulance	Distributed around the Island
Pay Detachment	Attached to RAPC
Nursing Detachment	Attached to Army Hospitals

Volunteers of Number Three Company seen working on a belt of machine gun ammunition in 1939.

A Volunteer motorcyclist with an armoured car in the background.

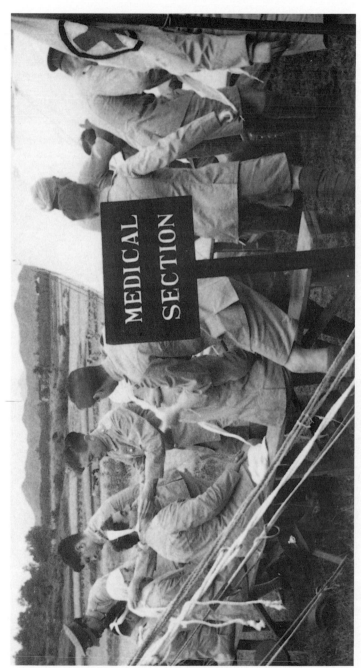

The Medical Section practising its skills at Fanling in 1939.

Volunteers inspected wire obstacles in 1940, as preparations for war continued.

In 1940, the Field Company Engineers stepped up their training. Their skill at demolitions was demonstrated by their success in delaying the Japanese advance. Here they are seen stuffing boreholes with gelignite.

Members of the First Battery, H.K.V.D.C. pictured in 1940 at Cape D'Aguilar, where the battery manned two converted four-inch naval guns, said to have seen service at the Battle of Jutland in the First World War.

Number Three Armoured Car known, not so affectionately, as 'Leaping Lena'.
Knocked out at Happy Valley in 1941.

With kilts swinging, the Scots of Number Two Company march past at the King's
Birthday Parade, on 8 June 1939.

Colonel H.B. Rose, Commandant of the Hong Kong Volunteer Defence Corps from 1938 onwards. On the death of Brigadier Lawson in the 1941 battle, Colonel Rose took command of West Brigade.

Mr. Kenneth Barnett commanded the Fourth Battery at Pak Sha Wan in the 1941 battle. He is pictured here at the battery during a visit made in 1987. The Kowloon hills, from which the Japanese guns shelled the battery, can be seen in the background. The harbour is obscured by the parapet.

Major H.R. Forsyth is seen leading Number Two Company to church on Sunday 31 December 1941. By the end of the month he, and many of his men, were dead. The parade was in commemoration of St. Andrew's Day, of which Major Forsyth was Vice-Chieftain.

Wong Nei Chong Gap, scene of much bloody fighting in 1941. Jardine's Lookout can be seen at the background.

The vital Wong Nei Chong Gap, seen from the Hong Kong waterfront.

Looking down over Wong Nei Chong Gap, with Hong Kong in the mid-ground and Kowloon beyond. Jardine's Lookout is to the right and Mount Nicholson to the left.

Looking along the ridge of hills of Hong Kong Island from Wong Nei Chong Gap to Mount Nicholson, with Middle Gap and Wanchai Gap beyond, and then Victoria Peak.

Wong Nei Chong Gap. The Hong Kong Cricket Club, tennis courts and residential buildings were erected after the war. The key road can be seen running to their right. Brigadier Wallis was killed in this area. The catchment path is to the left, while the Volunteer pill boxes were to the left of the three blocks.

St. Stephen's College, Stanley, site of the massacre by Japanese troops.

The Tai Tam area, south of the main ridge of hills on Hong Kong Island. Wong Nei Chong Gap is roughly where the three tower blocks can be seen.

Looking towards the south west of Hong Kong Island. The road from Tai Tam
Gap can be seen running down to the Tai Tam Tuk Reservoir on the right. Red
Hill is to the left while Notting Hill rises on the right. Beyond
is Stanley Peninsula.

The Stanley Peninsula, scene of much Volunteer action in 1941. The playing field
of St. Stephen's College can be seen in the middle ground, with Stanley Prison
beyond it on the opposite coast. Stanley Fort is at rear.

The narrow neck of the Stanley Peninsula, where the Volunteers fought bloody hand-to-hand engagements with the invading Japanese.

The Lei Yue Mun (Lyemun) Channel, seen from Devil's Peak on the mainland, with Mount Parker and Quarry Gap to its right, on Hong Kong Island. Lyemun Barracks and Pak Sha Wan Battery are just across the narrow stretch of water. Aldrich Bay, to their right, is filled with vessels.

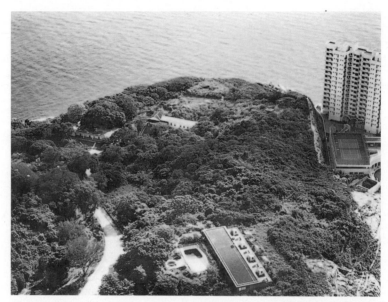

The Pak Sha Wan Battery is now almost overgrown by decades of vegetation, and the bay to its east has been completely reclaimed.

Sai Wan Hill, occupied in 1941 by Fifth Battery, with its anti-aircraft guns. Subsequently the site of slaughter by the Japanese.

Volunteers from Hong Kong are seen in 1946 on parade in London. They were inspected by King George VI and the royal family.

Continuing a long tradition, present day members of the Royal Hong Kong Regiment (The Volunteers) are seen on parade.

'Second To None In the Orient' — the proud boast on the cap badge of the Royal Hong Kong Regiment.

In addition there were the men of the Stanley Platoon, Fortress Signals, Reconnaissance Unit, and the Railway Operating Detachment Cadre.

There appears to be some confusion as to the total strength of the Volunteers at the outbreak of war. 'A Record of the Actions of the Hong Kong Volunteer Defence Corps in the Battle For Hong Kong, December, 1941', written by an officer who took part, and first published in 1953, gives some figures (see Table 12.2).

Table 12.2 Breakdown of Membership in the H.K.V.D.C. (1941)

	Officers	Other Banks
Corps HQ and S&T	11	43
Corps Artillery HQ	3	2
First Battery	3	65
Second Battery	3	83
Third Battery	3	75
Fourth Battery	3	94
Fifth AA Battery	2	65
Field Company Engineers	12	111
Corps Signals	2	38
Armoured Car Platoon	1	28
Number One Company	4	100
Number Two Company	4	94
Number Three Company	4	110
Number Four Company	4	74
Number Five Company	5	94
Number Six Company	5	91
Number Seven Company	3	38
ASC Unit	7	65
Stanley Platoon	1	28
Pay Detachment	3	14
Fortress Signals	2	15
Hughes Group	4	68
Field Ambulance	5	164

Adding up the figures in Table 12.2 gives totals of 94 officers and 1,566 other ranks.

However, figures given by Maltby in his despatch of November, 1945, give strengths of 89 officers and 1,296 other ranks. To further complicate matters, there are frequent references in Volunteer literature to there having been a mobilized strength of about 2,200 all ranks. The total destruction of all contemporary records during the Japanese occupation makes settling this point difficult.

News of the build up of Japanese forces was filtering through to Hong Kong in early December of 1941, with intelligence agents reporting considerable activity between Canton and the narrow mouth of the Pearl River. Although diplomatic telegrams remained calm, and military and naval intercepts showed normal activity, Maltby decided to recall those Volunteers who were at a training camp in the New Territories on 5 December.

Training had been intense throughout 1941, with the Volunteers training with their units at camps held on various dates:

Each camp lasts seven days and Officers and Volunteers are required to attend for a full period during which their units are under training unless a special exemption has been obtained by themselves or their employers. In special cases where exemption from a portion of the full period is sought employers should always request leave for their employees, in writing, as early as possible, from the Commandant, Hongkong Volunteer Defence Corps. Such applications should give full particulars as to the reasons for leave and the exact times during which it is required.

Leave will only be granted for the actual period during which it is required, and, except where the applicant is required for night shift work at his place of business, he will be ordered to attend camp from after office hours in the evening till the commencement of office hours the following morning ...

The very active cooperation of employers is requested so that each Officer and Volunteer may do his full time in camp, even if it means other employees doing extra work for that period. It is hoped that this co-operation will be more active than it has been in certain cases in the past. Telephones are installed in each camp for the use of Officers and Volunteers and it is preferable that a man be granted two or three hours leave from Camp to attend to any special business rather than he be exempted for the whole day on the off chance of his being required.

By the evening of 7 December, all troops were in their battle positions.

The Volunteers were at the very start of the battle on 8 December, for it was the H.K.V.D.C. Engineers who blew the bridge at the Shum Chun River and who started on their forward demolitions just before 5 a.m. A few minutes earlier, a broadcast message from Tokyo had been intercepted warning its nationals that war between Great Britain and Japan was imminent.

At 6.45 a.m., as the Volunteer engineers continued their work at the frontier, the garrison was formally told that war had started. For civilians, however, the first indication came at 8 a.m. when 36 Japanese fighters and 12 bombers were seen swooping down over Kai Tak airport and Sham Shui Po Barracks. Within a few minutes, all the R.A.F. machines were damaged or destroyed and eight civil aircraft were burnt out.

The border demolitions had proved to be no more than a minor irritant, and hundreds of Japanese troops had already crossed the border. Demolitions had been completed by 8.30 a.m., but the Volunteers reported that, as they blew the British bridge, they could see Japanese sappers building another bridge within rifle range.

The Japanese advanced on two fronts, each in battalion strength. One went westwards, towards the Yuen Long–Tuen Mun area, across Laffan's Plain, while the other thrust southwards towards Tai Po. Whenever the attackers encountered defending troops they quickly turned to the flanks.

After blowing obstructions at the border, the engineers fell back to a position about a mile north of Tai Po, near the present Hong Lok Yuen Estate, where the road passes through a narrow valley surrounded by hills on both sides. The flat countryside at the entrance and exit to the small pass was a sea of paddy fields. In danger from Japanese troops advancing alongside them to the west, the Volunteer engineers exploded several demolitions, including three bridges, at about noon. They then withdrew, with the Punjabi troops, through Tai Po Market, blowing up petrol stores as they went, to a position south of the town on what was then a causeway but is now buried beneath a multi-lane highway. There a defensive position was established with troops placed on the landward flank to the west. At about 6.30 p.m., a platoon of Japanese walked into a Punjabi position and was wiped out. The Volunteer armoured cars and bren carriers were also in action on the road at about 7.30 p.m. — killing a Japanese group which attempted to advance down the highway.

The Japanese then moved around the flanks of the position and the defenders withdrew along the causeway, but not before the Volunteer engineers had exploded three further demolitions. The next position was taken up at Cheung Shui Tan — where the Chinese University now stands. The enemy continued to push forward through the hills and there was a constant danger that the Punjabis and Volunteers would be outflanked. The Japanese had excellent knowledge of the terrain, accurate maps and experienced guides.

At 8.30 p.m., the Volunteer engineers blew up the Kowloon–Canton Railway tunnel which runs through a small hill to the north of Cheung Shiu Tan. This had the unfortunate effect of severing communications between some of the defenders.

The Japanese continued to advance, and at 10 p.m. a bridge on the road from Tai Po to Sha Tin was blown. A second bridge was demolished half an hour later. The long hours that the Volunteer engineers had spent in training were being used to good effect. There were two fuses on the second bridge, one a time fuse and the other electrical. The first was lit, but the Japanese managed to rush the bridge and cut the fuse. They had little time to celebrate their daring, however, for the Volunteers then completed the circuit to the electrical fuse and the bridge and Japanese were destroyed.

At 1 a.m. on 9 December, the defenders fell back to positions at the Fo Tan valley. The road then ran along the west side of Tide Cove. Today the entire area has been changed almost beyond recognition by the construction of the huge Sha Tin New Town. Tide Cove was a wide sea inlet which came about as far inland as the point at which the Lion Rock Tunnel Road now crosses the Sha Tin River channel. No trace of the cove now remains.

At 2 a.m., the Volunteer engineers withdrew to Kowloon Railway Station, leaving two demolition parties behind at Kowloon Reservoir. All the planned demolitions on the Tai Po Road had been completed.

At dawn, the Punjabis were at a position referred to as 'Monastery Ridge', which is the ridge where the Tao Fung Shan monastery now stands. They had almost been rolled up to the Gin Drinkers Line and the Shing Mun Redoubt was about three thousand metres away to the southwest. The Volunteer armoured cars continued to provide backup and to patrol the road leading to Tsuen Wan. Meanwhile, along the Castle Peak Road, leading from

Tsuen Wan to Tuen Mun, demolitions were also completed by the Royal Engineers, although a Japanese saboteur managed to disarm one of them. He was killed when he tried the same thing again at the next demolition. At 6 p.m. the last of the defenders in the Sha Tin area fell back to the Gin Drinker's Line.

In the opening phase of the battle, the Volunteers had performed well, successfully completing all their assigned tasks and delaying the enemy, with the armoured cars and bren carriers inflicting considerable casualties.

Throughout 9 December, the Japanese carried out aggressive patrolling and probing. The Royal Scots had several engagements and reported that the enemy patrols were often led by local guides, though it is not clear whether these were willing men or villagers pressed into service.

Part of the Gin Drinker's's Line extended from the sea at Tsuen Wan to the Shing Mun Redoubt. This was manned by the Royal Scots, many of whom were in poor health due to fever and who were very thinly stretched across a a straight line on the map which ran for about 3,000 metres. In particular, the redoubt was significantly undermanned. There was concern about the lack of strength where the Royal Scots area joined with that of the Punjabis, so a reserve company of the 5/7th Rajputs was moved to cover this area.

At 8 p.m. the last of the civilian planes which had survived the initial attack left Kai Tak for areas in China not occupied by the Japanese. On board one of them was Volunteer officer, Lieutenant Colonel H. Owen Hughes, who was to act as liaison officer with the Seventh Chinese Military Zone.

Just after 11 p.m., the Japanese were heard moving in the Shing Mun Valley below the reservoir and about an hour later the result was clear — the redoubt had fallen. 'This was calamitous,' wrote Maltby, 'for the Shing Mun Redoubt was the key to the whole of the left position.' Artillery was called in to shell the redoubt and confused fighting around the redoubt took place. Plans for a full counter-attack came to nothing and at 3.30 p.m. on 10 December, the order was given for the Royal Scots who had been pushed out of the redoubt to fall back on the Golden Hill line, which ran along a high ridge to the south of the redoubt. The remaining companies of the Royal Scots at northern Tsuen Wan, west of the redoubt, were now exposed. A reserve company of the Winnipeg Grenadiers was brought across the harbour and stationed at the junction of the roads leading west to Castle Peak and northeast to Sha Tin and Tai Po.

At about 9.30 a.m. on 10 December, the Japanese had pushed forward from the redoubt but were engaged by the Rajputs and artillery and were driven back with heavy losses. A counter-attack was ruled out on the basis that it would have left the Punjabis exposed and they were already facing Japanese probing and infiltration. By the middle of the day, the Royal Scots and Winnipeg Grenadiers in the west were under heavy attack as the Japanese attempted to separate the British centre and left sectors.

Demolition of a road bridge at Au Tau, just to the east of Yuen Long, had caused considerable problems for the Japanese advancing from that direction and no transport was able to cross. A battery of 5.9 inch howitzers was hauled onto the small airfield at Kam Tin and this shelled Stonecutters Island and the artillery fort at Mount Davis, on Hong Kong Island, where the three big 9.2 inch guns were harassing Japanese attempts to move along the Castle Peak Road, and firing at targets on the mainland. Shelling from HMS *Cicala* also disrupted Japanese attempts to move along the road and repair obstructions.

A counter-attack having been ruled out, it was decided that the Royal Scots, B and C Companies, in the Tsuen Wan area should be withdrawn from their exposed position and this was done during the night of 10–11 December.

Throughout the night, however, the Japanese were probing the Golden Hill position. Their attack went in at dawn and by 7 a.m. the position had fallen, despite a brave stand by the Royal Scots, who suffered heavy casualties, including two company commanders. A Royal Scots company stationed nearby counter-attacked and succeeded in regaining the hill for a short time, during which survivors were able to withdraw. The Royal Scots eventually had to fall back. The Volunteer armoured cars and bren carriers were called forward to cover the retreat along the Castle Peak Road towards Lai Chi Kok.

Staff officer, Colonel L.A. Newnham, reported: 'At about 10.00 hours on 11 Dec I visited Kowloon Infantry Brigade Headquarters in Waterloo Road. Here a very bleak position was painted to me i.e. that the Japs had broken through on the Castle Peak Road and would arrive in Kowloon at any minute.'

In a report written after the battle, he said that he telephoned to Kai Tak for the Volunteers' bren carriers which were the only reserves immediately available and left orders for the carriers and all men available to assemble at the junction of Prince Edward and Waterloo Roads. After about 20 minutes three carriers arrived. At about 10.45 a.m., the carriers and a small armoured car set off towards the fighting. Royal Scots were encountered and a Volunteer armoured car was then sent forward on reconnaissance.

After positioning the Royal Scots in the area, Newnham said he also sent one carrier forward with a platoon with orders to remove its guns and mount them on a spur. The second carrier was positioned to cover the approach from Lai Chi Kok. The third was ordered into reserve with the task of carrying out patrols in side streets.

The armoured car had returned with its commander, reporting that it had moved forward to Lai Chi Kok prison where there was a roadblock manned by about eight men of the Royal Scots. 'I told him that was not much of a recce, that he must go back, get the men to remove the road block so as to allow the Armoured Car to pass through and to go towards Castle Peak for at least one mile, definitely to draw the enemy's fire and to get information,' Newnham wrote.

The fall of the redoubt and of Golden Hill had placed the mainland defenders in a very serious position. The platoon from Number One Company, H.K.V.D.C., the bren carriers and two armoured cars were, with the remaining Royal Scots and the company of Winnipeg Grenadiers, stretched out along a line running back almost to Sham Shui Po — the area northwest of Boundary Street.

At noon, the decision was made to evacuate the mainland during the coming night. Once the order came through, further demolitions were started. The Volunteer engineers blew up the power station of the China Light and Power company and destroyed a cement works. Meanwhile, personnel at the docks wrecked the facilities there and other potentially valuable installations were also demolished. The engineers also had orders to save as many vehicles as they could and they moved these to the vehicle ferry pier.

Number One Company was heavily committed, with the platoon in action at Lai Chi Kok and its bren carrier platoon also in action. The remainder of the company was tasked with guarding against a surprise attack on Kai Tak, covering the withdrawal of troops being evacuated, dealing with looters, saboteurs and rioters, and, finally, being responsible for demolitions at the airport.

Throughout the long day there was constant shelling and bombing by enemy artillery. The West Fort on Stonecutters' Island, where the men of Number Three Company, H.K.V.D.C., were stationed with a battery of the Royal Artillery and some Royal Engineers, took 40 direct hits before noon. An attempt by the Japanese to land on Lamma Island was broken up by batteries at Aberdeen and at lower Mount Davis. A further attempt to land on Ap Lei Chau, where the Volunteers' Third Battery was stationed, was beaten off by machine gun fire. A fleet of about a hundred junks, seen off Lamma Island, was broken up by artillery fire.

The situation in Kowloon was chaotic, with fifth columnists active and looting breaking out. Civilian launch crews, lorry and car drivers, started to disappear, causing further strain on overstretched services.

There were two elements to the withdrawal from the mainland. The 5/7th Rajputs and the 2/14th Punjabis were ordered to fall back along the rugged line of hills above Kowloon towards the Devil's Peak peninsula in the east, where the former were to hold the defensive position known as the Mau Lau Tong Line while the latter withdrew to positions on the north-west of the island. This exercise was a remarkable operation, carried out at night, in very rough country and with the Punjabis fighting a full rear-guard action with the enemy all the way. The two battalions arrived at their destination intact and with their mules and stores.

The other withdrawal, involving the Volunteers, was from the Kowloon peninsula, where the vehicular ferry and certain other ferries were reserved for military use. Civilians flocked to the other ferries as the chaos mounted. The Volunteer bren carriers and armoured cars covered the withdrawal, only leaving shortly before midnight after the other elements had been evacuated. One of the armoured cars was knocked out during the fighting.

At Kai Tak, the remaining part of Number One Company completed its demolitions at the airport and then withdrew via Kowloon City ferry pier, being carried by an R.A.F. launch to the island.

The same night the Volunteers from Number Three Company, on Stonecutters' Island, were withdrawn along with the other troops there. Despite the terrible shelling and bombing, only four Volunteers had been wounded and none killed. The forts on

Stonecutters's Island, the remains of which can be seen today, are a rabbit warren of tunnels and galleries built in the 19th century. Before leaving, the Volunteers broke open a store and helped themselves to Thompson machine guns. With their heavy .45 calibre these weapons were to prove highly-effective in the coming battle at Wong Nei Chong Gap. Demolitions were completed on the island and the Volunteers left with all their stores and kit. However, soon after disembarking at the naval yard on the island, the boat which had ferried them across was sunk, taking the stores and kit to the bottom.

Meanwhile, over on the mainland, an element of the Punjabis, part of the headquarters company which was acting as the rearguard, became separated from the main body and found itself in Kowloon City where it became involved with fighting fifth columnists and advancing Japanese patrols. A private of the Volunteers' Number One Company linked up with them and led them through the chaotic streets of Kowloon to the Star Ferry Wharf which they held, allowing civilian evacuation, before withdrawing to the island themselves. During the morning, the last of the main body of the Punjabis passed through the Rajputs who had established themselves on the Mau Lau Tong Line, with a troop of 3.7 howitzers in support.

Throughout 12 December, the Japanese kept up the pressure on the Mau Lau Tong Line, with constant bombing and shelling. Heavy casualties were inflicted when a battalion-strong force attempted to break through the left of the line, but that and other attacks were beaten off. However, it became apparent that the position could not hold indefinitely and the order to evacuate was given, thus concentrating all troops on the island. The evacuation from the Mau Lau Tong line was another extremely difficult operation, carried out at night by small civilian craft, Royal Navy MTBs and HMS *Thracian*. At about 8.30 a.m. the last of men were seen leaving the mainland.

Maltby decided that, as the Royal Scots were in need of rest and re-equipment, they should be withdrawn into reserve from their current positions in the north-east sector of the island and replaced by the Rajputs.

At 9 a.m. on 13 December, a launch flying a white flag crossed the harbour with a demand from the Japanese for surrender. This was rejected out of hand and it was only a matter of time before the all-out assault on the island began.

Preparations were stepped up, with the Volunteer engineers playing a key part. All the pre-war exhortations about the need for training and experience were being proved accurate. A Hong Kong Engineering Corps was formed and about 200 workers, under the direction of Volunteers, built depots at Happy Valley, Kennedy Town, Pokfulam, Repulse Bay and Stanley. Much other work was done quickly, including the establishment of communications right along the waterfront from Shau Ki Wan to Kennedy Town. Facilities were destroyed and gun bases laid in the naval yard.

During the day a Japanese plane was hit and it crashed into the sea west of Lamma. One of the big guns at Mount Davis was knocked out by a direct hit. By the evening Belcher's Fort was in flames and major fires had also broken out in Kennedy Town and West Point.

A reconnaissance in force was made by the Japanese on the night of 12–13 December, but this was beaten off. On 13 December, the Fourth Battery, H.K.V.D.C., at Pak Sha Wan, Lyemun, at the east of the island, came in for particularly heavy bombardment.

Now that all troops were on the island, a new organization was drawn up. The island was divided into two brigade groups. East Brigade was commanded by Brigadier Wallis, who had commanded the mainland forces, and was made up of the Rajputs and the Royal Rifles of Canada. West Brigade was under the command of the Canadian Brigadier J.K. Lawson, and consisted of the Punjabis, the Royal Scots and the Winnipeg Grenadiers. There were, of course, also Volunteer, Middlesex Regiment, Royal Artillery, and other units within each brigade area.

East Brigade headquarters was established at the area where the road leading to Shek O runs off from the road to Stanley. The Rajputs were positioned along the eastern coastline from Causeway Bay to Sai Wan. The Royal Rifles of Canada were mainly spread around the coast from Sai Wan to Stanley. The Winnipeg Grenadiers covered the Repulse Bay–Deepwater Bay area, later being attached to West Brigade after the fighting began.

West Brigade headquarters was established at Wong Nei Chong Gap, about where a modern public tennis facility now stands. The Punjabis held the shoreline from the Royal Naval Yard to Telegraph Bay, in Pokfulam. The Middlesex Regiment covered the area from there to Stanley and was also responsible for the

coastline between the naval yard and Causeway Bay. The Royal
Scots were positioned in the area around Happy Valley.

Despite the massive changes which have been wrought by
Hong Kong's development in the years since the end of the last
war, many of the Volunteer, and other positions, during the battle
can still be seen.

At the opening phase, therefore, First Battery, commanded by
Captain G.F. Rees, was at Cape D'Aguilar. There there were two
9.2 inch guns, mounted at the top of the sheer cliffs, with Volunteers manning two converted four-inch naval guns, said to have
seen service at the battle of Jutland in the First World War. The
emplacements are well preserved inside the limits of the large
Cable and Wireless Ltd signal station which is now there, but there
is no public access.

Second Battery, commanded by Captain D.J.S. Crozier, was at
Bluff Head, Stanley. This was a six-inch battery on the western
ridge which runs down from the headland. Traces of the battery
remain, though the area is very overgrown. Three 9.2 inch guns
were on a nearby ridge and one of those emplacements remains.

Third Battery, commanded by Captain C.W.L. Cole, was
situated on what is today called Ap Lei Chau Island, Aberdeen.
Development has removed all trace of the gun sites.

Fourth Battery, commanded by Lieutenant K.M.A. Barnett, was
at Pak Sha Wan. The position was a part of the large Lyemun
military area at the eastern end of the island. The remains are in
reasonable condition and initial plans are being made to restore
the area as part of what is now Lyemun park.

Fifth Battery, commanded by Captain L. Goldman, was on the
top of Sai Wan Hill, again at Lyemun. The A.A. guns were
mounted within the fortifications built there during the last century and which can be seen today.

The Field Company Engineers, commanded by Major J.H. Bot-
tomley, were headquartered at Tai Hang, now a major residential
area. The Corps Signals, commanded by Captain A.N. Braude,
was headquartered at Peak Mansions. This impressive pre-war
building was earmarked for demolition in 1990, to be replaced by
a modern development.

The Armoured Car Platoon, commanded by Second Lieutenant
M.G. Carruthers, was headquartered at West Brigade Headquarters. The main headquarters buildings have been destroyed
but there are a number of smaller military buildings on the west

side of Wong Nei Chong Gap Road. There are also military buildings to the north of the road leading to the Parkview development, these played an important role in the battle for the gap.

The First to Seventh Companies were scattered around the island and there are many pillboxes, trenches, fire-steps, markers and other military remains to be seen today.

The A.S.C. Company was headquartered at Deepwater Bay.

The Hughes Group, commanded by Major the Hon. J.J. Paterson, was stationed at the North Point Power Station. No trace of this remains as the power station was dismantled several years ago.

The Field Ambulance Company, commanded by Lieutenant Colonel L.T. Ride, was distributed around the island, the Pay Detachment, under Major C. de S. Robertson, was attached to the Royal Army Pay Corps and the Nursing Detachment, under Mrs Braude, was attached to army hospitals.

The Volunteer headquarters stood where the Lower Albert Road Government Offices, east wing, now stands. On 14 December the headquarters staff moved from there to Peak Mansions. The Supply and Transport Section, commanded by Major H.G. Williams, was attached to headquarters.

On 14 December the heavy artillery and aircraft pounding of the island continued. Enemy warships were spotted steaming just out of range of the guns, although the battery at Cape D'Aguilar did engage a cruiser briefly before it moved out of range again. At Belcher's Fort, two 4.7 inch guns were hit and put out of action. Mount Davis suffered heavy bombardment.

Pak Sha Wan Battery came in for particular attention, being shelled, bombed and mortared. But still the Fourth Battery remained in action with its two six-inch guns. A third emplacement was filled with a dummy gun which was moved to give the impression it was real.

Mr Kenneth Barnett remembered during a 1987 visit to the remains of the battery:

I had got through to Douglas Crozier at Stanley and said that some of the chaps were getting a bit jittery. There had been a very old scheme for switching people around and I thought it would be a good thing to dig this one up. For him to send me some fresh men who hadn't been under fire in exchange for half a dozen or so of ours.

Mr Barnett had been wounded earlier and had been sent to

hospital for treatment. Through some misunderstanding, a portion of the battery went to Stanley without sufficient replacements being sent. But the battery remained in action. Maltby noted, 'In the general defence plan this battery had the role of a supporting one, but as the situation developed it found itself in the front line.'

Meanwhile, at Magazine Gap, artillery fire destroyed eight main signal cables, involving 195 circuits and severing communications between the Fortress Headquarters, situated deep underground within Victoria Barracks (about between present day Pacific Place and the Queensway Government Offices) and the southern side of the island. Within 20 hours the Royal Signals had restored the lines.

In the city, the situation was becoming increasingly confused, with the heavy bombardment causing fires and damage. However, the situation remained under control. During the night speakers mounted in Kowloon boomed demands for surrender across the empty harbour while fifth columnists were captured using primitive electrical signalling to notify the Japanese gunners of the location of key British posts.

On 15 December, The Japanese artillery continued to pick off the pill boxes along the northern shore of the island with accurate fire coming from a high-velocity, small-calibre gun hidden in one of the warehouses of Kowloon. Three pillboxes were completely demolished and two others badly damaged. One pillbox was found to have no less than 40 shell holes drilled right through it.

The Rajputs and the Royal Engineers worked feverishly to prepare 10 to 12 alternative machine gun locations in the north east sector and the shelling of this sector showed a marked increase. As night fell, all communications along the north east shoreline had been cut, but hasty repairs were made.

At noon on 15 December, mortar fire had begun to fall on the naval dockyard, fortress headquarters and other areas of Central. The Fifth Battery at Sai Wan was heavily shelled and one gun was knocked out. However, the Volunteer gunners there kept up their activity.

The Volunteers established a 'Command Observation Post', manned by its signallers, on the Peak, with the task of watching enemy activity in the mainland and reporting direct to Fortress Headquarters. This OP had to move several times as the enemy artillery persistently located it, thanks to fifth columnists, and put down accurate fire.

During the day, a large number of small craft was seen being assembled in Kowloon Bay but howitzer fire managed to set two craft alight with the remainder scattering. It was obvious that a landing was going to be attempted soon and orders were given for searchlights to be pointed downwards at night, if necessary, to illuminate the water.

At 9.15 p.m. Number Two Platoon of the Royal Rifles of Canada, opened fire from the West Fort at Pak Sha Wan. A searchlight of the Volunteer Fourth battery was depressed and a junk, a large number of small rubber boats, and improvised rafts, crowded with Japanese, were seen in the narrow Lyemun channel.

Mr Barnett said that he had considerable difficulty in convincing Fortress Headquarters that they were actually being attacked, the impression being that the Volunteers, as non-professionals, were rather jumpy. The Volunteers and the Canadians beat off the attack, killing the troops in the water before they had a chance to get ashore. Japanese batteries renewed their attacks on the area with howitzer and three-pounder fire. A searchlight was hit and considerable damage done to the Lyemun and Pak Sha Wan areas.

At about 10.45 p.m. preparations were seen being made for another attempt to cross the channel, but the searchlights were brought into play and four enemy craft were sunk. The Fourth Battery was commended for its action in fighting off the attacks.

During the evening, the anti-aircraft battery at Pinewood, on the lower slopes of the Peak, was knocked out by heavy shelling lasting four hours. Later that night, HMS *Thracian* made a raid into the harbour, making its way to Kowloon Bay where two ferry boats filled with troops were sunk.

During the day, two enemy aircraft were shot down, though it is not clear who scored the kills, with many units claiming credit. Certainly, the Volunteer anti-aircraft gunners remained active at Sai Wan Hill and they were particularly noted by the attacking Japanese.

On 16 December the shelling of the north shore continued, but the targets were more specifically military. The first air raid of the day arrived at 9 a.m. and continued for 35 minutes. During the afternoon, a large formation bombed the Mount Davis fort, which was also the target of heavy shelling. On 14 December, about 60 gunners had a very lucky escape, along with a future Honorary Colonel of the Volunteers, Dr Solomon Bard, who was serving there as medical officer. A huge shell smashed into the underground complex where they were sheltering, but it failed to detonate.

Bombing raids were also made by the Japanese on Shau Ki Wan, Shek O, Aberdeen and, of course, Lyemun. By the end of the day, more than half of the pillboxes from Wanchai to Lyemun had been knocked out and moves were made to alternative positions, but these depended on field telephone lines that were constantly cut by shellfire. Two more aircraft were shot down. Fifth columnists continued to be active. The shelling continued throughout the night of 16–17 December.

Dawn on 17 December saw yet another heavy air raid, after which a Japanese party made a further demand for surrender. This was again rejected. 'The Governor and Commander-in-Chief of Hong Kong declines absolutely to enter into negotiations for the surrender of Hong Kong, and takes this opportunity of notifying Lieutenant-General Sakai and Vice-Admiral Masaichi Nimi that he is not prepared to receive any further communications from them on the subject', said the Governor.

Maltby commented:

The envoys seemed surprised and somewhat consternated at the rejection of this call to surrender. The arrival of the second white flag within the short period of four days seemed to suggest either:–

(a) The Japanese disliked the prospect of attacking across the harbour.
(b) The Chinese threat to their rear was beginning to take effect.
(c) That it was an attempt to undermine our morale by offers of peace and a quick ending of hostilities.

Throughout the lull in hostilities produced by the surrender demand, communications were repaired. When hostilities recommenced, considerable activity was observed in Kowloon Bay as boats were readied for the attack. These were engaged by artillery and counter-battery work went on against hostile artillery on Devil's Peak, Gun Club Hill, and mortars on the Kowloon waterfront.

During the night of 17–18 December, fire at the large paint factory at Braemar Hill, above North Point, produced a dense pall of smoke over the area. So intense was the smoke that shore defence positions, and ammunition stores had to be moved. Shelling had resumed and many of the pillboxes had their communications severed. On the south of the island Aberdeen was shelled from the seaward.

On 18 December there were heavy air raids on the central district and the large oil storage tanks at North Point were set on fire. The waterfront defences along the northern shore were heavily engaged, several receiving direct hits, with two 18-pounder guns destroyed. The road from Causeway Bay to Shau Ki Wan was chaotic, a jumble of over-turned vehicles, rickshaws, dangling tramline power cables and over-turned trams. As the afternoon wore on, so the air raids became continuous with Sai Wan receiving particular attention and the artillery observation post there being dive-bombed, shelled and knocked out.

At 5 p.m. the enemy was seen advancing down Devil's Peak towards the waterfront. Just before dusk and afterwards, extremely heavy bombardment of the Lyemun area by artillery and mortars began. The fixed-beam light at North Point, which illuminated the harbour in that area was put out of action by the heat of the oil tank fire. At 7 p.m., Maltby despatched three Volunteer armoured cars to the Tai Tam headquarters of East Brigade and two cars to Leighton Hill, the headquarters of the Middlesex Regiment. These were to serve as reserves in case of an attempted landing. While the attack was gathering in Kowloon, the British commanders had still to keep in mind the threat to the south side of the island from the sea.

The stage was set for the attack on the island.

* * *

The Japanese Navy held supremacy at sea. The Japanese land forces were under the command of Lieutenant General T. Sakai, commander of the 23rd Army in South China. The task of attacking Hong Kong Island was given to the army's 38th division under Lieutenant General T. Sano, with certain additional units under his command. The force included the following.

Infantry —
The 38th Infantry Group: the 228th, the 229th, and 230th Regiments, each of three battalions. The 66th Infantry Regiment and attached troops, for protection against Chinese interference.
Artillery —
38th Mountain Artillery Regiment, of three battalions. Second and Fifth Independent Anti-Tank Artillery Battalions. One independent mountain artillery regiment. One heavy field artillery

regiment, plus one battalion. The 21st Mortar Battalion.

Siege Artillery —
One heavy artillery regiment with 24-centimetre howitzers. One heavy artillery battalion with 15-centimetre guns. One independent mortar battalion.

Engineers —
38th Engineer Regiment. One independent engineer regiment (two field engineer units, one landing craft unit)

Army Air Units —
45th Air Regiment with light bombers. One reconnaissance squadron. One fighter squadron. Detachment of the Fifth Air Division with 18 heavy bombers (from December 16). 47th Airfield Battalion. 67th Airfield Company.

A Japanese infantry regiment was larger than its British counterpart, usually consisting of a headquarters company, a machinegun company and four rifle companies. The total strength, including ancillaries, was about 1,100 men. The 38th Division drew its men mainly from Nagoya, the capital of Aichi Prefecture, 160 miles west of Tokyo, one of the largest cities in Japan. The 228th regiment was recruited from Nagoya itself, while the 229th came from Gifu and the 230th from Shizuoka.

For the attack on the island, the division, whose total strength was said to be over 20,000 men, was arranged as follows.

(a) The Right Flank Group consisting of two battalions of the 228th Regiment and the three battalions of the 230th Regiment;

(b) The Left Flank Group consisting of two battalions of the 229th Regiment with other attachments;

(c) The Right Artillery group which apparently included at least one Mountain Battery;

(d) The Left Artillery Group;

(e) The Kowloon Garrison Force, apparently consisting of second-line units and garrison elements;

(f) An Armoured Unit with light tanks; and

(g) Engineer, signal, supply and transport units.

General Sakai drew up a plan of attack for the night of 18 December. The three battalions of the 230th Regiment were to land at North Point and break through to Jardine's Lookout. The two battalions of the 228th Regiment were to hold a bridgehead at

North Point while supplies and other troops were landed. The two battalions of the 229th Regiment were to land in the Shau Ki Wan area and push onwards to the Tai Tam Valley.

At 7.30 p.m. the Fifth Anti-Aircraft Battery of the Volunteers on Sai Wan Hill was heavily shelled by artillery of all calibres up to nine-inch howitzers. Half an hour later three pillboxes in Wanchai were also the target of heavy bombardment.

The night was exceptionally dark, with an overcast sky and frequent showers of rain. The burning paint factory and oil tanks further obscured vision.

The Japanese launched their attack in three separate thrusts aimed at the north east coastline of the island. Each regiment left a battalion in reserve on the mainland. The attack went in in two waves with the first wave crossing the water at about 8.30 p.m. in inflatable boats. The second wave came at about 11.30 p.m. in landing craft and towed collapsible assault boats.

The 229th Regiment, under Colonel Tanaka, took the east sector. One battalion landed at Shau Ki Wan, the other battalion landed in the Aldrich Bay area, just west of Lyemun. The men of the Royal Rifles of Canada fought bravely, but were overrun, with a six-inch howitzer battery of the Hong Kong and Singapore Royal Artillery also being captured. The Fourth Battery started to fire into the Shau Ki Wan area. At 9.30 p.m. it was attacked by the invaders but they did not press the attack.

Lieutenant H.T. Buxton, of the Second Battery, was at Pak Sha Wan. He took a party of men up towards the parade ground at the Lyemun barracks above the battery. Fourth Battery commander, Kenneth Barnett explained, 'They were challenged in English. They replied in English then the Japanese opened fire and killed the lot of them quite quickly. Buxton went to report that we were out of rations and out of water and no word ever came back to the battery. There was one survivor and we found out later in the camp what had happened.'

But the Japanese subsequently paid little attention to the Lyemun area and Pak Sha Wan Battery and, instead, raced for Sai Wan Hill, where the H.K.V.D.C. Fifth Anti-Aircraft Battery was situated and then on towards the Tai Tam Gap.

A party of Rajputs later made their way into the Pak Sha Wan Battery from the West Fort, but on the morning of 20 December — the position being hopeless — the position surrendered.

Tanaka's men arrived at the summit of Sai Wan Hill at about

10.30 p.m. The Volunteers of the Fifth Anti-Aircraft Battery were not aware that the landing had taken place and were quickly overpowered. The prisoners were tied up and left for several hours, then the Japanese took them out and bayoneted them in cold blood, throwing their bodies down the side of the hill. Incredibly, two men survived after having been left for dead.

A further massacre took place at the Advanced Dressing Station at the Salesian Mission at Shau Kei Wan, below the hill fort. There, two wounded Rajput officers were killed and the doctors and orderlies were kept for some hours before being taken out to a large nullah, or drain, running along the hillside and bayoneted. Three men managed to survive, including Volunteer medical officer, Captain Osler Thomas. When the murder started he and two other men made a run for it. The other two were hit by shots. Thomas pretended he had also been hit and fell into a deep ditch. The bodies of the other two were thrown in on top of him.

Meanwhile, fierce fighting was going on along the waterfront as the rest of the attack force cut its way through the urban areas. The 230th Regiment, under Colonel Shoji, had landed at North Point — confusingly, the western thrust of the three-pronged attack. The 228th Regiment, under Colonel Doi, landed in the central section. The pill boxes in these areas were all badly damaged and the two companies of Rajputs along the shore line found themselves with the task of opposing a massed landing.

The 230th Regiment cut through the urban area and headed for the hills and the passes, or 'gaps' of the island. The 228th did the bulk of the fighting in the streets. Captured members of the St. John Ambulance Brigade and air raid precaution workers were beheaded. The big Taikoo Sugar Factory at Quarry Bay was attacked and taken. This factory stood in the area of what is now Tong Chong Street, or Sugar Factory Street, with its entrance on King's Road.

The Rajputs' 'C' Company ceased to function as a unit after heavy fighting, though individual groups in isolated pockets continued to resist. To the west, 'D' Company fought on, inflicting and receiving heavy casualties.

At the Power Station were the Volunteers, and an odd group of Volunteers at that. The Hughes Group, named after its veteran commander, Lieutenant Colonel H. Owen Hughes, who had been ordered to fly to China early in the battle, was composed of men who were too old to qualify for normal service as Volunteers. But their morale and enthusiasm was extremely high and many were excellent shots.

The group had a listed strength of four officers and 68 other ranks and it had been placed in the North Point power station which, it was thought, would allow it to remain out of the front line. In fact, the 'Hughesiliers' found themselves in the thick of the fiercest fighting, with the enemy finding the power station a hard nut to crack.

Their commander, Major J.J. Patterson, explained:

The Hughes Group was originally founded as a unit for internal, anti-sabotage defence and its personnel was found from British businessmen of over 55 years of age ... At the declaration of war the strength of the Hughes Group, which had been as high as 63, had fallen, through transfer to essential services and in a few cases failure to report, to 36, of which 22 were Hong Kong Electric. Because, however, of the difficulty in keeping the plant going through Chinese defection, seven marine engineers came from Taikoo and later when Kowloon had fallen 17 of the technical staff of the China Light and Power. To these must be added two officers, and six men of the Free French and any unit could count itself fortunate in getting so experienced a soldier as was Captain Jacosta who had seen service in both great wars and in Spain. For that matter, Captain Egal was wounded and taken prisoner in 1914–1918 and imprisoned in the present war and Captain Burch was in the South African and Great War.

Part of the Rajput 'B' Company came in from the west trying to push through towards Tai Hang where it hoped to link up with survivors of 'D' Company. Second Lieutenant M.G. Carruthers took a Volunteer armoured car along the King's Road in an attempt to reach the power station with a platoon of the Middlesex Regiment following behind. The car received a direct hit from a mobile anti-tank gun. Private H. Park and H.W. Smits were killed. Carruthers escaped. Half the Middlesex party was cut down by intense fire, but the balance managed to reach the power station and to strengthen the defences there.

At 1.45 a.m., Major Patterson reported that the power station was entirely surrounded. He was told to hold on and to act as a rallying point for remnants of other units which might be nearby. The Rajputs' 'B' Company tried to get through, one platoon making some progress and linking up with a group of survivors of 'D' Company, but eventually they were pushed back. Other members of the Middlesex regiment tried to make their way through from two pill boxes in Causeway Bay, but they too, failed.

Through the long, dark night the elderly men of the Volunteers, and the Middlesex party, fought on under constant fire. At about midnight, Captain Jacosta had suggested to Major Patterson that withdrawal be considered, but he refused to agree, saying he had been told of the importance of holding the position. Patterson considered that if they had withdrawn then, lives would have been saved but he did not think that his men 'would have cared to go so easily.'

At 10 a.m. the Japanese were in great force to the east and south of the power station and held the high ground above it. Patterson said:

It was then obvious that no help could get through and the position being complicated by women and civilians a withdrawal was unwillingly decided on ...

Nor did withdrawal look particularly hopeful for the lane of escape, if indeed it then existed, which it didn't, must perforce be very meagre. And so it proved to be, scattered parties of Japs were in the coal yard and on either side of Electric Road, the pill box in Causeway Bay had fallen and the Hughes Group coming under cross fire from machine guns was forced into the houses opposite the main gate of Ah King's Slipway. To cross King's Road was not possible for any considerable body of men, nor was it possible to rush the pill box held by one heavy, Vickers type, machine gun and two Jap brens.

It was hoped to cross Causeway Bay after dark but only could immunity from Japs be expected if something in the nature of a sustained counter attack developed. It did not, and late in the afternoon the Japs surrounded the houses concerned and threatened to fire them. They offered surrender which was taken.

One group remained in the office buildings of the power station, with Hughesiliers on the ground floor and men of the Middlesex Regiment on the first floor. 'These very brave men preferred to fight it out where they were and did so, although all were wounded, until the Japs rushed the place.'

When it was suggested to Private Sir Edward Des Voeux, who was in the nearby Government Store, that he make a dash for safety he replied calmly that he was to old to go dashing about and that he would far rather fire in comfort. He died, still firing. A scroll awarded to him was never presented, he was a bachelor and after the war the police were unable to trace his next of kin. The scroll reads:

This scroll commemorates Pt Sir E. Des Voeux, Hong Kong Volunteer Defence Force, held in honour as one who served his King and Country in the world war 1939–45 and gave his life to save mankind from tyranny. May his sacrifice bring the peace and freedom for which he died.

One engagement took place around an overturned bus in King's Road and this became known as the 'Battle of the Bus'. Private T.E. Pearce told Major Patterson that he thought it didn't make much difference whether or not he was killed under a bus or roasted alive in a burning building. 'At the time there seemed to be quite a bit in what he said — not much choice either way,' recalled Patterson. Pearce died at the bus, along with Private Vincent Sorby. Corporal R.P. Dunlop and Private J. Roscoe both fell, wounded by sword slashes. The last man, Private G.E. (or C.E.) Gahagan, drove off an enemy attack single-handed, killing an officer and four men with five rounds. He survived. The bus was abandoned.

On the morning of 19 December, while the Hughesiliers, and parts of the Middlesex and Rajputs were still involved in fighting in the shore area, all three battalions of the 230th Regiment were pushing into the hills, together with the second Battalion of the 229th Regiment. Facing them were two infantry companies of the Volunteers. These two companies, Number Three and Number One, had a very wide area to cover. The line of hills east from the Wong Nei Chong Gap to Mount Parker was their responsibility and the country was, and is, sheer and rugged. Jardine's Lookout is 433 metres high, Mount Butler is 436 metres high, while Mount Parker, at 532 metres, is only slightly lower than the main Island peak, Victoria Peak, which stands 554 metres. The line is pierced by Quarry Gap, between Mount Butler and Mount Parker.

Number Three Company, under Major Stewart, had the western part of the line. A contour path, known as Sir Cecil's Ride after a former governor Sir Cecil Clementi, runs around the lower slopes of Jardine's Lookout. On and around this path, occupying three forward posts, was Number Seven Platoon, under Captain L.B. Holmes. On the south-east slope of Jardine's Lookout, in the area opposite to where the large Parkview development now stands, were two pillboxes. These, though overgrown, can still be seen today. Lieutenant B.C. Field with Sergeant G.J. White and 18 men of Number Nine Platoon occupied them. The remainder of the platoon, and Number Eight Platoon were holding section posts north of Jardine's Lookout in the Blue Pool Road and Stubbs Road area, at Wong Nei Chong Gap, at Stanley Gap — along the road from Parkview — and at the south end of Sir Cecil's Ride. In the Wong Nei Chong Gap itself was Brigadier Lawson's West Brigade headquarters.

The whole of the Mount Butler area was undefended. Beyond Mount Butler was Number One Company of the H.K.V.D.C., with its headquarters in a building known as the Tai Tam Bungalow. This building was over the line of hills, down at the Tai Tam Reservoir, about 1,500 metres south of Quarry Gap. Number One Platoon, under Second Lieutenant B.S. Carter, was in the important Wong Nei Chong Gap. Number Two Platoon, under Lieutenant J. Redman, was at a feature called Repulse Bay View, too far away to support the platoon in the gap. Number Three Platoon, under Second Lieutenant R.S. Edwards, with its four bren carriers, was patrolling the Tai Tam Reservoir Road. (The terminology can cause some confusion. The Tai Tam Reservoir Road runs not from the Tai Tam Reservoir but from the Tai Tam Tuk Reservoir below it up to the Tai Tam Gap — where East Brigade Headquarters was situated).

To the east of the Volunteers was 'C' Company of the Royal Rifles of Canada who were holding the eastern slope of Mount Parker, and the 258-metre hill, Boa Vista, north of the Tai Tam Reservoir Road. The Canadians had made a brave attempt to retake Sai Wan Hill and had succeeded in reaching the walls of the fort, with nine killed in the process. A platoon of Number Two Company, H.K.V.D.C. had been brought up from Pottinger Gap to reinforce the Lyemun area. Much confused fighting followed, but eventually, the defenders had to fall back through the Tai Tam Gap.

Captain A.H. Penn, officer commanding Number One Company, had received a report of the Japanese landings at 10.30 p.m. He tried to get through to his platoon at Quarry Gap but the lines had been cut by shell fire so he went there in person. A platoon of Canadians which was meant to back up the position in the gap became lost, and by the time they found the guide sent by Captain Penn it was too late.

On arriving at the gap, Penn ordered up a section, under Sergeant F.L. Curtis, from Company Headquarters Reserve and sent it to a knoll on the eastern slopes of Mount Butler. Corporal F.M. Thompson and six men manned weapon pits near a pill box further down, close to the track leading to the Taikoo Sugar refinery. The remaining 15 men were spread across the gap itself, with the Vickers Guns, under Sergeant J.P. Murphy, on the right, and the light machine guns about 25 metres forward on the track.

As the Canadians had not arrived, Penn sent orders for Company Sergeant Major R.A. Edwards to move to the gap with the headquarters party. He had two officers and 29 men. Penn had intended to withdraw Thompson's party from its position near the pill box, but at 12.30 a.m. Thompson and his men were attacked from out of the pitch blackness. Without flares, the seven Volunteers fired on fixed lines until they were over-run. Three men, two of them wounded, managed to make their way back up to the gap and another returned via Mount Parker.

At 1 a.m., the main Japanese attack on the gap went in. Sergeant Curtis and his section had only just managed to get to the knoll, having to travel through difficult country in the darkness. They managed to get their gun into action and inflicted many casualties at point blank range before fighting it out hand-to-hand. Two men survived.

The enemy advancing up the path were, at first, thought to be Rajputs who were withdrawing from the fighting lower down. Carter, commanding the platoon, shouted, 'Who the Hell are you? Answer or we fire.' The reply was 'Banzai!', and a charge. For 10 minutes the Volunteers swept the path with Vickers and light machine gun fire, breaking up wave after wave of attack. In the darkness, however, the Japanese crawled in close to the Volunteer positions and threw grenades. Penn was hit on the helmet by a grenade splinter and stunned. The light machine guns were overrun. Carter moved across to the Vickers position to find that Sergeant Murphy had only three men left. Carter told him to put the guns out of action and fall back towards the Tai Tam Reservoir.

The Japanese were now through the gap and Carter was worried about the battery of Hong Kong and Singapore Artillery in the valley behind. He therefore withdrew with Murphy's party and two other survivors. Penn came around from his stunned condition and found three other men, one of whom he sent back down to the Bungalow with orders to bring up the Company Sergeant Major's party, but the messenger never arrived. Penn waited for about 20 minutes and during that time he was able to kill a Japanese officer about to fire a success signal to show that the gap had been secured. Penn then fell back to the Bungalow himself.

Carter informed the H.K.S.R.A. what had happened and it opened up on the gap immediately. Number One Platoon had lost 19 killed, wounded and missing in the fight at Quarry Gap. The survivors, the company headquarters party and a few Rajputs, about 30 men in all, took up positions to protect the battery and the Bungalow.

At dawn, the battery again started firing into the gap and the slopes of Mount Parker. Unsure of the forces facing them, the attackers paused in that area. Meanwhile, the Japanese began to bring heavy pressure against the two companies of the Royal Rifles of Canada holding the line from Mount Parker to Pottinger Gap, between Pottinger Peak and Mount Collinson, at the easternmost extremity of the island. On the flank of the Canadians were Volunteers of Number Five Company.

At the same time as Captain Penn and his men were battling, the three battalions of the Japanese 230th Regiment were heading for their objective — the Wong Nei Chong Gap which carried the vital road over the hills to the south side of the island.

News of the Japanese landings had been received by Major Stewart at 10.40 p.m. and he had immediately asked for reinforcements, which were supplied from the headquarters company of the Winnipeg Grenadiers. Four platoons came. One was stationed across Sir Cecil's Ride immediately below the pillboxes, and a second sent up Jardine's Lookout, but this proved impossible to climb in the rain and darkness. The third was placed in the gap between Jardine's Lookout and Mount Butler, and the fourth was stationed at Stanley Gap.

Lieutenant B.C. Field was in charge of the two pill boxes. He recalled:

We had six machine guns, one sub-machine gun and 48 hand grenades. We numbered 21 in all, including myself, Lance Sergeant G.J. White, Lance Corporal N. Broadbridge and Lance Corporal K.C. Hung. During the hours of darkness on December 15–18, we carried stores from company headquarters, dug weapon pits for local protection (with particular regard to night fighting) and thickened up the barbed wire. We checked all range cards for direction and elevation, lubricated the machinegun mountings, prepared guns for firing and practised fire orders, laying the guns etc., until I was satisfied that the guns could be handled efficiently. I prepared sketch plans for the Canadian infantry units operating in the area showing where the beaten zones would fall when carrying out the numbered tasks as detailed in the fire control charts.

On December 17 and 18 the North Point harbour front was shelled heavily and by December 18 I felt that the enemy might attempt a landing at any time. I was by no means happy about the provision for local protection but we did as much as we could in the time available. The men worked well.

At night fall on December 18, I deployed men in positions prepared for local defence, siting my headquarters centrally, behind pill box one, where I had two dozen hand grenades safely tucked away under a slab of masonry. I had two men with me and from there could throw beyond our inner wire and into nearby areas of dead ground. We had practised throwing before-hand with suitable stones.

The other Volunteers were also on the alert.

In all, there were about 230 Canadians and Volunteers at Wong Nei Chong Gap. There was also a party of Middlesex with four anti-aircraft light machine guns.

Just before midnight, the Japanese made contact with the section held by Lance Corporal D. Hung. The Volunteers opened fire, killing several of the enemy and giving the impression that the defenders were stronger than they were. About half an hour later, a stronger Japanese force appeared and Lance Corporal Hung withdrew his small force to a fallback position.

One Japanese tactic for locating such positions was to send ahead suicide squads who would sacrifice their lives to draw fire. A strong fight took place at this second position, with attack after attack coming along the narrow path and attempting to cut through the barbed wire obstacles. Eventually, through a barrage of hand-grenades and by crawling under the wire, some Japanese broke through and fierce hand-to-hand fighting took place. Captain L.B. Holmes was killed. Sergeant E. Zimmern, who had been wounded, gave the order to withdraw to the next position along the path and he was killed as he covered his men's withdrawal. Corporal E. Hing was killed at about the same time. Lance Corporal Hung and a few men tried to break off and get through to Stanley Gap, but were unable to do so, and therefore retired to Happy Valley.

The next position was not attacked, as the Japanese ascended the steep slopes of Jardine's Lookout in an attempt to outflank the defenders. (Today the whole area is a tangle of trees and other vegetation, but in 1941 the hillside was almost bare). Lance

Corporal F.R. Zimmern and his section withdrew from the position being outflanked and made their way to Stanley Gap where they joined the defenders there.

Volunteer, George Roylance, was on the road leading up to the gap and he saw the Japanese activity as dawn broke:

In the morning there was this mist arising from the valley. We were doing our job on the road, stopping vehicles and what have you. The mist lifted and we saw some uniformed chaps who we took to be our fellows, but all of a sudden a machine gun let fly at us.

We dashed across the road one at a time into a catchwater and that is where we did our little bit of fighting. It was nice and big, quite deep and had a tree growing above us which gave us protection. There was an airplane buzzing around trying to locate our positions.

The Japanese had a light machine gun. They had a short belt for it which contained 12 or 14 rounds. So you would get this burst of fire and then there would be a pause. After this first round of firing we noticed the regular breaks. So to get to the catchwater I sent my chaps dashing across the road one at a time during the pauses. By the time I went across the Japanese were up to what was happening. There was an abandoned truck and they saved four or five rounds after firing a burst. I dashed across and they fired, hitting the truck where I had jumped behind the rear wheel. Then when they really had to load I got to the catchwater.

The light was increasing. Lieutenant Field wrote:

I returned to Pill Box One in the half-light of dawn, and as I reached the pill box I heard a noise of confused shouting in a strange language in the valley to the south. I thought at first that the shouting came from our own Indian troops, but the sound of rifle fire from the same direction made it clear that fighting had begun.

In a few moments it was light enough to observe and identify a concentration of enemy troops near the southern end of Clementi's Ride, about 500 yards away. The Ride was crowded with troops for some 100 yards and there appeared to be about 250 men there while more were coming up to their rear and others had deployed towards the AA position and Stanley Gap and towards Wong Nei Chong Gap.

At about 6.30 a.m., the Japanese had hit the section post on the Ride held by Lance Corporal R. Ma. They, apparently, had not been aware of this position and halted, bunched, on and around the path.

There was a danger to our own troops in this area if fire were laid down carelessly, so in the first instance I manned the machine gun in the south west aperture of pill box one and fired three good bursts before the enemy scattered. There were two distinct heaps of dead and several others lying on the Ride all day, where I had fired.

Lance Corporal Ma and his men were attacked again and fought for 15 minutes, killing most of the lead platoon. The enemy suffered more casualties before it worked its way around the flanks and took the position in a bayonet charge. Of the nine men in the section, five were killed and three wounded.

Just before 7 a.m., a party of Japanese working up the stream bed, below the Ride, to avoid the machine guns of the pill boxes, rushed the Gap and drove back the section of Corporal M.S. Lau. But as they shouted in triumph, Field opened up and cut them down. Corporal Lau and three of his men held the gap until, at about 7.30 a.m., the enemy took the police station on the knoll at the summit. The three men were killed but Lau managed to fight his way through to Deepwater Bay Road and he joined up with B Company of the Middlesex Regiment there.

It was now light enough to identify enemy troops with ease at the short ranges to the targets offered, and I ordered the other two guns in Pill Box One to fire under gun control, but to be certain of their targets before firing. I carried on with my gun and we all observed excellent fire effect. So far as I could judge, we succeeded in breaking up the main assault on Wong Nei Chong Gap, although some enemy parties got through.

Private G. White, manning the south east gun, showed fine spirit. He appeared to be enjoying himself picking out the men carrying flags and those with white gloves. His manner generally struck a note very encouraging to his companions. About this time a section from Lt McCarthy's platoon, Winnipeg Grenadiers, joined pill box two and Lance Corporal Atkinson did some very useful work with a light automatic from a pit outside the pill box.

The Vickers guns in pill box two could not be brought to bear on Wong Nei Chong Gap as the pill-box was sited to fire east and north only. There could be no question at this stage of moving the guns from pill box two as I expected an attack at any moment, probably from the very approaches covered by the guns in the pill box.

From the gap, the Japanese now struck out up the road leading to Stanley Gap, which is now the access to the Parkview housing complex. It was held by a platoon of Canadians and two sections of Number Three Company, under Lieutenant D.J.N. Anderson. The attack was halted by Anderson's light machine guns and by pill box fire. But at about 7.30 a.m., another enemy attack came in from the east, the enemy coming along the slope above a path leading to the reservoir. The Canadians changed their front to meet this threat but the defenders were swamped by sheer numbers. Lieutenant Anderson and most of his men were killed. Major Stewart was wounded, and he and six others retired into the company head-quarters shelter. Company Quarter Master Sergeant E.C. Fincher, with a few other men, held out in a store-shelter until the Japanese blew in its front with a mortar round in the afternoon.

The force then turned its attention to the pill boxes, as Lt. Field described:

Pill box one was spattered with machine gun fire, and as I was firing my gun I could see pieces of the exterior camouflage rock-work falling away under bursts of fire. At 8.15 a.m., a burst of fire hit the metal shutter of the aperture through which I was firing and several small pieces of metal struck me in the face and left arm. I must have had my mouth open at the time because one piece hit a back tooth and shattered it.

Field was out of action for a few minutes, but his men carried on under Lance Corporal K.C. Hung. The attackers gradually worked their way up to about 150 yards from the pillbox and started pouring in fire through the apertures. The barrel casings of all three guns were soon perforated beyond temporary repair but they were still kept in action, even without their water cooling. Some type of armour-piercing bullet was being fired at the pillbox for the metal shutters covering the fourth aperture, which was not in use, were pierced clean through.

Coming to, Field considered moving the guns to positions away from the pill box but quickly decided this was impossible. Now mortar shells started to come in.

Their aim was accurate and some of the shells were very powerful, shaking the whole pill box, while any that burst on the platform of earth which sloped away from about window-sill level, threw blast and splinters into the gun apertures, inflicting casualties and damaging the guns. Private E.B. Young was killed in this way.

The pill boxes provided valuable protection against much of the effects of the mortar fire but the necessity for firing from loopholes which were clear aiming marks for enemy fire increased the casualty rate, as is borne out by the fact that before noon I had one man killed and seven wounded in pill box one out of a total of nine of us. During the morning a splinter entered my neck and damaged an artery. There was some loss of blood but it did not trouble me much at the time.

In the intervals between mortar bombardments small parties of the enemy came forward in dead ground to try to take the pill boxes. We had no difficulty in keeping them all, although they could get close enough under cover to throw hand grenades. I spent a good deal of time outside the pill-box, near the door. There was good cover but I wanted to be ready to throw grenades forward of the pill box if the enemy managed to creep up the steep hill-side unseen. I could not risk throwing grenades from the pill box apertures because, had I been knocked out after removing the pin, the grenade might have fallen inside and blown up the crew.

One party attempting to take pill box two betrayed its position and Private G.C. Jitts took the sub-machine gun and went out very pluckily on his own to deal with it. He came face to face with the enemy round a bend in the catchwater and succeeded in killing all five of them. He was hit badly but managed to collect their light automatic and return with it to pill box two. His example was very encouraging to his comrades in a trying situation.

Lance Corporal N. Broadbridge and Private T. Leonard were also involved in this action.

After the war, Major Stewart wrote to the widow of Private Jits:

The defence of the pill-boxes was a most magnificent effort; the defenders, though isolated, surrounded and outnumbered by a hundred to one, held the position for nearly twelve hours and inflicted heavy losses on the enemy. Subsequently, I sent the following report to Brigadier Rose:

'Commendation: I wish to bring to your notice the conduct of Private Jits, G.C., during the fighting on December 19, 1941. Private Jitts displayed the greatest courage and coolness during the defence of the pill boxes. On one occasion when a party of the enemy had moved up under cover of the catchwater to within grenade range of pillbox two, Private Jitts went out with a sub-machine gun and rushed their position, destroying the whole party. He was hit twice during this operation. Later, when Lieutenant Field sent away his walking wounded, Private Jitts refused to go, stating that he would need assistance in getting down the hill and would be an encumbrance to the others. He therefore remained and met his death when the Japanese finally took the position. Private Jitts' act enabled the defence to hold on for a longer period and thus delayed the enemy's attack on the Gap. I wish to recommend him.'

I cannot tell you how he was killed. I think it was in the final charge when the enemy overran the position. I know that he was killed quickly. He died a hero's death.

At about noon the Japanese managed to get on top of pill box one, said Field:

I heard the enemy chattering, apparently from on top of the pill-box. A party had evidently succeeded in coming unobserved from behind the pill-box. The lookout man, I discovered later, had been driven off by mortar fire and, finding himself unable to return to Pill Box One had gone down to pill box two. Lance Corporal K.C. Hung showed quick thinking and coolness in telephoning immediately to Pill Box Two and asking for assistance. I ordered everyone into the entrance passageway, which was screened from the pill box by a concrete wall, just in time to avoid two hand grenades which came through the east aperture. These did little damage but there was plenty of smoke.

I was standing by the doorway leading into the pill box and noticed a shadow moving outside the east aperture, then a hand groping for a rifle, the muzzle of which was resting on the sill. I went over and fired out at the man. Later his body was seen lying outside.

Five or six more grenades came in but the bursts were surprisingly feeble. Some machine gun belt boxes were pierced and three or four rounds exploded. Fortunately, there was no ammunition fire — there was no accommodation in the pill box for the safe storage of the main bulk of ammunition against such a possibility.

The smoke was almost unbearable. I thought at the time that they meant to smoke us out, but the crew remained steady, while I tried to work out some plan of action and kept an eye on the apertures in case further grenades came in at a more dangerous angle. I could have kicked them away into a corner, perhaps, if they fell too near the doorway leading into the passage. Pill Box Two organised a first attempt to relieve us. A party led by Private E.D. Fisher, tried to come up the main path but Fisher was wounded fatally and the attempt failed.

A second party of Canadians then approached from the rear and killed a number of Japanese, losing one of their own men but reaching the pill box. By this time, however, the guns inside were unserviceable and so Field decided to move to a position about ten yards to the rear, using the pill box merely as a shelter. Firepower consisted of one light machine gun and six rifles and he wished to forestall any attack from the south east. Attacks came in during the afternoon and were beaten off and regular sticks of half a dozen mortar rounds at a time were received. At about 2 p.m., five more Canadians joined the position, bringing with them a further light machine gun. These men were survivors from a unit which had been fighting on the slopes of Jardine's Lookout.

We continued to exchange fire with the enemy on the ridge. Lance Corporal Atkinson was wounded and I was hit again in the left arm. I felt very tired, but not particularly uncomfortable. My main problem was how, with one arm out of action, to get the pins out of the hand grenades. At the pill box I had hooked the ring over a metal projection on the door.

The afternoon wore on and it was decided to get away as many wounded as possible. They left, heading towards Tai Hang Road with an escort to deal with any small patrols encountered en route. The party lost two men on the way.

At 5 p.m., said Field, in what must rank as one of the greatest understatements of all time, 'I was feeling the effects of a strenuous day'. The loss of blood from another arm wound had made him unfit to carry on effectively. The Canadian corporal was wounded.

The situation appeared very difficult. Shots were coming from a wider angle on our front, and across from the slopes of Mount Nicholson. Lance Corporal Hung was shot in the back and killed by rifle fire from this direction. He had helped me very considerably throughout the action although he had been wounded in the head whilst in pill box one during the morning. The enemy was closing in as the light began to fail and at this stage my recollection of the course of events is rather hazy. At about 18.00 hours the position was overrun and I found myself a prisoner, together with four or five of my men.

Field noted, 'I was particularly impressed by the fine spirit and steadiness shown by the Volunteers under my command. They were all Eurasians, most with a British father and a Chinese or Eurasian mother, a type which in Hong Kong had not been credited generally with the character these men showed.'

The two sections of Number Three company, under Corporal J.F.C. Mackay and Lance Corporal Roylance, were west of the main fighting, in the area around West Brigade headquarters, as was the platoon of Canadians. Captain Bowden, officer commanding headquarter company of the Winnipeg Grenadiers arrived to take command, but was killed a short time later. At 10 a.m. the Japanese took West Brigade headquarters, killing the brigade commander, Lawson and all his staff. Several attempts were made during the fighting at Wong Nei Chong to counter attack, but all failed.

George Roylance did not know that the Brigade Headquarters had fallen. 'Eventually, I realised that we were the only ones firing. I knew the general was near and there would have been firing from the headquarters unit.' But all was quiet and in the evening he made his way to Wanchai Gap.

Major Stewart, with Company Sergeant Major V.H. White, Sergeant G. Winch, and four other ranks remained in the company headquarters shelter. The Japanese decided that it would be too difficult to dislodge them and made no attacks. Finally, on the night of 22 December, running short of ammunition, they evacuated the position and made their way, in pairs, to the allied line. Other Volunteer stragglers also made their way to other positions.

Number Three Company had fought with the utmost gallantry and tenacity, suffering 85 battle casualties in a mobilized strength of 115.

After the gap was overrun the Japanese indulged in their usual atrocities on wounded Volunteers and Canadians there. One man was kicked to death and others were killed by beatings and bayonets. Others, lying in the hills, died of gangrene and thirst.

The attempts to counter-attack had all failed. There was a great shortage of troops to mount an effective attack from the north. Those involved in the fighting at the waterfront and in the urban areas were fully committed. The only troops available, therefore, were the Royal Scots, and parts of the Punjabi and Volunteer forces. At 11 a.m. 'B' and 'C' Companies of the Punjabis moved to a position east of Leighton Hill to relieve pressure on the Rajputs. They then pressed on towards Tai Hang.

At 1 p.m. the counter-attack developed. The two companies of Punjabis were ordered to strike north east towards the power station at North Point, while 'B' Company of the Rajputs, which included survivors from 'D' Company, was to advance eastwards from Leighton Hill. 'A' and 'D' Companies of the Royal Scots were to attack from Middle Gap and the filter beds respectively, with Wong Nei Chong Gap as their objective. 'B' Company of the Winnipeg Grenadiers was to attack from the south.

The Field Company Engineers of the Volunteers at Tai Hang was formed into an infantry unit under Captain K.S. Robertson and Lieutenant I.P. Tamworth and attached to 'D' Company of the Royal Scots.

The Royal Scots and Volunteers pressed ahead, advancing along either side of Mount Nicholson. Unfortunately, they did not advance along the line from Tai Hang Road which Field and his machine guns had been keeping open all day. After the pill boxes had been overrun they managed to fight past the shelters where some Canadians were still holding out and one platoon actually reached Sir Cecil's Ride. But they had to fall back in the face of overwhelming numbers. An attempt to retake the police station knoll failed, with heavy casualties resulting. Among the wounded was Second Lieutenant A. H. Mackenzie, a former Volunteer, who had been commissioned into the Volunteers. 'D' Company fell back to Mount Nicholson at 10 p.m. and joined the platoon of Winnipeg Grenadiers there. Lieutenant Tamworth joined the grenadiers in the shelters and this party held out for another day before being forced to surrender. Two Punjabi companies fell back to a line northwest of Leighton Hill.

The Royal Scots 'A' and 'D' companies dug in as best they could on the slopes of Mount Nicholson. Their 'B' and 'C' companies were brought up on their left, then 'B' Company of the Rajputs then the two Punjabi companies. Leighton Hill was held by 'Z' Company, of the Middlesex Regiment, made up of about 35 men who had withdrawn from the pill boxes along the shore.

Throughout this time, the battle was continuing elsewhere. At about 7.30 a.m., on 19 December, six motor torpedo boats attacked enemy shallow-draft vessels which were ferrying troops from the mainland to the island. The boats made a rendezvous off Green Island and continued in pairs.

Motor Torpedo Boats 07, under Lieutenant R.W. Ashby, of the Hong Kong Royal Navy Volunteer Reserve, and 09, under Lieutenant Kennedy, Royal Navy Volunteer Reserve, succeeded in sinking one enemy landing craft, setting another on fire, and forcing a third to beach. 07 was hit by a shell in the engine room and had to be towed back by 09. The second pair then went in, but ferrying operations had stopped. MTB 18 received a direct hit, killing the commander, Lieutenant J.B. Colle and Sub-Lieutenant D. McGill, both of the H.K.R.N.V.R. Burning, the boat crashed into the sea wall alongside Chatham Road near Kowloon Docks. MTB 11, under Lieutenant J.C. Collingwood, R.N., was hit, but managed to return.

The Japanese were now shelling from both sides of the harbour and attacking the boats with light bombs and machinegun fire. The final pair were ordered not to attack, but apparently the signal did not reach MTB 26, under Lieutenant D.W. Wagstaff, H.K.R.N.V.R. The boat went in and was last seen lying off North Point under heavy fire. Wagstaff, Sub-Lieutenant J.C. Eager of the Naval Volunteers and all hands were killed.

Back on land, after the fall of the gap, stores which had been at Deepwater Bay were transferred to the junction of Pokfulam Road and what was known as Island Road. The Volunteer A.S.C. men were then formed into an infantry force under Major F. Flippance, with Captain D.L. Strellet and Captain R.R. Davies. They formed a mixed force with personnel from various other elements.

First, the force was sent to Bennet's Hill, to the west of where the southern entrance of the Aberdeen tunnel now stands. It was thought that a Japanese attack might develop there but it did not. There is a particularly fine pill box in this area, well worth inspection today. As the attack did not come, the force moved at midnight on the night of 19–20 December up to Postbridge, a large house just south of the Wong Nei Chong Gap, at the eastern side of the Deepwater Bay Valley, where there were five buildings, comprising the headquarters of the Royal Army Ordnance Corps. The Volunteers, and the others, joined a small number of men from the R.A.O.C., the Royal Army Service Corps and several Royal Navy men who had formed part of an abortive attempt to relieve the Gap, but who had been ambushed.

At daylight, the ridge was heavily bombarded by mortars. During the afternoon it was decided that the R.A.S.C. men should make their way back to the depot at Shouson Hill, but their advance party came under heavy fire as it attempted to do so, and suffered several casualties before returning to the ridge.

Throughout the afternoon, the enemy fire became heavier and at 4 p.m. the Japanese attack went in. After fierce fighting, the Japanese were repulsed, but the incoming mortar and rifle fire remained intense. Further attacks went in but the defenders managed to hold on. Finally, at about midnight, a mortar bombardment set fire to a house being held by the force, the front was demolished, and there were many casualties. The decision was made to withdraw, the wounded were lowered down a 50-foot slope and the party made its way to Aberdeen.

Thus, at dawn on 20 December, the Japanese were positioned as follows:

- On the eastern side of the island, two battalions of divisional reserve ready to advance south from the Tai Tam area and Sai Wan towards Stanley;
- At Stanley Gap, two battalions of the 229th Regiment, ready to advance towards Repulse Bay;
- At Wong Nei Chong Gap, one battalion of the 228th Regiment ready to advance towards Deepwater Bay;

- On the North Shore, the other battalion of the 228th;
- In Jardine's Lookout area, three battalions of the 230th regiment, ready to advance west along the line of hills.

First to move was was the 228th Battalion from Wong Nei Chong. This was the attacking force which hit Postbridge. Meanwhile, the 229th sent an advance party along the catchwater which runs along Violet Hill and this managed to reach a point directly above the Repulse Bay Hotel.

There had been much Japanese activity around the hotel and the garage had fallen. (This garage remains today, as a petrol station. The hotel was razed for property development some years ago, though a poor pastiche was erected in its place). In the hotel were a platoon of the Middlesex Regiment, a few Royal Navy men from the mine-control station at Chung Hom Kok and few members of the H.K.R.N.V.R.

East Brigade decided to attempt to relieve the hotel and then to try to get up to Wong Nei Chong Gap. The party sent consisted of Number Six Platoon of the Volunteers, under Lieutenant D.L. Prophet, and Number Five Platoon, under Lieutenant W. Stoker, from Number Two Company (the Scottish company). There was also 'A' Company of the Royal Rifles of Canada.

Six Platoon advanced along the road from Stanley to Repulse Bay while Number Five Platoon engaged the enemy force which was moving down from Violet Hill. On arriving at the hotel the Japanese were successfully cleared from the grounds and Number Six Platoon and the Canadians attacked and took the garage, freeing five prisoners. Twenty-six Japanese were killed.

The Canadians pushed on along the road towards Deepwater Bay, but ran into heavy fire and were forced to fall back to the large house, 'Eucliff', which used to stand at the western edge of Repulse Bay. Some occupied the house while others took up positions nearby. The position then remained fairly static for a period at Repulse Bay, with the Japanese across and above the road and on the steep hillside above the hotel.

There was also fighting to the west, where the Japanese had succeed in getting down to the road at Deepwater Bay. A group of Punjabis was taken from the pill boxes in the urban areas and sent to attack the enemy via Aberdeen but this attempt was unsuccessful as they ran into a strong force. After engaging the enemy they were eventually compelled to pull back.

A Canadian force attempted to relieve the Wong Nei Chong Gap by moving across country from Violet Hill, south of the gap, but were unable to do so due to the difficult nature of the country, their unfamiliarity with the terrain and fire from the enemy who held the high ground.

Following the death of Brigadier Lawson, the Commandant of the H.K.V.D.C., Colonel H.B. Rose, M.C., was made West Brigade Commander and the command of the Volunteers were taken over by Lieutenant Colonel E.J.R. Mitchell.

From the gap, the Japanese made attempts to gain the high ground of Mount Nicholson, to the west, which was held by the Royal Scots and Winnipeg Grenadiers. They succeeded in getting to the main ridge but could not secure the summit. The Grenadiers sent a company from Wanchai Gap along Black's Link but were unable to dislodge the Japanese. Still, the summit was held.

There was a party of defenders at a group of houses on the ridge about a quarter of a mile south of Wong Nei Chong Gap, on the east side of the Deepwater Bay Valley. Today there are several residential blocks on the site. On 21 December a platoon of the Royal Rifles of Canada managed to get through to them, but their other platoons, and the two platoons of Scottish Volunteers were unable to join them and the position remained isolated.

During the night, the Japanese had moved in force to Stanley Mound, between Repulse Bay and Stanley and the defending forces at the former were in danger of being cut off. Also during the night, a party was sent out from the Ridge, heading for Repulse Bay. In the pitch black, men became lost or stumbled into Japanese patrols. Some managed to find their way to the Repulse Bay Hotel area but less than a dozen made it to the hotel itself. The men rounded up in the hills, and other prisoners, were taken to Eucliff, which was then in Japanese hands, where they had their hands tied behind their backs, were roped together in threes and slaughtered. The only survivor was one of the men from the Ridge, Company Sergeant Major Hamlon, R.A.S.C., who was shot in the face and left for dead but who managed to crawl away.

On 21 December, it was decided to make another attempt to get through to Wong Nei Chong by going up through the Tai Tam Valley. However, by this time the valley was in the hands of the Japanese.

The force which made the attempt was made up of Number One Company of the Volunteers and two companies of the Royal

Rifles of Canada. The first phase was to advance east along the road from Stanley to the Tai Tam Tuk reservoir dam area, where the old road which leads up to Wong Nei Chong Gap branches off. Then the force was to push across country, around Violet Hill, and occupy the Stanley Gap. It was hoped that this would then allow the troops at Repulse Bay to break out and join the force in a combined attempt on Wong Nei Chong Gap.

Captain A.H. Penn, of the Volunteers, knew the country well and he suggested that the features, Notting Hill and Bridge Hill should be first secured. These two hills are on the north side of the road to the reservoir and completely dominate it. Once they were taken, the area around the dam, including the road junction, could be kept under observation and fire. Second Lieutenant B.S. Carter, who also knew the area well, was to lead the advance with ten riflemen from Number One Company of the Volunteers, followed by a platoon from the Royal Rifles of Canada. They were also strengthened by a section of Vickers guns from Number Two Company of the Volunteers under Lieutenant E.M. Bryden. The attacking force to advance along the road consisted of the Volunteers' bren carriers, of Number Three Platoon, the balance of Number One Company and the headquarters company of the Royal Rifles.

Both groups started out at about 9.15 a.m. The bren carriers soon came under heavy fire, one man being killed and another badly wounded. The Japanese were on Red Hill, which is on the east side of the road, directly opposite Notting Hill.

A section of Canadians tried to take Red Hill, but the strong force there killed two men and the attackers were thrown back. Meanwhile, Captain Penn had taken his light machine guns forward to bring fire onto a bungalow occupied by the enemy. However, these guns themselves came under heavy fire, with Penn and Second Lieutenant J. Redman hit. Sergeant N.L. White also received a wound from which he died. A request for reinforcements to take Red Hill was sent back to Stanley.

However, Volunteer bren carriers, had meanwhile been able to get almost up to the road junction. With them were some of Number One company and some Canadians. There was an enemy artillery position on the other side of the reservoir and the carriers were able to mow down the crew. Second Lieutenant Richard Edwards and some riflemen advanced, under cover of the carriers, but as the party advanced further it received heavy fire and

Edwards and Corporal J.M. Houghton were killed. The remainder fell back to the carriers. Sergeant G. Lemay took charge and decided to hold the position and wait for a covering party to come in from the party which was advancing over the hills.

Carter and his ten men had been able to take the first of the hills, Notting Hill, without any problems, but they ran up against stiff resistance from Bridge Hill, right above the junction, which was in possession of a strong party of Japanese. The platoon of Canadians closed up and a fight developed over several hours with the enemy finally being driven off the summit when the vegetation was set on fire. Lieutenant Bryden then brought up his machine guns and, at 2 p.m., they were able to target the road junction, but by then the carriers and riflemen had been forced to fall back. At about 4 p.m. tanks were seen across the valley and these were engaged. By 5 p.m. the Japanese on nearby Red Hill had greatly increased in strength and about an hour later the attack was over.

Once back at Stanley the two remaining Volunteer carriers were ordered to move to Repulse Bay to assist in the defence there. Meanwhile in the west, the Japanese, by 4 p.m., were attacking the Brick Hill area, held by the Middlesex Regiment. The gunboat HMS *Cicala* shelled the attackers and succeeded in breaking them up temporarily.

At Shouson Hill a party consisting of about 20 men of the Royal Navy Volunteers held two houses, and continued to do so until the surrender. The R.A.O.C. Depot at Little Hong Kong was held by about 50 men of the R.A.O.C. About 50 men from various units held another position in the area.

The Japanese succeeded in taking the Middlesex position on Brick Hill — the hill where Ocean Park is today — and beheaded any prisoners. Further along the hill, about where the sealions now frolic was a position of the H.K.S.R.A. which held out bravely before being overrun. Some of the original buildings can still be seen.

West of the Wong Nei Chong Gap, the Japanese were fighting their way against the Royal Scots along Mount Nicholson and Black's Link. Further north, the Japanese drove back the defenders, exposing the flank of 'B' Company of the Punjabis which was filling a gap between the Royal Scots and the Rajputs. The forces were repositioned and this was remedied.

A further counter-attack was arranged for 7 a.m. and the

Winnipeg Grenadiers struck out from Middle Gap. But the Japanese were well dug in on the slopes and at 8.15 a.m. the Canadians fell back, with the enemy then attacking and securing the hill top from where they could cover the western hillside, Middle Gap, and the eastern slope of the next hill, Mount Cameron. The Winnipeg Grenadiers were driven back still further to the next holding position, Mount Cameron.

Men of 'D' Company, the Winnipeg Grenadiers, were withdrawn from their pill boxes in the urban areas and moved to Wanchai Gap, east of Mount Cameron to act as a reserve. The headquarters of the Grenadiers was situated at this gap, together with West Brigade Headquarters.

Down by the waterfront, the Japanese pushed along towards Central and another major landing of troops took place at about 10.30 a.m. The Japanese had reached the area on the east side of what is now Victoria Park. An anti-aircraft gun manned by men of Number Six Company, of the Volunteers, at the Watson's Factory in Causeway Bay was knocked out. Heavy mortar fire rained on the naval yard and every gun was put out of action.

All medium machine guns were withdrawn from the south west sector and formed into two mobile platoons, with one being sent to the Aberdeen–Bennett's Hill area and the other joining the Middlesex at Leighton Hill. Fire from mortars and high-velocity guns continued to take out the pill boxes along the north shore.

Maltby tells how he received a telegram at 4 p.m. from the Military Attache at Chungking saying that a main Chinese counter-attack could not start before January 1 but that it was hoped that Chinese bombers would operate against Japanese airfields, a forlorn hope. Many involved in the fighting believed that a Chinese force would come to their aid. Later that night, Maltby received another telegram, from the War Office this time, telling him to destroy all oil storage and other important installations.

The defender's line now ran from the west side of Causeway Bay (Victoria Park) through Leighton Hill, the south end of the Happy Valley racecourse, up to Mount Cameron and then down to Bennet's Hill.

From north to south, the line was held by 'C' Company of the Punjabis, 'Z' Company of the Middlesex Regiment, 'B' Company of the Rajputs, 'B' Company of the Punjabis, Royal Scots companies, 'C' Company of the Winnipeg Grenadiers on Mount

Cameron, 'D' and 'B' Companies of the Grenadiers holding from Mount Cameron to Bennet's Hill inclusive, then mixed units of 'A' Company of the Middlesex, Royal Engineers, naval ratings, officers and men of the H.K.R.N.V.R. and others. There was no connection with the other force in the east at Stanley, nor the group at Repulse Bay as the Japanese had cut the island in two.

Repulse Bay was held by the two platoons of Number Two Company of the Volunteers, the two bren carriers from Number One Company, 'A' Company of the Royal Rifles of Canada, a platoon of the Middlesex Regiment and a naval party. At Stanley there were the First and Second Batteries and the remainders of Number One and Two Companies of the Volunteers, 'C' and part of 'D' Company of the Middlesex Regiment, and the remainder of the Royal Rifles.

Number Three Company of the Volunteers had practically ceased to exist after its stand at Wong Nei Chong. Some survivors linked up with the Middlesex element at Leighton Hill. Some had made it to Stanley. Some were with Number Six company in the urban area on anti-aircraft defence. Number Four and Number Seven Companies, which were well below strength, were forming a second line of defence behind Mount Cameron. Number Five Company was in the Mount Davis area as the threat of landings in the west could not be discounted. The Third Battery remained on Ap Lei Chau. Number Four and Number Five Batteries, at Pak Sha Wan and Sai Wan Hill had been written off. Two armoured cars remained serviceable and these were operating in the North Sector, having taken part in attempts to re-take Wong Nei Chong Gap.

At about 5 a.m. on 22 December, a message was telephoned to the men at the Ridge from the Repulse Bay hotel saying that they should make for the hotel after dark. But at 10 a.m., a Japanese attack came in which was, eventually, repulsed with considerable loss. Another attack was expected at any moment and headquarters said the position could either fight on, try to withdraw, or surrender.

There was no food or water, and at 3 p.m. mortar and shell fire intensified. A white flag was displayed but this was fired upon. When Lieutenant Colonel Macpherson went to the door holding the flag he was shot and fell wounded. When darkness fell, therefore, two men remained behind to take care of the wounded while 40 people split into two parties and left for the hills. The Japanese almost immediately entered the house where the 30 or so wounded were and murdered them.

One of the two retreating parties surrendered on the morning of 24 December, after having been surrounded. The other made for Repulse Bay, but when they arrived it was in Japanese hands and they were fired on from Eucliff. At 7.30 p.m. on 23 December that party, and some Canadian survivors, joined by Company Sergeant Major Hamlon, the only survivor of the Eucliff massacre, entered the sea to attempt to swim along the coastline to Stanley. The phosphorescence in the water gave away their plan, and several were hit, with others dying of cold and exhaustion. At 5 p.m. on 24 December three men reached Stanley after nearly 22 hours in the water. Hamlon and a few others who were incapable of swimming remained behind. Hamlon, Volunteer Company Quarter Master Sergeant J. Meyer and an officer, later reached Lamma Island.

A Canadian attempt, during the night, to push forward to cover the withdrawal from the Ridge had failed and the Canadians had retreated to the hotel. Heavy artillery fire was stepped up during the morning, coming in from positions at Middle Spur, at the western side of Repulse Bay. The two Volunteer bren carriers went into action against these positions and Number Six Platoon engaged them with machine gun fire from the ridge south west of the hotel. The guns at Stanley also fired and the position was improved a little. But the enemy continued its attacks and one of the carriers received a direct hit near the hotel, while the other was disabled near the road bridge at South Bay. The bren carrier men then joined up with Number Six platoon and the Volunteers held the area immediately above the hotel while the Canadians fell back to the hotel itself.

It became quite clear that a withdrawal would have to be made and, initially, the plan was that the civilians, including women and children, would withdraw with the soldiers. Number Six platoon was to guard them. But then it was felt that their presence with troops would actually increase their risk as they tried to make their way to Stanley, so it was decided that they should remain in the hotel.

It should be borne in mind that many millions of dollars have been spent in recent years in improving the drainage system at Repulse Bay and a major extension of the sand area has been carried out. The beach, in 1941, was nothing like as big as it is now, though of course the east-west dimensions have not changed. In 1941, a large pipe ran from the hotel down to the Lower Beach Road and then up to the road to Stanley. The plan was to make the withdrawal through this tunnel but, if it was to work, it was essential that the Japanese be prevented from moving down to the Lower Beach Road area. Number Six platoon was, therefore, ordered to move towards the Violet Hill area to forestall this, and throughout the afternoon they fought off enemy attacks. Again, the undergrowth was set on fire, to drive back snipers. At 4 p.m. the platoon withdrew, leaving a section under Sergeant T. Stainton to hold on.

At 7.30 p.m. the Volunteers went out with orders to hold the South Bay bridge at all costs, from 8 p.m. until 3 a.m. the following morning. A few Japanese snipers were eliminated and the bridge secured. Then the difficult withdrawal began. The moment that a position was vacated by troops pulling back to the hotel it would be overrun by the Japanese.

One enemy patrol managed to enter the north wing of the hotel, but was driven back with hand-grenades bowled down the corridors which had hitherto echoed only to the merry tread of holidaying guests.

The plan to withdraw through the tunnel proved impractical on grounds of noise. It was decided after the first three men had entered the tunnel that even though the men had removed their boots, the clanking of their weapons and equipment would have quickly given the game away. The remainder of the party made for the road. Lieutenant 'Benny' Prolux, of the Naval Volunteers, came back up the tunnel to see where the rest of the men were and found that the Japanese were already in the hotel.

The soldiers who had decided against escaping through the tunnel went to the bridge and then broke into small parties which successfully made their way to Stanley. Nearly all the wounded were taken with the withdrawing group. However, two Volunteers had to be left behind and they owed their lives to the courage of the hotel's nursing sister who stood between them and the invading Japanese.

The bridge had been heavily attacked at about 10 p.m., but the Volunteers had managed to hold on. One section was overrun, but bayonets and machine gun fire pushed back the attackers. Over the next five hours many more assaults were made and it was not until the ordered time, 3 a.m., that the Volunteers eventually withdrew back along the main road. On their way to Stanley they ran into a Japanese patrol and drove it off with grenades and a burst from a Thompson sub-machine gun.

At Stanley, the troops who held the bridge joined up with Four and Five Platoons who were in a forward part of the area, at Stanley View. The Volunteers, under Lemay, moved on southwards, through the village, and linked up with the remnants of Number One Company, now commanded by Second Lieutenant B.S. Carter.

Throughout 22 December, the Japanese had been attacking strongly all through the island. Since the failure of the attack on the dam the previous day, they had been pouring reinforcements into the Tai Tam Tuk area and from the morning onwards had been shelling from there. The Canadians in the forward area fought very bravely against repeated attacks throughout the day, inflicting heavy casualties, but steadily the Japanese advanced, despite the stiff resistance. Stanley Mound, the 386-metre peak at the landward end of the peninsula, north of the road, fell.

Maltby realized that it was highly improbable that the forces of the two brigades would be able to link up again. That evening, he recorded: 'I realised that the force under the command of Brigadier Wallis (East Infantry Brigade) was unlikely to have any effect on the outcome of the battle and all that could be expected of it was to fight a defensive action with its back to the Stanley Peninsular.'

The Japanese continued to pour reinforcements across the harbour and onto the island, while on the front from Causeway Bay to Bennet's Hill were the remains of the 228th and 230th Regiments and another newly landed regiment. Two battalions of the 229th were at Bennet's Hill and Repulse Bay. In the Stanley–Tai Tam area was the divisional reserve, together with another regiment.

During the morning of 22 December the Canadians on Mount Cameron were heavily dive-bombed and mortared, while the Royal Scots on Stubbs road were being heavily mortared from the western slopes of Jardine's Lookout. By the early afternoon, the Japanese were attacking the lower slopes of Mount Nicholson to within 100 yards of the Royal Scots there. Bombing raids, with a high degree of accuracy, were almost continuous.

Rose, the former Volunteer commandant, now in charge of West Brigade, assessed the situation at 1 p.m. The enemy was concentrating large numbers of troops on a front three-quarters of a mile long, in the area between the lower southern slopes of Mount Cameron and Little Hong Kong. It seemed possible that an attack would come from that area towards Wan Chai Gap, avoiding the defensive position on Mount Cameron by passing to the west of it. Rose, therefore, brought up Numbers Four and Seven Companies of the Volunteers to a line running from Wanchai Gap to Mount Kellett. Lieutenant G.H. Calvert brought all remaining troops from Volunteer headquarters to the line. Rose also drew up a plan of defensive artillery fire.

During the afternoon there was a very strong attack on the area held by the 'B' Company of the Punjabis, who were near the Royal Scots. They beat back the attack, but were reduced to eight men. A gap was, however, opened between the left flank of the Royal Scots and the right flank of the Punjabis. 'B' Company of the Rajputs attacked the Japanese flank and prevented the gap being developed and men of the Middlesex regiment were moved up. An attack south of Mount Cameron was driven off by 'D' Company of the Grenadiers.

Artillery was used to destroy the big oil installations at Tsun Wan, Tai Kok Tsui and the Royal Navy tanks about a mile south of the Cosmopolitan Docks, but the tanks at Lai Chi Kok could not be fired on as they were near to a prison hospital.

The situation was increasingly grim.

Headquarters received notification at 1.20 a.m. that the water supply from the Tai Tam reservoirs had been cut off. The supply from the Aberdeen reservoir had been out of action for at least two days and only a trickle of water was coming through from the Pokfulam Reservoir. 'The town is now helpless,' it was reported. Shortage of water was affecting both troops and the civilian population.

Ten minutes later, headquarters was informed by Rose of the loss of Mount Cameron, with troops coming back in disorder and efforts being made to rally them at Magazine Gap and at Mount Gough. However, the Wan Chai Gap, the gap just east of Mount Cameron, was still in the hands of 'A' Company of the Royal Scots, marines and some engineers.

Mount Cameron was held by 'C' Company of the Winnipeg Grenadiers and a few others. Soon after midnight, the Japanese had made a strong attack and, in a series of fanatical charges, disregarding heavy losses, had broken up the overall position of the outnumbered defenders into small pockets fighting individually. Some survivors had made their way back to Magazine Gap, the next gap from Wanchai Gap, while others tried to fight on. A reinforcing party of about 40 or 50 Royal Marines was sent to the Royal Scots at Wanchai Gap. There was a lot of confused fighting in the darkness, but at dawn it was found that the Japanese held the summit of Mount Cameron. Though Wanchai Gap held, the West Brigade headquarters was pulled back to Magazine Gap. The Japanese were seen to be reinforcing their positions.

At 9 a.m., the mixed detachment in the Little Hong Kong magazines reported that the enemy was advancing in strength upon the area and on Bennet's Hill. The attack on the latter developed and there was considerable bombing from the air of Aberdeen and other areas. However, the hill was still held. At 1.30 p.m., Wan Chai and Magazine Gaps were both heavily attacked by dive-bombers.

During the morning, the situation at the northern urban areas of the island had also become critical. The Rajputs, who were on the right of the Middlesex stationed at Leighton Hill, had suffered greatly from constant attacks and were few in number and with little ammunition. They fell back at about 8 a.m., exposing the right flank of the Middlesex party. At 9.22 a.m., the Middlesex commander reported that he was down to 40 effective men and six Vickers guns but that he was still managing to hold on. With the Middlesex were seven survivors of Number Three Company of the Volunteers. The enemy was infiltrating the area around them. About 40 minutes later, the position was heavily shelled and a further bombardment by artillery and mortars came in at about 11 a.m. All the positions of the platoon were destroyed. A party of about 50 men was collected from Fortress headquarters consisting of gunners, spare signallers and some Royal Scots who had returned from hospital treatment. This party went to the Lee Theatre. At 3 p.m. the Leighton Hill and Lee Theatre positions were still being held against fierce attack.

By noon on 22 December the defenders' line ran from a pill box on the north shore, to Leighton Hill, to Canal Road, to Wanchai Gap and down again to Bennet's Hill.

At 5.30 p.m. the Royal Scots made a counter attack on Mount Cameron and managed to secure a foothold on the western slopes. They held this through the night. During the early evening an ammunition convoy managed to get through to the magazines at

Little Hong Kong but two of the eight lorries were knocked out on the return journey and had to be abandoned.

Meanwhile, at Stanley, the opportunity was taken while the Japanese paused after their considerable losses on 22 and 23 December, to organize the defences around Stanley Village.

On 23 December, Stanley Mound changed hands twice but eventually it was the Japanese who held it. A party of Number Two Company of the Volunteers, held a position on a feature known as Stanley View. The Japanese assaulted the forward portion of this position but they came under flanking fire from a Volunteer position which was only about 150 yards away and the attackers were almost wiped out. During the afternoon, more attacks were made, most of which were against the section which held the ground overlooking the main road to Stanley. Lance Corporal W. Sharp was killed and several men were wounded. The Volunteers fell back on a ridge which ran from Stanley View to the Chung Hom Kok peninsula where they beat off infantry attacks, despite being exposed to harassing fire from the higher ground of Stanley Mound above and immediately to the north of them.

Brigadier Wallis decided that he could no longer hold the line of hills overlooking the Stanley Peninsula and he therefore made the decision to concentrate his resistance on the flatter ground. There were to be three lines. The first was to the north of the Stanley village itself, the second ran immediately south of the main buildings of St. Stephen's College and the third ran from the preparatory school to Tweed Bay. Orders were sent to the Volunteers at Stanley View to fall back to the village. Major H.R. Forsyth, took command of the advanced area as forward commander.

The men of the three platoons of Number Two Company were later ordered to move to Chung Hom Kok, where there was a party of Canadians, and to defend that peninsula. Stanley Village itself was held by the 10-men of the Number Two Company Headquarters, who were just southeast of the old police station. At the east of the village were the Volunteers of the Stanley Platoon — the prison officers' unit — with a Middlesex machine gun section in support. The platoon was in the area just to the north east of the old police station, while the Middlesex machine gunners were in a building known as Number One bungalow — just in the fork where Stanley Village Road splits into Tung Tau Wan Woad and Wong Ma Kok Road. On the right was a company of Middlesex with part of 'A' Company of the Royal Rifles of Canada. The ridge known as Monastery Hill was defended by a section of Number One Company of the Volunteers, under Corporal E.C. Drown, and a platoon of the Middlesex.

The second line of defence, immediately south of Saint Stephen's College ran north-east at an angle of about 30 degrees from about the smaller, more northerly, of the two piers at St. Stephen's beach to a pillbox on the coast of Tai Tam Bay. This line was defended by the First Battery of the Volunteers, which had come from Cape D'Aguilar, with a section of Number One Company, north-east of the prison, while the remainder of the company and a platoon of Middlesex were in the area of the preparatory school. Of course, there were members of the Royal Artillery and other units from the fort at Stanley among the defenders.

The remnants of 'A' company, headquarters of 'D' company and the headquarters company, and all of 'D' Company of the Royal Rifles of Canada were also at Stanley Village. The headquarters of the Stanley Force was moved to the Officers' Mess at the prison.

As the men of Number Two Company of the Volunteers who had been ordered to move to Chung Hom Kok moved out, they ran into the right flank of the attacking force. Hand-to-hand fighting took place and they fought their way through, capturing some Japanese equipment. However, the Japanese counter-attacked and Number Six Platoon was forced to fall back. Number Five Platoon was cut off, but managed to fight its way back to join the defenders at the third line of defence. During the night the other two platoons held their ground, though under constant attack. Sergeant T.F. Stainton was badly wounded by a Japanese officer who was 'dealt with' by Corporal W.E. McFarlane.

An attack at Stanley came shortly before 11 p.m., when three Japanese tanks advanced along the road. A light anti-tank gun made two direct hits on the first two, while the third retired. A strong infantry attack followed, with the main thrust coming in on the left flank. The Stanley Platoon, the small headquarters element of Number Two Company and the Middlesex machine gunners stood firm and beat back each wave.

At 10.30 p.m., Major Forsyth, the forward area commander was again seriously wounded and he was moved into the school house next to the police station. Other Volunteers were going down and

Lieutenant Fitzgerald, commanding the Stanley platoon called for reinforcements. Just after midnight, the platoon was forced to fall back to the area of the Number One bungalow being held by the Middlesex. The Japanese had taken the beach at the east of Stanley Bay and were able to bring heavy machine gun fire to bear. The Middlesex guns had been hit, as had 14 of the 28 men in the Stanley Platoon. All members of the company headquarters unit had also been wounded.

At 1 a.m. on Christmas Day, the decision was made to withdraw to the next position. The survivors of the Stanley Platoon and some Middlesex men made a dangerous withdrawal along Wong Ma Kok Road, being joined by some survivors of Forsyth's unit. Forsyth himself was too badly wounded to move and so he and Company Sergeant Major T. Swan stayed behind to fight to the finish. The retreating party made it through to the preparatory school.

Meanwhile, on the right, the Japanese had fought their way along the road from Stanley Main Beach, in the west, and were pouring fire on the remaining Middlesex who continued firing until they were overrun. The remaining elements of the Royal Rifles, exhausted, were ordered to fall back to Stanley Fort, and did so via Tung Tau Wan Road.

The Japanese were now at the narrow neck of the Stanley Peninsula, with the defenders on the St Stephen's College line. Isolated elements of Volunteers and Middlesex still held Monastery Hill but these were no real threat to the enemy's rear.

At the defensive line, a platoon of Middlesex held the centre of the ridge, while the First Battery of Volunteers held the line between Wong Ma Kok and Tung Tau Wan Roads (then known as Fort and Prison Roads). At the extreme right, the Volunteer section of Sergeant H.J. Millington lined Tung Tau Wan Road, Second Lieutenant H.S. Jones had a section covering the entrance to the college from that road. To his left was a section under Second Lieutenant H.G. Muir, near a bungalow known as Barton's Bungalow, and a section which held the lower slopes at the south end of the large sports ground. Other troops were also in the area.

At about 2 a.m. the Japanese pressed an attack along Tung Tau Wan Road and the section on either side of the road found itself in a fierce fire fight. The next attack went in on the other side, across the football ground, where the machine guns mowed down the advancing enemy. The attack then developed right across the line.

The section on the Tung Tau Wan road where the attack was pressed home most strongly was badly mauled.

Throughout the night the fight went on, with the enemy losing many dead and wounded, and the defenders being steadily thinned out. Captain G.F. Rees, of the Volunteers was badly wounded and put out of action. Shortly before daylight, the enemy stormed the ridge just south of the tennis courts and two of the Middlesex guns there were overrun, the enemy succeeding in breaking through the centre of the line. The two Volunteer sections on the eastern flank were pushed back towards the prison and Sergeant Millington was killed. Second Lieutenant Jones, whose section was at the school entrance, brought his men to the rescue and they tried to retake the positions, but failed against very heavy enemy superiority. Jones was killed in the attempt, along with half his men. The remaining Volunteers were pushed back.

In the east, the enemy was also attacking strongly and the two sections were forced to withdraw. They fell back on the preparatory school and rallied with the Middlesex men there to maintain the fight. At Barton's Bungalow the Volunteers managed to fight off heavy attacks but were eventually forced out by an enemy flame-thrower. However, the Volunteers counter-attacked and succeeded, in a fierce hand-to-hand fight, in retaking the area. Still the attacks went on, and eventually Second Lieutenant Muir and his men went down in a hail of gunfire and flashing of bayonets and swords. There were no survivors.

The Japanese casualties in the battle for the ridge, held by about 70 Volunteer gunners and 30 Middlesex, were very high indeed. The civilian soldiers and their Middlesex comrades had held off to the last a force of highly-trained, tough and experienced Japanese fighting men. Of the three officers and 65 men of the battery, 35 were killed and five were wounded.

As the cold light of dawn broke that Christmas Day, the position at Stanley was confused. Some Volunteers and Middlesex had managed to get back to the fort from Monastery Hill. So had the remainder of the Stanley Platoon which was ordered as head-quarters guard for the last stand. The Canadians, with some others, had been ordered to hold the ridge behind St. Stephen's College, and had been involved in a brave but deadly counter-attack. The survivors of First Battery and Number Five Platoon had made their way to the fort. At the preparatory school, the last part of the Middlesex and Volunteer force hung on but the Japanese had pushed through to the Tweed Area. Second Lieutenant Carter of the Volunteers and his counterpart subaltern decided that they had no option but to withdraw. The Volunteer section from Monastery Ridge and the section that was north east of the prison had withdrawn with their guns and equipment.

The final line was set up on the steep ridge which leads up from the flat land of St. Stephen's College.

The Japanese did not, in fact, make a major infantry attack at Stanley on Christmas Day, but a large body of troops could be seen gathering across Stanley Bay on the Chung Hom Kok Peninsula, getting ready to attack there. Mortar and artillery fire, together with air raids on the Stanley line went on all day. The two six-inch guns of Bluff Battery, manned by the Volunteers, opened up on the enemy at Chung Hom Kok and, in return, received heavy counter-bombardment which crippled one of the guns.

Exhausted after constant fighting, with little food and scarce water, with all Volunteer and Middlesex machine guns knocked out, few mortars and no mortar bombs, the defenders stuck to their lines and awaited the final attack.

Over at Chung Hom Kok, the two platoons of Number Two Company of the Volunteers had been by-passed and the Japanese had taken the two six-inch guns at the fort on the headland. A counter-attack was decided on and a fighting patrol of 12 men attacked the enemy which was at the summit. They got within 50 yards of their goal before being forced back, with Private I.F. Grant actually reaching the summit, where he was killed. Half the men were hit and the patrol pulled back.

The main defensive positions were in a very precarious position, under constant mortar and machine-gun fire and it was decided to attempt to fight a way through to Stanley. A plan to attempt to locate sampans came to nothing and it was decided that at nightfall every man should try to make his own way through. The bombardment continued throughout the afternoon and, after darkness fell the breakout was made, with some swimming Stanley Bay and others travelling overland. However, by the time they arrived, the surrender had been ordered.

Early on Christmas morning, as fighting was still going on, the Japanese stormed the main building of St. Stephen's College where an emergency hospital had been set up. The hospital was under the Command of Lt. Col. G.D.R. Black of Volunteer headquarters. With him was a captain, named Whitney, from the Royal Army Medical Corps, a sister from the Military Hospital, and European and Chinese nurses, including those of the Nursing Detachment of the Volunteers. There were also nurses of the St. John Ambulance Brigade.

On rushing into the hospital, the frenzied Japanese troops started bayoneting the wounded men, driving their bayonets clear through the wounded and the mattresses underneath. When Lieutenant Colonel Black tried to stop them by blocking a doorway, he was immediately shot and bayoneted dozens of times as he lay on the floor. The same thing happened to Whitney. Soon all the 56 patients in the main hall had been slaughtered. Some managed to hide, including Company Sergeant Major Begg who had been one of the three survivors of the Eucliff massacre.

The following day, the surviving wounded and the orderlies, about 40 in all, were confined to a small upper floor. As the day went on, a few died, while the remainder were taken out and killed. At about 5 p.m. a Japanese officer told the survivors that Hong Kong had surrendered, which was lucky for them. The walking wounded were made to carry the dead bodies to a large fire which had been made during the evening out of school desks.

The women were raped repeatedly, three Volunteer nurses being amongst those who died. Again a Japanese officer told those who managed to survive that they were lucky that Hong Kong had surrendered.

Back in the Western Sector, the situation on 23 and 24 December was worsening.

On 24 December, Leighton Hill fell to the attackers. The Middlesex Regiment had held the area, including the hill. The line then ran south of the race course to the Morrison Hill area and Mount Parrish on the south side of Queen's Road East, near the Stubbs Road junction, where the Wah Yan College stands. This area was held by surviving Punjabis and Rajputs, including men collected from hospitals. Near Mount Parish were the Royal Marines. A number of houses near the junction of Morrison Hill Road and Queen's Road East were held by a small party of Middlesex and some Volunteers from Number Three Company who had been involved in the fight up at the Wong Nei Chong Gap.

The situation on Mount Cameron had stabilized, with the Royal Scots holding their slope positions. But it was reported during the morning that the Japanese were reinforcing with an estimated 400 men.

The line which ran from the St. Albert's Hospital up to Wanchai Gap was also held by the Royal Scots and then the area down to Bennet's Hill was held by the Winnipeg Grenadiers, with elements of the Royal Navy, the Royal Navy Volunteer Reserve and the Hong Kong Royal Navy Volunteer Reserve. Little Hong Kong was still in British hands and a Hong Kong Navy Volunteers' party held the top of Shouson Hill.

The Japanese built up their attack on the Leighton Hill area throughout the morning, with the positions there been severely harassed by artillery and mortar concentrations and by dive-bombing from the air.

An initial attack went in at about the middle of the day but was beaten back with heavy losses. At 3 p.m. the Middlesex Regiment reported that they were being attacked from three sides; they were being surrounded and most of the houses in the area were on fire. At about 4.45 p.m. orders were given that the position should be abandoned and two officers and 40 other ranks pulled back, suffering about 20 per cent casualties in the process. They joined up with the party of Royal Artillery and Royal Scots in the Lee Theatre and Canal Road area. However, eight men remained behind at Leighton Hill as their retreat was cut off. They included two members of Number Three Company of the Volunteers, Privates L.A. Fox and H. Wong, who both eventually escaped. Fox later made his way to Chungking and subsequently fought in Burma.

The Japanese had turned their attention to Morrison Hill and the shelling and mortar fire was directed at the Middlesex party there. All the seven machine guns were destroyed, but most of the crews survived as they had moved to cover ready to rush out and man the guns as the enemy infantry came in. A 30-strong party was sent out from Fortress Headquarters, made up of headquarters personnel, such as military police, clerks and signallers. The hill was held until the surrender.

Large fires broke out in the urban areas and these severely restricted movement. One large fire was near the China Fleet Club, while other targets, such as the naval yard, Victoria Barracks and Fortress Headquarters, were under constant artillery attack. The exhausted civilian firefighters asked for military assistance but there were no men to spare.

On 24 December, the Japanese also turned their attention to two other hospitals. The Jockey Club buildings at the racecourse housed an emergency hospital and the Japanese arrived there in the evening. Four nurses were raped, but a massacre was prevented by the bravery of Dr J.A. Selby who got the victorious troops drunk. At St. Albert's Hospital, a massacre was prevented by the fact that the attackers found one of their own wounded officers in bed, being well cared for.

It was said that, throughout the battle, there was only one case of a wounded British soldier being cared for by the Japanese. This was Private J.E. Mogra, of Number Three Company of the Volunteers. He had been shot at Wong Nei Chong Gap but he knew Japanese, having been born and brought up there. An officer ordered that he be picked up with the Japanese wounded and given water, however, he refused Mogra's appeal for the same to be done for other wounded. Mogra died on 10 January, but told his story to other prisoners.

Fighting was, of course, going on at Stanley on the night of 24–25 December. In the early hours of the morning, the Japanese also attacked the line in the Bennet's Hill area and established positions on the north east slopes. At 3 a.m. they pushed forward, trying to work their way around to the west, but were held up by the H.K.R.N.V.R., whose only support was a single 4.5 inch howitzer.

At about 8 a.m. the Japanese managed to advance east of Bennet's hill. 'B' Company of the Winnipeg Grenadiers prepared to attack, but an impromptu local truce occurred and when this was over the opportunity had passed. More Japanese were thrown into the attack and, by 2 p.m., the hill was completely surrounded and surrendered. This meant that other members of the Grenadiers, of the H.K.R.N.V.R. and other units, lower down in the area were forced to withdraw and Aberdeen was in real danger.

In the Happy Valley area, the problems intensified. Holding the line from the Lee Theatre to the sea were the remains of 'B' and 'C' Companies of the Punjabis, with a mixed force of British and Indian gunners, and wounded men of the Royal Scots from the hospitals.

Part of 'B' Company of the Middlesex Regiment and a collection of stragglers held Morrison Hill. The houses nearer the racecourse were held by the remainder of the Middlesex company and some Volunteers. 'B' Company of the Rajputs was on Mount Parish to the south of which were the marines. The Royal Scots held the line from the marine positions to St. Albert's and up to Wanchai Gap. The decision was taken to remove the remaining Middlesex men from their pill boxes and send them to back up the Punjabis. The whole of the shore line was therefore the responsibility of Number Five Company of the Volunteers.

Just before dawn, a Bofors gun dispersed an enemy concentration at the the area now occupied by the Royal Hong Kong Regiment headquarters. The enemy continued to move ahead, infiltrating the area around Canal Road and by 7 a.m. it was reported that certain units had made it as far west as the China Fleet Club. At 8.30 a.m. it was reported to Fortress Headquarters that new line was organized, running from the Royal Naval Hospital (now the Ruttonjee Sanatorium) through Wanchai Market to the junction of Hennessy Road and O'Brien Road in Wanchai. Fighting in the urban areas was difficult for the defenders who were unable to make full use of their artillery because of the danger of innocent casualties — a restriction which did not bother the Japanese.

The battle was moving to its close. At 9 a.m. on Christmas Day, two civilians who had been captured at the Repulse Bay Hotel by the Japanese came across the harbour, bringing a verbal message that the enemy was in great strength. However, according to the messengers, the Japanese intended not to initiate any hostile activity between 10 a.m. and noon while surrender was considered. A meeting was called by the Governor and it was decided to take no action on the message. Although the infantry attacks did appear to halt, some bombing and shelling apparently continued elsewhere.

Promptly at noon a huge barrage began, while hand-to-hand fighting was taking place at Mount Parish and nearby. At 1 p.m., the Middlesex and Rajputs successfully fought off a Japanese advance and the Wanchai market was held, although Mount Parish was reported to have fallen. The junction of Kennedy Road and Queen's Road East was now in Japanese hands, opening an advance to the rear of Victoria Barracks and Fortress Headquarters. Ironically, the original conception of this road, decades before, had been to allow defenders to move easily along behind Victoria Barracks to repel attackers. The road was obstructed and, further along, a platoon of Punjabis moved up to the road.

At 1.40 p.m. there were only six guns from the defenders'
mobile artillery in action. Reinforcements of about 50 Punjabis
reached the Middlesex, but pressure was increasing and, at 2.30
p.m., a further withdrawal was necessary. At the same time,
Wanchai Gap and Magazine Gap were being pounded by dive-
bombers and the vegetation was alight. The Royal Scots had been
forced off Mount Cameron and were at Wanchai Gap which was
also under heavy bomb and mortar attack. A Japanese infantry
attack at noon was beaten off, but it was reported soon after 2.40
p.m. that the gap had fallen. Magazine Gap appeared to be holding but was in serious difficulty.

Ten minutes later, the Middlesex group reported that their line
was breaking up but that they would withdraw to a line along
O'Brien Street, just to the east of the Southorn Playground in
Wanchai. Maltby recorded:

As far as is known Major Marsh's detached force in the Little Hong Kong
area was still holding out, but there had been no communication with him
for some time. Bennet's Hill had been seriously attacked, had been completely surrounded, and by 15.00 hours had been forced to surrender.
With Stanley I had no communications and no information. The
Canadian Line north of Bennet's Hill had been forced to retire. This
advance by the enemy along the line of gaps, the possession of those gaps
by him, thus giving him an open road to the Central District, the fall of
Bennet's Hill, the isolation of such superior forces and armament, the
exhaustion after 16 days of continuous battle with no reliefs for any
individuals, our vulnerability to unlimited air attack, the impossibility of
obtaining more ammunition for the few mobile guns I had left, the serious
water famine immediately impending — these were the factors which led
to the inevitable conclusion, namely that further fighting meant the useless slaughter of the remainder of the garrison, risked severe retaliation
on the large civilian population and could not affect the final outcome.
The enemy drive along the North Shore was decisive.

I asked Lieutenant Colonel Stewart, OC First Middlesex, how much
longer in his considered opinion the men could hold the line occupied. He
replied: 'One Hour'. The Commodore with every officer and rating at his
last post, agreed with my conclusion.

At 15.15 I advised H.E. The Governor, that no further useful military
resistance was possible and I therefore ordered all commanding officers
to break off the fighting and capitulate to the nearest Japanese Commander, as and when the enemy advanced and opportunity offered.

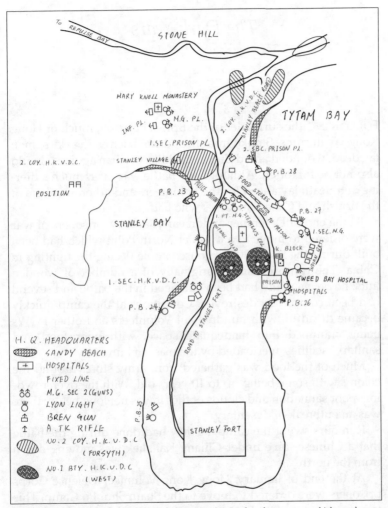

This map illustrates the position of the Volunteers at Stanley. It is based upon a map which was drawn on a silk handkerchief by a survivor shortly after the battle.

13

The Dark Years

FOLLOWING the surrender of the British garrison, much of Hong Kong lay in ruins. Smoke from fires drifted across the skies, men lay dead, wounded and dying in the hills. Civilian agonies should also not be forgotten. Although the battle was over, much suffering and death lay ahead for the Volunteers and other members of the British and Canadian forces who had survived.

At the end of December and in early January, prisoners of war were ordered to move to a camp at North Point which had been built during the late 1930s to house people fleeing the fighting in China. The camp consisted originally of a number of wooden huts, however, many had been damaged in the battle and several had been completely destroyed. Conditions at the camp quickly became dreadful, with hundreds of Volunteers and other POWs being crammed into inadequate space, with poor food and sanitary facilities overloaded by the mass of humanity.

Much of the food was gathered from army stores around the colony, with some being up to 10 years old. With the overcrowding, poor sanitation and clouds of flies it was not long before there was an outbreak of dysentery.

Rumours swept the camp, as they had done during the battle that a Chinese force under Chiang Kai-shek was moving down from the north.

At the end of January, Hong Kong Volunteer Defence Corps prisoners were ordered to move to the Sham Shui Po Camp. This large camp, opposite Stonecutters Island had been constructed during the 1920s as a main base in Kowloon. It consisted, in fact, of three main camp areas; Jubilee, Hankow and Nanking. The Volunteers crossed the harbour by ferry and then walked through the streets of Kowloon to the camp. They were initially placed in the Jubilee Building, an accomodation and office block on the waterfront at the soutern end of the camp. The building had been thoroughly looted and there was no furniture, beds or bedding, the plumbing had been badly damaged and there was no water.

Instead of the bully beef and occasional biscuits that had been the fare at North Point, rice became the staple diet at Shamshuipo. As the months past, the Volunteers, through their ties to the outside community, started to receive additional food brought to the camp fence, often at great risk, by family and friends. However, the diet was never adequately balanced and it was not long before cases of beri-beri, dysentery and other diseases began to appear. Sanitation was very poor with no flushing system and this added to the miseries of the prisoners. Deaths became more frequent.

Despite the poor condition of the prisoners of war, work parties were a key element of life in the camp. Each day, the prisoners paraded for work parties, with the Japanese receiving much help from a British major who quickly turned collaborator. A large work project was the extension of the runway at Kai Tak Airport. Each day, prisoners rose at about 5.30 a.m. for a bowl of rice and a parade, before marching out to labour with hand tools and wicker baskets, shifting earth and toiling in the summer heat. When it became apparent that these simple methods were slow, the Japanese provided narrow-guage rails and wheeled boxes. Dynamite was used to shatter the rock or hard soil and the prisoners then had to work to meet their punishing quotas. Other work parties were used in various back-breaking projects elsewhere.

By the middle of the summer, the Japanese had decided to ship what they considered the 'trouble makers' from Sham Shui Po camp to Japan, where they would be used as slave labour. This first batch of 'Undesirables' was selected and its 600 members were loaded onto a small Japanese freighter. With no toilet or medical facilities, dysentery caused many deaths during the journey.

The second batch of prisoners of war sailed from Hong Kong on 27 September; 1,800 prisoners loaded into the cargo ship, the *Lisbon Maru*. The POWs were crammed deep in the holds of the ship. Above them were loaded about a thousand Japanese troops, and stores which had been looted from the colony. There was virtually no ventilation and only a few buckets for sanitation. In addition to dysentery, diptheria broke out and spread rapidly.

At about 7 a.m. on 1 October, there was a sudden explosion and the ship rocked violently; it had been hit by a torpedo fired by an

American submarine. The *Lisbon Maru* had displayed nothing to indicate that it was carrying prisoners. Those prisoners who did manage to escape were fired on by the Japanese and many were killed in the water. Soon about 840 of those who had sailed were dead and another 200 were to die in the following weeks.

Those POWs who arrived in Japan after surviving the hellish journey from Hong Kong, in either these or later batches, were put to work in railway yards, factories and warehouses where they were used as slave labour.

Those remaining behind at Sham Shui Po continued to suffer the miseries of incarceration. Outside the wire the suffering was also intense. Shortly after the end of the battle, the Japanese had ordered a high proportion of the Hong Kong population to leave the territory and much suffering and death had resulted. For those left behind the situation was grave.

Escapes were few, but one that was to have a significant effect in leading to the setting up of the British Army Aid Group took place on 9 January 1942. Lieutenant-Colonel Lindsay Ride, commander of the H.K.V.D.C.'s Field Ambulance, escaped with Lance Corporal Francis Lee Yiu-piu, also of the Field Ambulance, and Lieutenant D.W. Morley and Sub-Lieutenant D.F. Davies, both members of the Hong Kong Royal Naval Volunteer Reserve. After a hair-raising journey, the party arrived at Waichow (now Huizhou) on 18 January. They then set out for Kukong, where they met with Lieutenant-Colonel Harry Owen-Hughes, of the Volunteers, who had been ordered to leave Hong Kong during the battle in an attempt to link up with the Chinese Nationalist forces and thus threaten the attackers from the rear. Orders were received from Chungking that Morley and Davies were to proceed to Burma, and Lee was to attend guerrilla training school. Ride was ordered to report to the British Embassy at Chungking, which he reached on 17 February. A few months later, the British Army Aid Group was set up and this became a key part of the anti-Japanese resistance, carrying out intelligence, counter-intelligence, rescue and resistance operations throughout the rest of the war.

In his book, *BAAG, Hong Kong Resistance 1942–1945*, Lindsay Ride's son, Edwin Ride recorded that, by the time it was disbanded,

The BAAG had rendered assistance to 33 escapers belonging to the British and Allied services; to over 400 Indians, 140 of whom were in the forces and whose escapes were wholly engineered by it; and to nearly 40 American evaders, who were brought to safety through the BAAG network. It passed into the prison camps medicines, messages, information and escape aids, giving comfort and hope to those who had been forced to endure the horrors of internment. It provided relatives with news of prisoners. It helped nearly 1,000 Chinese members and civil employees of the British services and supported them, and in many cases their families also, in China. It assisted nearly 120 Europeans and over 550 Chinese civilians out of enemy territory. It founded and trained a China Unit which later served with distinction in Burma. It planned and supervised the spending of over three million Chinese dollars of British funds for famine and refugee relief; and its food and hosptial services saved the lives of thousands in famine, epidemics and air raids. Through its information service it maintained pro-Allied morale among the guerrilla forces and civilian population in South China. It helped the Chinese armies with demolition operations during the battle for Kweilin. It set up an intelligence service when information from Hong Kong was entirely lacking and provided data vital to air and naval operations in the China threatre. Above all, through the BAAG an active British resistance was maintained in Hong Kong and South China in defiance of the Japanese occupation.

Chinese enrolment in the defence forces had greatly increased in the run-up to 1941 and, in December of that year, the government had decided to form a unit of Regular soldiers, all Chinese, to be known as the Hong Kong Chinese Regiment. At the outbreak of war, this unit had not been recruited up to strength but many of its members took part in the fighting. After the surrender, Chinese members of the Volunteers and of other units, including the Chinese regiment, were informally advised that they could 'slip away.' Many, therefore, escaped into China and linked up with the British Army Aid Group, continuing on to its headquarters at Kweilin. Colonel Ride recalled:

Buildings were rented and converted into barracks and all service personnel put under strict military discipline. Courses in Infantry Training, small arms and signalling were conducted by officers and the camp supplied the daily guard at BAAG Headquarters, and special guards of honour for any official British function in Kweilin. This incidentally had a great deal to do with raising British military prestige, for the daily changing of guard ceremony at BAAG Headquarters became a very popular spectacle with the Chinese.

Most of our agents and Chinese staff were recruited from amongst these people, and many of them obtained employment with the US Airforce and with other British organisations, but a large number still remained on our strength. A scheme was put forward that they should be formed into a unit and sent to India and Burma for further service. The 127 who joined this unit (later known as the Hong Kong Volunteer Company) afterwards served with distinction in India and Burma.

A signal of 16 November 1942, from the C-in-C India to the War Office referred to approximately 100 members of the Hong Kong Volunteer Defence Corps, about 49 Chinese members of the British Army and about 50 Auxiliary, transport, air raid precaution and other personnel.

In early 1943, after a short period of training, the first groups were flown over the 'Hump', by R.A.F. aircraft, to Assam. From there they travelled to Calcutta. The first two groups to arrive were enlisted in the 9th Battalion, Border Regiment, stationed at Fort William. Two groups arriving three to five months later joined the First Battalion, the Gloucestershire Regiment, which had taken over from the Border Regiment. Hard training ensued, with a good measure of sporting activity thrown in. Then came a move to Deolali, where morale slumped as the feeling grew amongst the Hong Kong men that no one quite knew what to do with them.

Fortunately, Brigadier Michael Calvert stepped onto the scene. He was familiar with Hong Kong people, having commanded Chinese members of the Royal Engineers in the colony before the outbreak of war. He called for volunteers to fight the Japanese in Burma. All those present quickly stepped forward and so they became members of Wingate's Chindits. Hard jungle training followed for many months at Jhansi, Chindit Headquarters and, on 14 February, the Hong Kong Volunteer Company was put into the war establishment and served with great distinction until the end of hostilities.

When Admiral Harcourt sailed into Hong Kong for the liberation on 30 August 1945, the colony lay in ruins. The suffering prisoners of war were freed and given every attention. The work of reconstruction of the city began. The task was slow and arduous but a start was made. Preparations began for the war trials that were to deal with Japanese criminals from Hong Kong and throughtout Asia. Slowly, life began to return to normal. But inevitably, that return to normality involved turmoil across the border in China.

14

The New Challenge

By 1949, the situation in China was looking very serious as the Communists continued to ride the tide that was to take them to control. As ever, the government in Hong Kong regarded events across the border with a wary eye and passed several ordinances which increased its power to deal with any threats to law and order by use of registration, curfew or deportation.

The opportunity was taken to put the Volunteers of Hong Kong on to a new footing and, on 15 December 1948, the Governor, Sir Alexander Grantham, rose in the Legislative Council to explain the new plans. In a format unusual in the Empire's volunteer forces, there was to be a single force which would include naval, army, air, civil defence and essential services units. Sir Alexander explained that the new Hong Kong Defence Force was to be made up of six components: The Naval Force, which was the old Naval Volunteer Force; the Hong Kong Regiment, which was the old Hong Kong Volunteer Defence Corps, the Hong Kong Air Force, which was an expansion of the Air Arm of the former H.K.V.D.C.; the Hong Kong Auxiliary Force, which would be divided into a Home Guard and an Essential Services Wing; the Hong Kong Women's Volunteer Force; and a Headquarters Force. 'The Force is so organized that there is a place in it for every citizen who wishes to offer his services in peace or in time of emergency,' said the Governor. 'It is open to persons of all nationalities, and the Oath is so worded that non-British citizens may join without endangering their own national status.' However, the system of national groupings was to remain 'because of its clear advantages.' But Sir Alexander was quick to stress that all Volunteers were equal:

A platoon, or even a company, if recruiting is successful enough to allow it, will consist of Non-Commissioned Officers and men of one race, but the officer may not necessarily be of that same race; thus a company composed mainly of English other ranks may well have some Chinese officers or a predominantly Chinese company may have Portugese Officers.

The pay was to be the same as that of the regular forces and, except for the naval and air units, Volunteers could state on joining whether or not they would be willing to serve outside the colony. The command of the overall force and its components was to remain in the hands of Volunteers, assisted by regular staff officers.

The force was to be built up in two phases, with the first phase anticipated to take about six to 12 months. This would consist of a Force Headquarters with a strength of about 50; a Depot (part of the Force Headquarters) with a strength of about 500 — mostly recruits; an Infantry Battalion of the Hong Kong Regiment of about 1,000; A Specialists' Cadre of about 200; a Home Guard Wing of the Auxiliary Force of about 500; and an Essential Service Wing of about 2,250. This would give a total of 4,500 men.

Phase two, which was to overlap phase one was to see the addition of auxiliary units, such as engineers, signals and medical, with a strength of 270; a Heavy Anti-Aircraft Battery of 260 members; an Officer Cadet Cadre of 50; the 300-strong Military Wing of the Women's Volunteer Force; and the Essential Service Wing of 350. The total would then stand at 5,730. In addition, there would be about 350 men in the Naval Force and about 100 in the Air Force. Grantham added, however, that the plans were flexible and might be amended in the light of future circumstances or and conditions.

Grantham stressed that the Volunteers should be treated fairly: 'These men and these women who join the Force are going to give up much of their time, and maybe even their lives in the defence of Hong Kong. We know the quotation from Kipling: "It's Tommy this, an' Tommy that, an' 'Chuck him out, the Brute!" But it's 'Saviour of 'is country' when the guns begin to shoot".' The Governor gave further assurances to the Volunteers, stating that, as well as ensuring that pay and allowances were adequate, there would be provision of facilities such as a gymnasium, a theatre or concert hall, reading rooms, messes and canteens.

Sir Alexander closed by remarking, 'The plan I have laid before you is no panic scheme drawn up in a hurry.' It had been developed after a great deal of thought by both the Hong Kong and British governments and with the benefit of advice from a committee under the chairmanship of the Commandant of the Hong Kong Volunteer Defence Corps. He trusted that young men and women would come forward to join: 'They will be the inheritors of the fine tradition built up by the former Hong Kong Volunteer Defence Corps and the former Hong Kong Naval Volunteer Force.' Applause greeted this inspiring statement.

On Friday 17 December, the Hong Kong Defence Force Ordinance was gazetted. This involved the repeal of the Volunteer Ordinance of 1933 and the Naval Volunteer and Defence Ordinances, 1933 and 1939. As forecast, the new ordinance provided for the establishment of the Hong Kong Defence Force. The organization was to be divided into:

- The Hong Kong Naval Force;
- The Hong Kong Regiment;
- The Hong Kong Air Force;
- The Hong Kong Auxiliary Force;
- The Hong Kong Women's Volunteer Force; and
- The Force Headquarters, which was to consist of the Commandant and his staff, the Depot, the Officer Cadet Cadre and the Specialist Cadre.

The subject of calling out was dealt with in the ordinance: 'In case of an emergency the Governor may by proclamation call out the Force or any part thereof.' Failure to report within seven days without good excuse could lead to a charge of desertion. Provision was made for pay and allowances, for compensation for wounds, injuries or illness and for widows and orphans. A Welfare Fund was established and rules laid down as to discipline. The oath, and alternative declaration, were laid down for both British and non-British subjects.

On 23 December the ordinance was enacted. On 28 February 1949, the Hong Kong Volunteer Defence Corps was disbanded and the following day, 1 March, the Hong Kong Defence Force was established. It was reported that every member of the former force joined up with the new one and so the long Volunteer tradition continued uninterrupted.

The Communists continued their success in China and, on 1 October 1949, the establishment of the People's Republic was formally declared. During the year the garrison in Hong Kong was strengthened but, although Communists troops had closed up to the Sino-British border by October, no incidents occurred.

The first Volunteer unit to be set up under the new arrangement was the Hong Kong Regiment, which was formed on 1 March 1949, the same day that the H.K.D.F. was established. On 10 June, the first batch of men passed out from the Depot at Murray Barracks and was posted to the regiment. The first section of the first platoon of the Infantry Battalion was said to have consisted mainly of ex-officers — including one who was a graduate of the Imperial Defence College.

Colonel L.T. Ride, the distinguished Volunteer who had seen much action against the Japanese, was appointed Commandant of the H.K.D.F. He reported at the close of 1949 that training had advanced very well and that a good standard of efficiency had been established. Camps, cruises, exercises and a rifle meeting had been held and enthusiasm had been high.

The Volunteers were playing an important part in the build-up of the garrison which was taking place against the background of the triumph of the Communists in China. Britain was determined to defend its colony. On 31 August 1949, the General Officer Commanding in Chief, Lieutenant-General F.W. Festing, gave a press conference and he painted a confident picture. A number of units were on the high seas, he said, including the South Staffordshires and the King's Own Shropshire Light Infantry, anti-aircraft, field and medium artillery, a regiment of Royal Engineers, field ambulance, detachments of Signals, R.A.S.C. and R.E.M.E. and a number of other units. Two Spitfire squadrons were in the colony with additional R.A.F. reinforcements on the way. Naval strength had also increased. 'You chaps may think I am trying to teach my grandmother how to suck eggs by saying these things which you already know, but you can put two and two together about it,' said the general.

The point of the reinforcements was to resist any aggression, he explained. A 40th Division was being built up in the New Territories, he said, with troops coming from the Middle East and Germany. The Division was based mainly around the Fanling area. The Third Commando Brigade was also in the colony. 'Some were in Haifa,' said Festing, 'Many of the lads have never been further east than Charing Cross.'

There was little chance of a repeat of 1941, he felt: 'To my mind there are three obviously vital basic differences between the present moment and 1941.' He continued, saying that in 1941 the Japanese had complete command of the sea, they had command of the air, and the defences were inadequate. Additional troops had arrived at the last moment 'and there was uncertainty to put it lightly.'

Thirty-six camps for large-sized units were now under construction, reconnaissance and other exercises were being stepped up. New roads were being built, including the one linking Yuen Long and Tai Po, so that troops could move quickly. Social needs were not overlooked, with a dance laid on at Government House. 'The young officer, like the soldier, is a chap who does very much appreciate getting to know the civilian population.'

In the newspapers the following day there was a column of crammed small print giving the routine orders for the Hong Kong Defence Force. These covered officers' appointments, honours and awards, training, zeroing of rifles, weapons instruction, equipment, drills, kit and allowances. For the Hong Kong Regiment the entry read: '(a) training — Week ending September 10, 1949. No 1, 2 and 3, platoons — Type of Dress. Fitting of Clothing and Equipment. Organisation and Equipment of the Platoon. (b) Drill. Each platoon will carry out 10 minutes drill prior to commencing training on each parade.'

The Hong Kong Government printed a small booklet, entitled 'Why Hong Kong?' which it distributed to all members of the garrison. The booklet set out the reasons Britain should stand by Hong Kong. 'It does not need much political insight to know why you were sent to Hong Kong and not to Timbuctoo.' Britain had a duty to defend the people of Hong Kong from any aggression. The colony was successful due to the nature of its people and its geographical position: 'But none of these advantages would have been turned to much account if it had not been for the stability, security and initiative which a century of British rule and traditions has provided.'

Tribute was paid to the people of Hong Kong.

There can be no doubt that we owe them much. When our country was in danger in 1914 and 1939 they sent fine contributions of money and goods as well as men who were both Chinese and Europeans. Local factories were turned over to the production of war essentials, and the local shipyards devoted their whole efforts to the production of ships whose importance to Britain in the early years of the last war could hardly be exaggerated. And when the Japanese attack came we were in no position to do much for their defence. Our Navy and Air Force were withdrawn, but 2,000 local volunteers fought alongside the Canadian, British and Indian regular battalions with the utmost courage and loyalty and skill. They suffered the occupation period with fortitude. In the face of tyranny and terror of the Japanese rule they sent gifts to the prisoners of war and internees, and they sheltered those who escaped and led them to safety. And there was no doubting the sincerity of the welcome we received when we came back.

The presence of a British Government and of British troops in Hong Kong is alone responsible for the city's present flourishing condition and its maintenance as a free port which in fact constitutes its value as a commercial centre.

By autumn, the Communists had closed up to the border, the first of their advance forces arriving at 3 a.m., on Monday 17 October. 'Some were mere boys, and could not be much older than 14 or 15,' noted a reporter. 'There was one girl aged about 23. She also carried a wicked looking Mauser.' The *Daily Telegraph* commented, 'Sooner or later, and sooner rather than later, Anglo-Chinese relations will have to be based on political realities.' A British government official was quoted as saying, 'We can only repeat that we do not intend to be talked or jostled out of the Colony. We would resist a military assault and we have no intention of withdrawing.'

The strength of the garrison stood at about 40,000 men, with Volunteers an important component. In November, elements of the Hong Kong Defence Force attended annual camp at Sai Kung and recruiting was said to be going well. In the following year the Volunteer movement continued to grow in strength and a signal honour was announced in the *London Gazette* of 1 May 1951: 'His Majesty the King has been pleased to approve the change of title of the Hong Kong Defence force to be, in future, 'The Royal Hong Kong Defence Force''.'

This award was made in recognition of the heroic defence of Hong Kong by members of the Hong Kong Volunteer Defence Corps and its news was welcomed with great pride in the colony. For a Volunteer force to be granted such a title in its own right was extremely unusual. Earlier that year the Hong Kong Regiment had paraded for another emotive occasion — the presentation of new colours. The original King's Colour and Regimental Colour had been buried during the battle for Hong Kong in 1941 and, at that time, had not been recovered. The replacement colours were made by the Royal School of Needlework in the United Kingdom.

The parade, on 14 February, was held on the ground of the Hong Kong Cricket Club, under the command of Lieutenant Colonel H. Owen-Hughes, Commandant of the Hong Kong Regiment. It was reported

The adjutant's heart was truly gladdened when over 200 Volunteers paraded in H.M. Dockyard at 14.30 hours for a final 'spit and polish' and preliminary arms drill under the R.S.M. and the 'first today drill' impressed even that doughty warrior.

All this augured well and the march to, and line up on the Chater Road ground where there was a final pep talk by the C.O. brought favourable comment not only from the civilians, but also from our regular Service confreres who who were gathering for the ceremony.

The Reserve Company under Major J.C.M. Grenham graciously 'lined the ground' and a new note was struck when members of the Hong Kong Women's Volunteer Force acted as 'usherettes'...

Music was provided by the Volunteers' old comrades in arms, the First Battalion of the Middlesex Regiment. The Bishop of Hong Kong and South China, The Rt. Revd R.O. Hall carried out the consecration itself and the Governor presented the Colours and addressed the parade before moving to the saluting base for the march past to the Volunteers' tune, 'the Leather Bottel'. The civilian soldiers then marched off, with the G.O.C. personally holding up traffic for them to pass and the day ended with celebrations in the drill shed and officers' mess.

In his speech at the ceremony the Governor, Sir Alexander Grantham, reviewed what was known of previous Volunteer colours:

Although we know that a Volunteer Corps existed in Hong Kong in the 1850s, the first definite information we have about Colours is that on February 16, 1863, almost 88 years ago to the day, Colours were presented to the Hong Kong Artillery Volunteer Corps by Mrs Mercer, wife of the then Officer Administering the Government. We have no knowledge of what happened to those Colours, nor whether any of the succeeding volunteer units had Colours until we come to the period of the Hong Kong Volunteer Defence Corps.

In May, 1928, Sir Cecil Clementi presented the King's Colour and Regimental Colour to the Hong Kong Volunteer Defence Corps, and it is interesting to note that the officer who received the King's Colour was Lt E.J.R. Mitchell, who today has sponsored the new King's Colour.

The Colours presented in 1928 were buried by officers of the Corps after the hostilities in 1941, but they must have been discovered by the Japanese, for despite extensive search after the reoccupation of the Colony they could not be found.

In fact, they were later discovered.

The Governor said of the new colours, 'They represent long years of faithful service to the Colony by former generations of volunteers, and also they represent the supreme sacrifice of over 280 members of the Hong Kong Volunteer Defence Corps in the last war.'

In another ceremony that day, Lieutenant Colonel H. Owen-Hughes gave up command of the regiment. To mark the occasion, Colonel Lindsay Ride, Commandant of the Hong Kong Defence Force, presented the regiment with a bugle which had been one of the prized possessions of the British Army Aid Group. 'It is doubly fitting that this should be done, because not only was the B.A.A.G composed largely of H.K.V.D.C. personnel, but Colonel Owen Hughes was intimately associated with its work both in China and India.'

Further pleasant news came on 14 August, when the King granted a formal alliance between the Hong Kong Regiment and the Middlesex Regiment. The first result of this was an inter-regimental swimming match, won by the Volunteers. While training was intense, there were many social events, including a June ball and sporting engagements.

However, internationally, the situation was tense, with war breaking out in Korea and the start of the Malayan Emergency. Though the stalwarts of the Volunteers remained as keen as ever, an insufficient number of people had come forward to bring the force up to the required numbers. The Hong Kong Regiment reported that its strength at the end of the year stood at 21 officers and 318 other ranks.

On 7 September, the Compulsory Service Ordinance 1951, was published. The ordinance applied to all citizens of the United Kingdom and the Colonies ordinarily resident in Hong Kong who were between 16 and 60. Under the ordinance, people were liable to be called up for service with the Royal Hong Defence Force if they were aged up to 45. Call up for the Special Constabulary or Essential Services Corps was to apply to men aged up to 60 and women aged up to 50. Provision was made for grounds of objection to selection for service, including conscientious objection. Members were unable to leave the colony without a written permit.

At the same time, a new Royal Hong Kong Defence Force Ordinance 1951, was published. The organization was to consist of:

- A Force Headquarters and staff;
- The Hong Kong Royal Naval Volunteer Reserve;
- The Hong Kong Regiment, consisting of:
  - An Artillery Battery, comprising a Gunnery Troop and a Control and Reporting Troop;
  - One or more Infantry Battalions;
  - An Intelligence Unit.
  - The Hong Kong Auxiliary Air Force.
  - The Hong Kong Home Guard.
  - The Hong Kong Women's Naval Reserve.
  - The Hong Kong Women's Auxiliary Army Corps.
  - The Hong Kong Women's Auxiliary Air Force.

Two other ordinances were also introduced, the Hong Kong Royal Naval Volunteer Reserve (General Service) Ordinance 1951, and the Essential Service Corps (Amendment) Ordinance 1951.

The introduction of compulsory service was greeted with mixed feelings by men who were Volunteers, and protests were heard. The reality of the situation was that compulsion was necessary. However, the Naval Reserve, the Home Guard and the Women's Services remained voluntary.

By 1953, the Royal Hong Kong Defence Force had greatly expanded. Research by Michael Leung, a serving Volunteer, explains the set-up. The Force Headquarters consisted of the headquarters staff, and an artillery battery comprising a Field (Training and Reinforcement) Troop and a Control and Reporting Troop. These troops had no guns and they were used to backup the regular Royal Artillery units based in the territory. In addition, there was a Reconnaissance Platoon; an Intelligence (Interrogation and Interpretation) Platoon; a specialist staff; a pay section; a records section; a Depot responsible for the 16-week training of recruits; and a Light Troop, which was operational in 1956, and was equipped with six 4.2 inch heavy mortars mounted on a wheeled carriage.

The Hong Kong Royal Naval Volunteer Reserve consisted of an executive and sea-going branch, together with engineering, electrical, supply and secretariat, plotting, cryptography, ordinance artificers and communications branches. The Volunteers had a depot ship, with extra craft being loaned by the Royal Navy for training and exercises. During annual camp, personnel went aboard Royal Navy ships of the Hong Kong flotilla. The H.K.R.N.V.R. was commanded by a civilian and came directly under the Commodore-In-Charge, Hong Kong.

The Hong Kong Regiment was made up of a Battalion Headquarters, with a Headquarters Company including a Three-Inch Mortar Platoon, a Machine Gun Platoon, an Assault Pioneer Platoon and a Defence Platoon. There were four Rifle Companies, equipped — except for minor modifications — as regular army units.

It was laid down that the Commanding Officer of the Hong Kong Regiment could be either a regular officer or a civilian. Regular staff were attached to fill such posts as adjutant, R.S.M., permanent staff instructors and a signal instructor. The regiment was responsible for its own internal organization and routine training, with Force Headquarters, R.H.K.D.F., responsible for administration. However, for operational matters and general training direction, the regiment came under the G.O.C. Land Force, Hong Kong, who was its Service Commander.

The Hong Kong Home Guard was a unit of about 100 men, mainly ex-members of the Hong Kong Regiment or its predecessors, who were aged over 45. They were commanded by a civilian Major and had a reduced training obligation.

The Hong Kong Auxiliary Air Force was the air arm of the Defence Force and was a self-contained unit, under the Air Officer Commanding, Hong Kong, (its Service Commander) for general direction in operation and training matters. All matters of administration came under the Force Headquarters of the R.H.K.D.F. The air force was commanded by a Wing Commander, a civilian ex-R.A.F. officer, who had two regular R.A.F. officers to assist. Ground crew, aircraft servicing and maintenance staff consisted of regular R.A.F. N.C.O.s with some auxiliaries.

At one stage, the H.K.A.A.F. had 16 aircraft of its own: four Austers, four Hawards, and eight Spitfire Mark XXIVs. The aircraft were loaned by the R.A.F. The Hong Kong government paid their freightage to Hong Kong and operated, maintained and supplied them. The auxiliary air force had as its object the training and maintenance of an additional fighter squadron to back-up the R.A.F. fighter defences of the colony. Later, as the fighter role was reduced, the force took on an air spotting role.

In 1953, the H.K.A.A.F. consisted of a Headquarters Unit, a Fighter Squadron and a Control and Communications Unit, supported by training flights.

The three female organizations were an important part of the defence forces. The Hong Kong Women's Naval Volunteer Reserve was complementary to the H.K.R.N.V.R. with its women working in roles relating to plotting, signalling, telegraphy, secretarial services, cryptography and meteorological duties.

The Hong Kong Women's Auxiliary Army Corps worked in support of the Hong Kong Regiment, being involved in cooking, nursing, driving, signalling, telephone and pay duties. The corps provided half the plotters in the regiment's Control and Reporting Troop. The Hong Kong Women's Auxiliary Air Force, supported the H.K.A.A.F., working in the Administrative and Control and Communications Units.

In 1953, the forces' strength stood at 1,521, broken down according to Table 14.1.

Table 14.1 Breakdown of Hong Kong Defence Forces (1953)

Force Headquarters	199
H.K.R.N.V.R.	201
H.K.R.N.V.R. Women's Services	25
Hong Kong Regiment	787
Hong Kong Regiment Women's Services	33
Hong Kong Auxiliary Air Force	178
H.K.A.A.F. Women's Services	18
Home Guard	80
Total	1,521

This total was made up of 207 officers, 131 Warrant Officers and Non-Commissioned Officers, and 1,183 other ranks. The Force continued to be a melting pot of nationalities, as is shown by the breakdown relating to the Hong Kong Regiment in Table 14.2.

Table 14.2 Nationality Breakdown of Hong Kong Regiment (1953)

Chinese	45
Portuguese	23
British	16.5
Eurasian	5.3
Indian	2.5
Pakistani	1.8
Philippino	2.5
Others	3

The breakdown of the 'Others' category revealed members who were American, Dutch, Greek, Mexican, Indonesian, Malay, Bolivian, White Russian, German, Jamaican, Ceylonese and stateless. It was even reported that one member of the regiment was an ex-soldier of the Japanese Army who was half-Chinese and half Japanese and who had been drafted after the occupation of the colony.

The year 1954 was a milestone — marking the 100th anniversary of the formation of the first Volunteer organization in Hong Kong. Celebrations took place throughout the year, but the Honorary Colonel of the Hong Kong Regiment, long-time Volunteer, Colonel H.L. Dowbiggin, still noted in an anniversary message: 'Each year progress has been made, but there is still a lot more than can still be done to improve efficiency.'

In honour of the original Volunteers, a new toast was introduced for the Royal Hong Kong Defence Force — 'The Ninety-Nine' — and this toast is still drunk today by members of the Royal Hong Kong Regiment. Introducing the toast, at the 'dining out' of Colonel H.B.L. Dowbiggin, Colonel L.T. Ride, explained:

Our thoughts naturally go back to the 99 residents of this Colony who in 1854 first initiated our Volunteer movement; a movement which has been justly described as 'one of the healthiest and most useful movements that was ever inaugurated in Hong Kong.' To those 99, Hong Kong — and especially we volunteers — owe much, and while it is true that we should also not forget those who have carried on the tradition that they initiated, to them should go the pride of place. I have, therefore, decided in order to keep continuously before the members of the volunteers the great debt we all owe to those 99, that we should introduce in this Centenary Year the custom of drinking a Toast immediately after the Loyal Toast at every Mess Dinner to 'The 99.'

The Hong Kong Regiment had inherited the motto of the Hong Kong Volunteer Defence Corps: 'Nulli Secundus In Oriente.' But the Defence Force lacked a motto and a search had been carried out for previous mottoes which might be suitable. It seemed that the 1862 formation had adopted 'Caelum Non Animum Muto' — 'I have changed my skies, but not my spirit', a quotation from Horace. The motto remained apt and so an order was issued adopting it as the official motto of the Royal Hong Kong Defence Force.

On 27 and 28 March the Hong Kong Regiment, for the first time in its history, provided a Guard for Government House. On parade for the first time since its formation was the Band and Drums of the regiment which headed the march to the gates of Government House to take up duty. In May, the Hong Kong Royal Naval Volunteer Reserve also mounted guard.

Among the events organized during this 100th anniversary year was a cricket match, held in April, between Pre-War members of the Hong Kong Volunteer Defence Force and the Shanghai Volunteers. On 30 May, a Centenary Parade was held at the Hong Kong Cricket Club ground, with the Governor taking the salute. The *South China Morning Post* reported the following day:

The sky was dark and overcast. Fans and programmes fluttered as the ladies struggled to keep cool. The ground was splashed with colour. The lush green of the Peak, rising to form a superb background to a scene which few will forget. The fighting men of the Colony, men who work as bankers, as electricians, in offices, during the day but who train in the arts of war at night, went through the arms drill with a precision worthy of their long history.

A message from the Queen was read out to the parade. The H.K.R.N.V.R. lined the north side of the ground, the Hong Kong Regiment was in the middle and on the south stood the H.K.A.A.F., the Women's Services and former Volunteers. A fly-past was provided by the H.K.A.A.F., consisting of four Austers and four Harvards. Finally, three Spitfires zoomed past, peeled-off and dived over the ground.

The following evening, a grand centenary ball was held at the Defence Force's new headquarters at Happy Valley. attended by the Governor and 800 other people: 'Hundreds of bemedalled officers and their bejewelled partners gathered round the huge dance floor' and sang Happy Birthday to the force. A Centenary Exhibition was held at the St John's Cathedral Hall with many photographs and items illustrating the history of Hong Kong's Volunteers.

The members of the Defence Force continued to be active throughout the 1950s. In 1957, the remnants of the original colours of the H.K.V.D.C. were unearthed at a building site in Central District, on Hong Kong Island, and they were paraded by 72 veterans in the 1958 Annual Review of the Royal Hong Kong Defence Force. At that parade the battle honour 'Hong Kong' was also worn for the first time on the new colours of the Hong Kong Regiment. The original colours are now housed at St John's Cathedral.

In 1961, the government announced that it no longer felt that there was a requirement for compulsory service and this was abandoned. The Volunteer movement became voluntary once more. It had earlier been found that many of the people serving with the Defence Force had no legal obligation to do so and that many of those who were, on paper, serving by compulsion would have done the same as Volunteers.

The Force had given much assistance during recent natural disasters. Helicopters, which had been in use for some time by the H.K.A.A.F. had proved particularly useful.

Reorganization came again, in 1961–2, with the decision to disband the Force Headquarters of the R.H.K.D.F., individualizing the component elements. The Hong Kong Regiment was also reorganized, and it started training for a reconnaissance role. Three Company became initially an Infantry Company and then a Recruit Company. Its role was to provide an Assault Infantry Platoon to support each of the Reconnaissance Squadrons which had now been formed. The Light Troop was disbanded, mainly because of the cost of ammunition. The M.M.G. Platoon was given a mobile role as a light reconnaissance patrol. The Home Guard Company and the Women's Auxiliary Army Corps were integrated as part of the regiment.

Training was aimed at producing Reconnaissance Squadron groups, each consisting of a Reconnaissance Squadron, a platoon of Three Company and detachments of mortars and M.M.G.s. The two groups used Land Rovers and worked to improve mobility and observation of enemy movements. In early 1962, the First and

Second Reconnaissance Squadrons took part in regular army exercises in their new role, in place of annual camp.

A major recruiting campaign was launched in 1962 as it was desired to establish a Third Reconnaissance Squadron as soon as possible. The standard Self-Loading Rifle and the Sterling Sub-Machine Carbine became the regiment's weapons, and 1958 pattern equipment was made to replace the assortment that was currently being worn. More Land Rovers were given to the regiment.

In addition to the squadrons, work continued in the regimental headquarters, the Intelligence Platoon, the Band and Drums, the Medical Section and the Women's unit. Six British Ferret armoured cars, equipped with .30 inch machine guns were handed over to the regiment on 15 January 1963 and the Fourth Reconnaissance Squadron was formed, with two troops, each of two Ferrets and two Land rovers.

On Liberation Day, 30 August 1962, the formal opening of the Volunteer Garden of Remembrance, Shrine and Memorial Gates at the City Hall took place.

By 1964, the Hong Kong Regiment was almost fully established, trained and equipped for its new role in Reconnaissance in support of the Regular Army. The regiment was the first unit in the colony to receive the new 7.62 mm General Purpose Machine Gun.

In 1965, it was reported that the regiment was settled into its new role of reconnaissance. 'This is a good role for us since it makes particular use of one of the most valuable of the regiment's characteristics, which is an intimate knowledge of the territory and people of Hong Kong,' said the Commanding Officer, Lieutenant-Colonel J. Laurence-Smith. The set-up at that time consisted of: Regimental Headquarters; Headquarters Squadron; Band and Drums; Intelligence Troop; Medical Troop; M.T. Troop; Pay Section; Quartermaster's department; Signals Troop; Sniper's Section; Women's Auxiliary Army Corps; Recruit's Cadre; First Reconnaissance Squadron; Second Reconnaissance Squadron; Three Company; Fourth Reconnaissance Squadron; and the Home Guard Troop.

However, while the new Volunteer organization was settling down, events across the border in China boded ill for Hong Kong. The Great Proletarian Cultural Revolution was in full swing and the Red Guards were on the march.

15

Soldiering On

IN the mid-1960s the turmoil in China was spilling over into Hong Kong. In April 1966, the Hong Kong Regiment was called out to help with the suppression of rioting in Kowloon. At least 97 per cent of the regiment answered the call which came at 1 a.m. The call-out lasted for five days.

The regimental diary recorded that, as strikes and demonstrations occurred during May 1967, the regiment stepped up its training. Disorder continued during June and there was rioting in Kowloon and on the island. The police dealt with the riots, and curfews were imposed at night in some areas of Kowloon and on the north coast of the island. The regiment continued with its training, paying particular attention to internal security drills.

In early July, further trouble was felt to be brewing and the First and Second Recce Squadrons were warned to prepare for operations in support of the police. On 12 July, the authorities exercised the power of Limited Call-Out for the regiment. This enabled the whole regiment to be called-out for a period of up to 25 days, or allowed parts to be called out for limited periods.

That evening, the First Recce Squadron joined regular forces and stood ready for operations. The Second Squadron stood by for escort duties. At 11 p.m. a joint police-military search of Communist premises in Wanchai was undertaken, with the involvement of the First squadron. The two squadrons were stood down the next day. A 24-hour guard was posted at Regimental Headquarters. On 14 July, the regiment was again in action, when members of the Fourth Recce Squadron assisted the authorities with a cordon and search operation in Queen's Road West. On 15 July a bomb was thrown at the eastern end of Sports Road, near the Regimental Headquarters.

The Volunteers were busy over the following weekend. The First and Second Recce Squadrons met at Wong Nei Chong Gap and then joined up with regular forces at Lyemun Barracks. At noon on 16 July, a large cordon and search operation was carried out in Shau Kei Wan, with many suspects being detained and several weapons found.

On 25 July, it was the turn of Three Company for operations in the New Territories. Platoon-strength ambush parties were laid out in the Lau Fau Shan area. These ambushes were withdrawn on 28 July and the company moved to cover the Chik Hang area in Sai Kung, Kat O Island, and Shatin. The opportunity was taken for a 'hearts and minds' operation, with the regiment's medical officer flying in by helicopter to provide aid to local villagers. On 29 July, the company was stood down. That same day the regiment assumed responsibility for providing two 'anti-intimidation' patrols each night. Each patrol consisted of eight men mounted in two Land Rovers. Each patrol was tasked with preventing workers in public transport from being intimidated. One patrol worked in the Causeway Bay and North Point area, while the other covered Shau Kei Wan and Chai Wan. Each night, the officer commanded one patrol and the troop sergeant the other. The patrols lasted from 6 p.m. to 6 a.m.

Despite the problems during July, with regular civil disturbances, Volunteer morale remained high, with members of the regiment reporting for their normal work after their all-night military duties. Police raids on Communist premises were having some effect, weapons and documents were seized and many leaders went into hiding.

In early August, the Second Recce Squadron was called out for operations in the New Territories — with 94 per cent attendance. The squadron was based at a government primary school at Tai Po. Village patrols were carried out — 48 hours on patrol and 24 hours back at camp. Every village between Ma On Shan and Tai Long, Sai Kung Peninsula, was visited. Most patrols included a medical officer or orderly who gave treatment to villagers. It was reported that, 'In general, villagers showed great friendliness towards the patrols and talked freely to all ranks. Village problems concerning amenities were the main topic of conversation and very little political interest was shown.'

The Volunteers also provided road patrols. At the same time members of the Intelligence Troop were active, providing translations of broadcasts from China. Morale was said to be excellent.

The Second Recce Squadron was relieved by the Third on 12

August 1967, with the detachments from the medical and intel-ligence units also being changed. The area for the village patrols was changed to the Yuen Long and Frontier Divisions: 'As before, the villagers were very friendly and talked freely. They welcomed medical assistance and even accepted calmly the discovery of an illicit still. The fact that many members of this squadron were speakers of the Hakka dialect was a big plus factor'.

On 19 August, the Third Company was relieved by the Fourth Recce Squadron and detachments from the Medical and Intel-ligence Troops were also changed. Village patrols concentrated on the Pat Sin area with border patrols being increased. A typhoon struck during the week and the squadron was involved in relief operations. The squadron also assisted the police by providing the cordon party in a raid on Communist premises in Yuen Long.

The First Recce Squadron relieved the Fourth on 26 August, with patrols concentrated on villages in the Castle Peak, Pat Sin and Sai Kung Peninsula areas.

August had been a busy month for the regiment. One squadron was maintained in the field throughout the month and, at the same time, guard was mounted on the regimental headquarters with nightly vehicle patrols continuing. During the month, Com-munist tactics changed as counter-measures taken by the police began to take effect. Rioting died down to be replaced by an effort to cripple the port and reduce food imports from China. Bomb explosions became more common. All stocks of fireworks were called in by the government, but there remained sufficient ex-plosives in circulation to make many devices. Simulated bombs were placed with real ones. The task of the nightly road patrols changed from the protection of transport workers to operations against the bombers and much work was done in assisting the police.

Village patrols continued in September throughout the New Territories, including Lantau Island where the Volunteers were frequently mistaken for Gurkhas.

Trouble was expected for the important Communist anniver-sary of 1 October. By 2 p.m. on that day, the whole regiment was standing by, with two of the squadrons reporting 100 per cent attendance. The Commander, British Forces, inspected the regi-ment before it deployed. The First Recce Squadron went to Stan-ley, Victoria Barracks and Lyemun; the Second to Gun Club Hill Barracks; the Fourth to Kai Tak; Three Company, Headquarter

Squadron and the Home Guard Company remained in reserve at headquarters. However, the day passed without incident and the regiment was stood down at 11 p.m.

Bomb planting had continued throughout September and the road patrols were kept very busy each night. One morning, 48 bombs were found in North Point between 7 a.m. and 8 a.m. During an evening patrol, bombs were thrown from a high building at a patrol investigating a bomb in the street below. However, the bombing campaign, which had caused casualties both to the security forces and the public, engendered a feeling of revulsion against those responsible.

By mid-October, the nightly road patrols were stopped, two having been provided each night since 29 July. Although bombs continued to be found, the regiment started to resume its normal pattern of training — although no autumn camp was held in view of the recent activity. Bomb attacks reduced during November and had virtually ceased by the end of December. As the regimental diary recorded, 'It had been a very busy and testing year for the Regiment, as for the Colony. We had fulfilled part of the task for which we exist and there was a deserved feeling of accomplishment amongst The Volunteers.'

As the troubles died down a close look was taken at the organization of the Volunteer forces in the colony. As a result of this, in 1967, the Hong Kong Royal Naval Reserve was disbanded. The Hong Kong Women's Royal Naval Reserve and Hong Kong Women's Auxiliary Air Force had already been disbanded.

In 1962, the Force Headquarters of the Royal Hong Kong Defence Force had also formally disbanded and the post of Commandant was abolished. This followed a careful consideration of the situation of the Hong Kong Regiment and the Hong Kong Auxiliary Air Force. Each unit then became more closely associated with the army and with the Royal Air Force.

It had, apparently, always been the intention, since the abolition of the Headquarter Unit of the Defence Force to make the Hong Kong Regiment and the Hong Kong Auxiliary Air Force separate legal entities. One of the problems which had prevented this formally taking place had been 'difficulties' over the succession to the 'Royal' title.

In 1969, proposals were drawn up for the final disbandment of the Defence Force and for the formal establishment, by separate

ordinances, of the Hong Kong Regiment and the Hong Kong
Auxiliary Air Force. At the same time, formal application was to
be made for both to bear the title 'Royal' as carrying on the historic
Volunteer tradition. This request was granted and both units carry
the title today.

At a Regimental Foundation Day dinner on 30 May 1961, the
Governor, Sir Robert Black, had conferred the added title of 'The
Volunteers' on the regiment, to acknowledge its descent from the
earlier units and to mark the end of conscription. This was to
continue.

The question of the colours was somewhat vexed. The regimental colours were, in fact, presented to the Defence Force and
handed to the regiment for safe keeping. Strictly speaking, they
belonged to a unit which no longer existed. Application was,
therefore, to be made for the regiment now to be presented with a
guidon, which is the standard normally carried by a reconnaissance regiment. Eventually, a guidon was granted and this is
carried by the regiment today.

The Volunteers continued their busy schedule throughout the
1960s and into the 1970s and 1980s. In 1975, a review was carried
out of the Royal Hong Kong Regiment and it was reported in the
official yearbook of the following year that this had confirmed the
light reconnaissance role. The regiment was now made up of three
reconnaissance squadrons, one infantry squadron, a headquarters
squadron and a home guard squadron. There was also a junior
leaders squadron of 135 boys aged between 14 and 17. The
regiment operated in support of the British Armed Forces in
Hong Kong both in internal security and reconnaissance roles.
The Royal Hong Kong Auxiliary Air Force was the only remaining operational auxiliary air force squadron in the Common-
wealth.

Other volunteer organizations also existed, the Essential Services Corps, the Civil Aid Services, the Auxiliary Medical Service
and the Auxiliary Fire Services.

In 1977, the Royal Hong Kong Regiment was stated to have
four reconnaissance squadrons, a headquarters squadron and a
home guard squadron, together with the junior leaders squadron.
During 1976, the regiment had been called out to assist with
fighting serious hill fires which had occurred over the Chinese
New Year.

The regiment was busy in 1979, due to a large influx of illegal immigrants from China. The regiment was asked to assist the British army in its operations and, in June, this involvement increased when the regiment was placed on limited call-out for active service under the Royal Hong Kong Regiment Ordinance. Volunteer soldiers participated in border patrols and acted as guides and interpreters for the regular forces during the year. The regiment performed in a professional manner and was praised for its enthusiasm, military efficiency and approach. During the year, the regiment celebrated its 125th anniversary and many events were organized to mark the occasion of the gathering of the Ninety-Nine, back in 1854.

The present Volunteer headquarters at Happy Valley opened in 1980 and this greatly helped in improving standards of training. Throughout that year, the regiment was again called on to stem the flow of illegal immigrants from China — though this work was confined to weekends to reduce the demands on employers. In October, the regiment was deployed on the border, in lieu of annual camp, and did much valuable work stopping illegal immigrants and the people aiding them. The same week-long commitment took place in following years.

In 1982, the regiment was expanded to some 860 Volunteers. Its role was officially said to be primarily one of internal security, but it also included reconnaissance, anti-illegal immigrant operations and assistance to other government departments in the event of natural disasters. During the year, the regiment was re-equipped with a new Clansman communication system, which, being fully compatible with the equipment used by the regular army in Hong Kong, enhanced the regiment's capability in its reconnaissance role.

In 1983, the women returned to the Volunteers when a women's troop was established to provide supporting services in internal security and anti-illegal immigrant operations as searchers and interpreters. Further expansion came in 1984, with the establishment growing to 946 Volunteers. Throughout the 1980s the regiment continued to attract a flood of applications at each recruitment drive, allowing it to be highly selective. Volunteers travelled overseas for training and all officer cadets were trained at the Royal Military Academy at Sandhurst in Britain. The regiment continued to play an important part in the life and prosperity of Hong Kong.

The Regiment Today

Although the return of Hong Kong to China in 1997 will have implications for the Regiment, at the time of writing, no final decision on its future has been announced.

The modern Regiment is organized along the lines of a reconnaissance regiment in the British Army, with a number of special characteristics of its own. It consists of a Regimental Headquarters and four sabre squadrons, each sabre squadron having four troops. There is also a Headquarters Squadron, a Training Squadron, a Home Guard Squadron, and a Junior Leaders Corps.

The Headquarters Squadron includes a number of smaller units. The Escort and Liaison Troop specializes in duties such as establishing long term observation points, insertion techniques and searching. The Boat Troop operates small motor boats which are particularly important in view of the extensive coastline of Hong Kong and its many islands. The Women's Troop has a strength of about 50, with its members involved in interpreting, radio, intelligence, administration and first aid. The Regimental Aid Post provides medical support and the Quartermaster's Deprtment looks after the armoury, stores, transport, guards, general duties, and administration.

There is also a Reserve for Officers and Senior NCOs who, while they wish to remain Volunteers, find that work or other commitments prevent them, temporarily, from taking part fully in regimental activities. These Reservists assist with training whenever they can and provide a valuable source of experience.

Membership of the Home Guard Squadron is open primarily to those aged 45 or over, who have previous service as Volunteers, and who wish to maintain an active role. The squadron consists of two troops and the regimental band.

The Junior Leaders Corps is a very active unit with a membership of about 300 boys aged between 14 and a half and 18. The Corps is not heavily oriented to military training, but aims to give an active and challenging experience to young people by providing leadership training, outdoor activities and participation in the Duke of Edinburgh's Award Scheme.

Operationally, the Regiment comes under the command of the Commander British Forces (C.B.F.). Its roles include guarding key installations, investigating incidents, providing a light recce force

with excellent local knowledge and supporting 48 Gurkha Infantry Brigade. In addition, for a short period each year, the Regiment takes over responsibility for border patrols from the Regular
Army or, in the future, from the Royal Hong Kong Police.

An important task for the Regiment is providing assistance to
the civilian community. One example is work to help cope with
the influx of Vietnamese boat people; in 1988, 600 Volunteers were
provided over a period of seven weeks. Assistance is also given in
the form of emergency relief work, and in situations such as
typhoons and other natural disasters.

The Regiment maintains a strong sense of identity, with an
active programme of sporting and social activities, and a large
association which links former Volunteers around the world. Although the future of the Regiment may be unclear, one thing is
certain — the spirit of community service established over almost
150 years by generations of Volunteers will carry on, in one form
or another, well into the next century.

Sources

MANY of the sources used in the preparation of this book are identified in the text. Research was carried out in Hong Kong and it is no doubt true that further valuable material rests in official and other archives in the United Kingdom and elsewhere.

One result of the Japanese invasion and occupation was the destruction of almost all official records in the colony. Newspapers, therefore, have proved a valuable resource and have been used extensively.

The Hong Kong Public Records Office has been a key facility with its copies of the CO/129 series of files, containing correspondence from Hong Kong to London, being of particular interest. *Government Gazettes*, official announcements, and ordinances have also been used.

The chapter on the battle itself draws on the report made by General Maltby after the war, and held by the Imperial War Museum. The publication, *A Record of the Actions of the Hongkong Volunteers Defence Corps in the Battle for Hong Kong, December 1941*, first published in 1953, and the recollections of survivors were also valuable sources.

The photographs in the book form part of the collection in the regiment's own archives.

Many people have assisted with the preparation of this book and to them all I am deeply grateful.

PHILLIP BRUCE

Index

Hong Kong Volunteer Reserve Association, 102, 104, 106, 109
Hong Kong Volunteer Rifle Corps (1878–82), 49, 50
Hong Kong Volunteers (1862–65), called out, 38–9; colours, 37; composition of, 37; equipment, 35; establishment of, 32–4; regulations, 36; visit to Macau, 37–8; wound up, 40
Hong Kong Women's Auxiliary Air Force, 289, 291, 300
Hong Kong Women's Auxiliary Army Corps, 289, 291, 295
Hong Kong Women's Naval Volunteer Reserve, 291, 300
Hong Kong Women's Volunteer Force, 282, 283, 287
Hoolmany, William, 14
Houghton, Corporal J.M., 257
Hsu, Immanuel C.Y., 155
Huffam, Frederick Sowley, 14, 21
Huffum, F.S., see Huffam, Frederick Sowley
Hughes Group, The, 80, 97, 207, 218, 219, 230, 237, 238, 239, 240
'Hughesiliers', see Hughes Group, The
Hughes, Lieutenant Colonel Harry Owen, 130, 207, 223, 237, 278, 288
Hung Hom Battery, 111
Hung, Lance Corporal D., 244
Hung, Lance Corporal K.C., 243, 247, 249, 250
Hunt, H.H., 14, 18
Hunt, William Henry, 18
Hyndman, Joao, 14, 22

ILLEGAL IMMIGRANTS, 301–2
Imperial Japanese Navy, 118–19, 120, 140–1
Improvised Battery, 189
Indian Medical Services, 216
Infantry Company, 96
Inniskillin Fusiliers, 188
Internees, 113, 115
Irwin, Thomas, 14
Ivanovitch, Stefan, 14, 21

JACK, SERGEANT, 144
Jacosta, Captain, 238, 239
Japan, at Versailles Peace Conference 123; attack on China, 163, 188–9, 191–2; attack on Hong Kong, 198–200, 216, 221–74; expansion of, 118–20; in First World War, 117, 121;

in South China, 209, 213; increasing power of, 110, 177; occupation of Manchuria by, 155; threat to Hong Kong, 181, 183; war with China, 74, 119; see also Imperial Japanese Navy, Japanese land forces
Japanese land forces, 234–5
Jardine, D., 11
Jardine Matheson and Company, 15, 104
Jarvis, Lieutenant S., 137
Jerrard, F., 71, 75
Jitts, Private G.C., 248
Jones, 2nd Lieutenant H.S., 267, 268
Jordain, Captain S.J., 169
Junior Leaders Corps, 303

KAI TAK, 178
Kane, William, 35
Kanji, Admiral Kato, 141
Kellett Island, 4, 9
Kennedy, Lieutenant, 252
King George VI, between 218 and 219 (Plate 52)
King's Own Royal Lancaster Regiment, 86
King's Own Shropshire Light Infantry, 284
Korea, 74, 119, 120
Kowloon City, 5, 25–6, 88, 89–91, 97
Kowloon Dock Battery, 47
Kowloon Golf Club, 141
Kumaon Rifles, 187
Kuomintang, 124

LAMMERT, LIONEL, 80
Lamont, John, 14, 18
Lane, Thomas Ash, 14, 15–16
Lane Crawford and Company, 15
Langley, Mrs R., 193
Lapraik and Company, 18
Lapraik, Douglas, 14, 18
Lau, Corporal M.S., 246
Laurence–Smith, Lieutenant Colonel J., 295
Lawrence, Frederick William, 14, 17–18
Lawson, Brigadier J.K., between 218 and 219 (Plate 36), 228, 241, 250, 255
Layton, Vice Admiral Sir Geoffrey, 213
League of Nations, 163
'Leaping Lena', between 218 and 219 (Plate 34)
Lee, Lance Corporal Francis, Yin-piu, 278

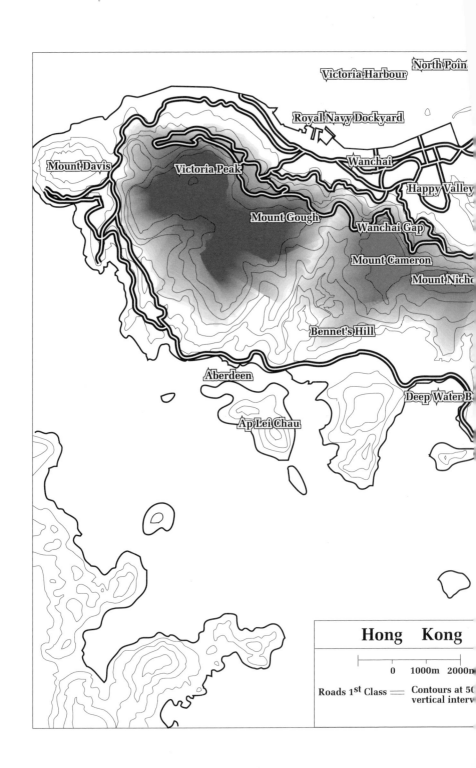

North Point

Victoria Harbour

Royal Navy Dockyard

Mount Davis

Victoria Peak

Wanchai

Happy Valley

Mount Gough

Wanchai Gap

Mount Cameron

Mount Nicho

Bennet's Hill

Mount Nicho

Aberdeen

Deep Water B.

Ap Lei Chau

Hong   Kong

0   1000m   2000m

Roads 1ˢᵗ Class ═══   Contours at 5(
vertical interv